Developmental Literacy Inventory

Developmental Literacy Inventory

CHARLES TEMPLE
Hobart and William Smith College

ALAN CRAWFORD
California State University, Los Angeles

JEAN GILLET

Boston • New York • San Francisco
Mexico City • Montreal • Toronto • London • Madrid • Munich • Paris
Hong Kong • Singapore • Tokyo • Cape Town • Sydney

Executive Editor: *Aurora Martínez Ramos*
Editorial Assistant: *Kara Kikel*
Executive Marketing Manager: *Krista Clark*
Marketing Manager: *Danae April*
Production Editor: *Janet Domingo*
Editorial Production Service: Kathy Smith—*Publishers' Design and Production Services, Inc.*
Composition Buyer: *Linda Cox*
Manufacturing Buyer: *Linda Morris*
Electronic Composition: *Publishers' Design and Production Services, Inc.*
Interior Design: *Publishers' Design and Production Services, Inc.*
Cover Administrator: *Linda Knowles*
Illustrator: *Deborah Schneck*

For related titles and support materials, visit our online catalog at www.allynbaconmerrill.com.

Between the time website information is gathered and then published, it is not unusual for some sites to have closed. Also, the transcription of URLs can result in typographical errors. The publisher would appreciate notification where these errors occur so that they may be corrected in subsequent editions.

ISBN-13: 978-0-205-45833-2   ISBN-10: 0-205-45833-5

Printed in the United States of America

▶▶▶ Contents

▶ ▶ ▶ Preface

The authors are delighted that the *Developmental Literacy Inventory* is finally in your hands. Two of us first dreamed of creating this work thirty years ago, as we worked on the first edition of the textbook on reading diagnosis, *Understanding Reading Problems*. The actual writing and field testing of the *Developmental Literacy Inventory* was done over the course of four years. The instrument can stand alone, or it can be used along side any of several books on reading diagnosis and special instruction.

The *Developmental Literacy Inventory* is made up of an informal reading inventory, complemented by informal assessments of emergent literacy and phonics knowledge. These devices are constructed to display the reading behaviors of students confronted with materials at different levels of difficulty.

The *Developmental Literacy Inventory* is informal as opposed to standardized, because it has not been normed through testing with thousands of students under controlled conditions. But because the instrument allows a teacher to look closely at an individual student's performance in a variety of reading tasks at many levels of difficulty, the portrait of reading that is revealed by the *Developmental Literacy Inventory* is richer and arguably more authentic than what is gained from standardized tests, making the device more informative for diagnostic purposes.

▶ How the *Developmental Literacy Inventory* Was Created

When Emmett Betts designed the first informal reading inventory 60 years ago (Betts, 1946), most reading instruction in the United States used basal textbooks written at carefully controlled levels of difficulty. But after the 1980's, basal textbooks relaxed their emphasis on controlled reading levels (Hiebert, 2002; Hiebert and Fisher, 2004; Hoffman, et. al., 1994), and basal readers are no longer promising sources of passages for informal reading inventories.

In preparing the *Developmental Literacy Inventory,* the authors rewrote science and social studies passages from textbooks in those subjects provided by Scott Foresman publishers. The narrative passages were all written expressly for the *Developmental Literacy Inventory* by a published children's author, and patterned after literature that is typically read at their respective grade levels.

The text passages in all informal reading inventories are tested with readability formulas to estimate their difficulty and assign them to grade levels. Several readability formulas have been developed over the years for the English language, but most of them have surprisingly limited accuracy beyond a few grade levels. One system that does reliably measure the difficulty of texts written at levels from grade one through the adult level is the Lexile system, developed by MetaMetrics, Inc. Every text passage used in the *Developmental Literacy Inventory* from grade one through high school was tested by the technicians at Meta-Metrics, Inc. and was assigned a Lexile score. The Lexile scores are excellent indicators of the reading level of each passage.

We note with affection and gratitude the many old and new friends who helped us bring the *Developmental Literacy Inventory* into being. The late Edmund Henderson at the University of Virginia was and still is a bedrock inspiration, and classmates from Virginia's McGuffey Reading Center have kept up a lively conversation about literacy over the last 30 years: Darrell Morris, Shane Templeton, Elizabeth Sulzby, Bill Teale, Tom Gill, Jeannie Steele, Marcia Invernizzi, Richard Gentry, Donald Bear, Jane Cooke—what a crew! Darrell Morris generously allowed us to borrow from his insights about early literacy assessment. Hallie Kay Yopp offered her test of phonemic segmentation to all of us. Dr. Jane Cooke supervised field-testing drafts of the instrument in the Greenwich, Connecticut Public Schools. Chrystne Wood helped assemble the word lists and assisted with the logistics of field testing while at Hobart and William Smith Colleges. Ana Balibanu tweaked the text passages with consummate skill. The teachers at West Street School and North Street School (both in Geneva, New York) field-tested the word lists. Special thanks to Joseph DeMeis and Nina McCarthy, their respective principals. We thank the staff of the Fluvanna County, Virginia, Public Schools for their help, and Professor Ron Cramer, of Oakland University, for early encouragement. Carolyn Pluchino of William Smith College helped out with final proofreading. Thanks also to Julie Crawford for field testing the *DEMTUP Names Test* and also many of the passages and accompanying questions. Lauren Kiehm Whitehead at MetaMetrics, Inc., shepherded our text passages through the Lexile process with enthusiasm and care. The authors are especially grateful to Kathy Smith for going far beyond the call of duty with her extensive editorial assistance and brilliant help with the formatting and to Deborah Schneck for her beautiful illustrations. Thanks is perennially due to Aurora Martínez for her enthusiastic support of our projects, *en dos idiomas.*

Thank you to our reviewers: Rhea A. Ashmore, University of Montana; Yvonne W. Bouknight, Glen Ridge Public Schools/Linden Ave School; Diana L. Carr, Elgin Junior High School; Candice T. Chandler, University of Texas-Dallas; Susan L. Hampton, Virginia Middle School; and Donna Schweitzer, Forwood Elementary School.

▶ ▶ ▶ About the *Developmental Literacy Inventory*

The *Developmental Literacy Inventory (DLI)* is a set of informal instruments that offer a detailed profile of the reading ability of students from kindergarten through middle school. The *Developmental Literacy Inventory* is administered to individual students, and will report the students' **reading levels**—independent, instructional, and frustration, and listening comprehension levels—in terms of both grade equivalents and Lexile scores. The *DLI* also assesses students' strengths and weaknesses in the most important aspects of literacy, including **word recognition**, **comprehension**, and **fluency**. It focuses on **emergent literacy concepts**, including **phonemic awareness**, and it tests **phonics knowledge** and **vocabulary**. It includes **oral and silent reading**, as well as reading in **different genres**.

At the core of the *Developmental Literacy Inventory* is an informal reading inventory with word lists and text passages arranged from late kindergarten through high school levels. Two sets of graded word lists are provided at each of these levels:

Pre-Primer [pronounced "pre-primmer"](late kindergarten)

Primer [pronounced "primmer"](early first grade)

Grade 1 (second half of first grade)

Grade 2.1 (first half of second grade)

Grade 2.2 (second half of second grade)

Grade 3

Grade 4

Grade 5

Grade 6

Middle School (grade 7.5)

High School (grade 10.5)

There are three levels of texts at the early first grade level. Six text passages are provided at each of the levels from grade 1 through grade 6, middle school, and high school. These are accompanied by assessment tasks and scoring frameworks that enable the teacher to assess students' oral and silent reading rates, their oral reading accuracy, and their reading comprehension and listening comprehension (including recall, making inferences, and knowledge of vocabulary).

The *Developmental Literacy Inventory* also includes assessments for the main aspects of **emergent literacy.** The *DLI* offers two different assessments of emergent literacy: first, a sampling of core components of students' preparation for beginning reading instruction that includes **alphabet knowledge,** the **concept of word, phonological awareness,** and **early word recognition** (including environmental print and decodable words), and second, a lower level observation of children's **print concepts.**

In addition, there is a separate instrument that further explores students' **phonics knowledge.**

When all of these factors are considered in relation to each other, the *DLI* provides a detailed profile of each student's strengths and needs. This profile provides a **diagnostic assessment** that can guide teachers in designing an instructional plan for each student, including those who are at risk of failure at the early stages of reading, those who have fallen behind expectations, and those who need more advanced instruction than their classmates.

The *DLI* can also be used for **screening assessment.** Instructions are given for a sampling of measures that will yield sufficient data to make an informed decision on a child's initial placement for instruction—early intervention? remedial instruction? placement in an advanced reading group?—but the sampling of measures from the *DLI* can be administered relatively quickly when many children must be screened.

The *DLI* can also be used for **monitoring assessment.** Along with the two sets of word lists at each level, six reading passages are provided at most reading levels. Instructions are given for taking a few key measures of a student's reading performance and comparing them across time to observe that child's progress in learning to read.

▶ Why Should You Administer the *Developmental Literacy Inventory*?

Informal reading inventories such as the *Developmental Literacy Inventory* show us two kinds of information.

1. They show us in great detail how an individual student reads. These informal assessments may be the most comprehensive devices available to indicate the levels of a student's reading, as well as the strengths and weaknesses of the most important aspects of the student's reading ability. Thus, classroom teachers may use the *Developmental Literacy Inventory* to place students in appropriate reading materials. Classroom teachers, special educators, and school psychologists also may use the *Developmental Literacy Inventory* to gain the information they need to provide fine-tuned instruction to a student who requires remedial instruction, or enrichment to one who is reading above grade level.

2. They show us how the reading process works. Administering a good diagnostic instrument such as *the Developmental Literacy Inventory* provides a window into the reading process, showing us how word recognition, comprehension, fluency, vocabulary, and other factors interact to produce competent reading. Students in reading courses need such a view, whether they are undergraduate or graduate students. Classroom teachers, too, may administer the *Developmental Literacy Inventory* in order to better understand the reading process, or aspects of it. For example, when the *DLI* authors work with teachers in overcrowded classrooms in developing countries, we recommend that the teachers administer elements similar to the *DLI* (in the local language, of course) to a small number of students, so that they will see, by extension, the needs that all of their students have, and think about the best ways to teach the whole class.

▶ ▶ ▶ Before You Begin . . .

T he following pages contain important information about assessing readers with the *DLI*. This section will tell you what you need to know to get started. At the end of this book are instructions on interpreting results and using the information in teaching.

> ### Suggestion for the Examiner
>
> You will want to know your way around the *DLI* before you administer the assessments to a student. Take a few minutes now and browse through the testing instrument beginning on page 42. Note that the instrument begins with two levels of assessments for early literacy, and these include both testing procedures and recording sheets. The *DLI* next contains an informal reading inventory, which consists of word lists and text passages. These are presented in two versions: the first for students and the second for the examiner. The text passages contain complete sets of narrative, social studies, and science texts. The word lists and the text passages come in two versions (called Form A and Form B—they are meant for pre-testing and post-testing). The last part of the test is the *Demtup Names Test* (yes, that's what it's called!), a device for assessing students' ability to decode new and unknown words. The last section of the *DLI* shows how to interpret the results of the test.

▶ Why Are You Testing This Student?

Many teachers use assessments of literacy for four purposes: screening, diagnosing, monitoring, and assessing the achievement of learning outcomes.

- **Screening assessment** is used to determine the level of instruction each student needs.
- **Diagnostic assessment** is used to identify each student's strengths and needs, so instruction can be planned with the right emphases.
- **Monitoring assessment** is done periodically through the year, to ensure that a course of instruction is effective and to make adjustments if it needs to be improved.
- **Measuring achievement of learning outcomes** is done toward the end of a year to determine if grade level expectations for learning have been met.

The *Developmental Literacy Inventory* can be used for all of these purposes. Since most states and school districts employ their own year-end tests to assess the achievement of outcomes, however, the *DLI* is most likely to be used for the first three purposes. Let's look now at ways of using the test for each purpose.

▶ Using the *DLI* for Screening Assessment

When teachers use assessments to screen students, they use the information to place each student in appropriate instruction. For example, many first graders are identified early in the school year for Reading Recovery© tutoring, or for some other kind of early intervention help in reading. Because teachers often need to screen many students in a short amount of time, screening assessments must be done as quickly and as accurately as possible. Thus, screening assessment usually focuses on a few telling variables. Later, more detailed assessments can provide the information needed to plan specific instruction for the student.

To use the *Developmental Literacy Inventory* for screening assessment, we recommend that the following instruments be used.

IN LATE KINDERGARTEN, AND THE FIRST HALF OF FIRST GRADE

Begin with the first group of emergent literacy assessments. This section tests **alphabet knowledge**, **concept of word**, **phoneme segmentation**, and **early sight word recognition**.

WHAT TO LOOK FOR. As a rule of thumb, the children who score in the bottom 20% to 25% of the class on an average of the first group of emergent literacy assessments should be considered for special reading services, such as one-on-one tutoring by a reading teacher or a trained and supervised tutor. (See Darrell Morris's *Howard Street Tutoring Manual* [Morris, 2000], or Marcia Invernizzi and Connie Juel's *Book Buddies* program [Invernizzi and Juel, 1999]) for more information.)

If a child scores below 50% on an average of the measures in the first group, you are advised to administer the second group of emergent literacy measures: the concepts about print assessments. These assessments are aimed at a less advanced emergent reader than the first group. These measures will show if students understand the nature and layout of print. Children who score below 50% on these measures need much holistic exposure to written language and to the acts of reading and writing.

IN MID-TO-LATE FIRST GRADE

When children have been in first grade half a year or more, you may begin assessing with the Pre-Primer section of the *DLI*. The first step is the word list on page 60. If the child makes ten or more reading errors, make a note of the child's score, stop testing on this part of the *DLI*, and assess on the emergent literacy measures instead, beginning with the first group of measures.

If the child reads ten or more words correctly, continue administering word lists until the child misses two or more words. Administer the text passage that corresponds to the grade level where the child first read two words incorrectly. Continue administering text passages until the child scores at the frustration level, according to the scoring guidelines included on the teacher's version of that passage (see Box 1.1).

Box 1.1: Three Reading Levels

The *Developmental Literacy Inventory* will reveal not one reading level for a student, but three: the **independent level**, the **instructional level**, and the **frustration level**.

The Independent Reading Level

If the student is to read material on her own, without the support of a teacher or other more skilled readers, then the material should fall within the student's *independent level* of reading ability. Material written at the student's independent level will be such that the student encounters no more than three of four unknown words in a hundred, and enjoys nearly total comprehension.

Books that should fall within the student's independent level include those that are chosen for pleasure reading, or textbooks that are read independently for homework. Regardless of the student's grade placement, if the books are written *above* his or her independent level, then the student should be provided with support for reading, such as buddy reading, study guides, or tape-recorded text.

The *Developmental Literacy Inventory* will show the level or levels of text that a student can read at his or her independent level. Especially for students beyond the first two grades, the independent reading level may span more than one grade. For example, normally developing sixth graders are able to read independently any books written at levels up to the fifth or sometimes the sixth grade. In that case, teachers periodically have to prod students to read more challenging material that falls toward the upper end of the range of students' independent levels. On the other hand, younger or less developed readers may find only one grade level of text, or none at all, that they can read independently.

The Instructional Reading Level

In the classroom, teachers often work with students in text that is moderately challenging for them, so they will learn from supported practice reading the text. Text used for this purpose should fall within the student's *instructional level* of reading ability. This text presents the student with unknown words at a rate of up to one in ten, and language and concepts that are not fully comprehended—at least not at first. The intention is that with guided practice in materials written at the instructional level, students will learn the unknown words and come

(continues)

to comprehend the once-challenging language and concepts. The instructional level corresponds to psychologist Lev Vygotsky's concept of the *zone of proximal development* (Vygotsky, 1976), the area of moderate challenge that is just at the threshold of a reader's growing abilities. It is here that teachers most often practice *scaffolded instruction*, providing temporary support, including the teaching of strategies, that will help the student learn on her own in the future.

A particular student's instructional level often falls above or below that student's grade placement level. Because of the value of working in moderately challenging materials when teaching a student to read, it is very important to locate a student's instructional level, wherever it may fall. The *Developmental Literacy Inventory* will show the level or levels of text that a student can read at his instructional level. Note that for a more developed reader, the instructional level may span more than one grade level. By definition, the instructional level occupies the range between the independent reading level and the frustration reading level, which is described below.

The Frustration Level

If the material is too challenging—that is, if it contains more than one unfamiliar word in ten, as well as language and concepts that substantially resist a particular reader's comprehension—it is said to be written at the student's *frustration level*. The *Developmental Literacy Inventory* will reveal a student's frustration level, which means that it will show the upper limit of that student's instructional level. The frustration level is not actually a reading level because students do not practice successful reading there. Teachers may assign reading material during closely supervised instructional tasks that approach, but do not cross into, the frustration level.

As the name implies, frustration level text is so demanding for a student that the challenge of reading it is burdensome and disagreeable. Even before testing, teachers often recognize that students are trying to read text at their frustration level when they observe finger pointing, squinting, body movements (such as rocking in the seat, swinging the foot), wrinkling the brow, and struggling with the text in oral reading tasks (Gillet, Temple, & Crawford, 2008; Temple, Ogle, Crawford, & Freppon, 2008; Gipe, 2006).

Emergent Readers

If a child turns out not to have a reading level yet—that is, she recognizes few words on the earliest reading list and struggles to read the lowest level reading passage—we turn to the emergent literacy assessments of the *Developmental Literacy Inventory*. Even when children cannot yet read many words or lines of text without support, there are still other things these emergent readers may or may not know about reading. These include concepts about print—knowing that it is print that "talks" and not pictures, being able to follow the direction of the print on the page, and knowing what words and letters are. They also include the awareness of sound units in words and knowledge of the letters of the alphabet.

The emergent literacy assessments in the *Developmental Literacy Inventory* can be used to screen young readers and identify those who will need special help. They also can yield diagnostic information that can guide instruction for emergent readers.

WHAT TO LOOK FOR. You should have established the top and bottom ranges of the child's reading ability: If you find an **independent level**, you will know the level of books the child can read easily. The **frustration level** will show you the outer limits of the level of books the child can read with much support. In between lies the **instructional level.** If the child does not have even an instructional reading level, she or he will need to develop more emergent literacy concepts.

WITH STUDENTS BEYOND FIRST GRADE

After first grade, the general rule is to begin testing the child a year below grade placement. Thus, you begin testing a second grader at the first grade level, a third grader at level 2.1, a fourth grader at level 3, a fifth grader at level 4, and so on. Begin testing a first grader at the Pre-Primer level.

Begin by administering the word lists. Since reading word lists is faster for a student than reading and answering questions about text passages, your goal is to use the word lists to find the appropriate text passage to use to test the student.

If the child misses three or more words on the word list, drop back to an easier list, and keep dropping back until the child makes no more than two errors. However, if the child reads all of the words on the first list correctly, administer higher level lists until the child reads more than six words incorrectly. As before, administer the text passage that corresponds to the grade level where the child read two words or fewer incorrectly, and continue administering text passages until the child scores at the frustration level according to the scoring guidelines found on the teacher's version of the passages.

WHAT TO LOOK FOR. Since you are doing a screening assessment, you are probably interested only in establishing the student's reading levels at this point. These procedures will establish the student's independent, instructional, and frustration levels. Knowing these levels will enable you to place the child for instruction with students at similar levels. You may also find a group of books that the child can read independently and another group of books that can be used with the child for face-to-face instruction.

MATCHING STUDENTS WITH BOOKS

Once a student's reading levels are known, this information can be used to match him with some books he can read at his instructional level during reading lessons and others that he can read independently. In the *Developmental Literacy Inventory*, reading levels are reported two ways: as grade equivalents and as Lexiles. Grade equivalent scores can be used to match students to books, usually without much difficulty. Trade books for young readers often report their reading levels ("RL") as grade equivalent scores. For example, Kate McMullen's *As Far as I Can See*, from Scholastic's *My America* series, is identified as "RL3" in small characters on the back cover, which means that a child who is an independent reader at grade 3 could read the book with nearly complete understanding.

Because the passages in the *DLI* have been leveled according to the Lexile framework, it is also possible to match students to books using Lexile scores.[1] Assume, for example, that the *DLI* shows a child's independent reading level at grade 2.2 (second half of second grade), and her instructional level at grade 3. The passages in the *DLI* at grade 2.2 have Lexile scores of around 450, and the passages at grade 3 have Lexile scores of around 600. So you may assume that this child could read independently in books written at around Lexile 450, or from about 400 to 500. She should be able to read books written at around Lexile 600, or from about 500 to 700, with support from the teacher—that is, at her instructional level. Note that these levels are approximate. A particular child's age, interests, and background knowledge may make any book easier or harder to read than the Lexile score would predict.

The developers of Lexiles, MetaMetrics, Inc., maintain a large database of books ranked according to their Lexiles. On the Lexile web site (http://www.lexile.com), you may go to the educator's page and enter the Lexile Book Database and find the Lexile scores of tens of thousands of books from first grade through high school level. You may search the database for books by title, author, or keyword.

There are other systems of assigning reading levels to texts besides grade level equivalents and Lexiles. Irene Fountas and Gay Su Pinnell's system of leveling books for guided reading is one popular system. Reading Recovery© is another, and DRA or Developmental Reading Assessment is still another. Individual publishers such as the Wright Group have their own proprietary systems. All of these book leveling systems make very fine gradations in reading levels in the earliest grades, usually through grade 2. You can use the correlation chart in Table 1 on page 418 in the Appendix to make approximate matches between the independent, instructional, and frustration reading levels obtained from the *Developmental Literacy Inventory* and these other book leveling systems.

---

[1] MetaMetrics, Inc., the developers of the Lexile framework, have certified the Lexile levels of the passages in the *Developmental Literacy Inventory*, grades 1 through high school. MetaMetrics did not review the questions or the testing procedures employed in the *Developmental Literacy Inventory*. The suggestion that a student's observed and evaluated performance in reading any of the passages in the *DLI* predicts the level of challenge that student will encounter when reading another text written at a particular Lexile level is solely that of the authors of the *Developmental Literacy Inventory*. Information about the Lexile system can be found at www.lexile.com.

Using the *DLI* for Diagnostic Assessment

Diagnostic assessment is done when a teacher wants to know what a student can and cannot do as a reader, in order to prepare a plan of instruction. Diagnosis reaches greater breadth and depth than screening assessment, and it takes more time. We recommend that every child in the first through the third grade be given a diagnostic assessment within the first weeks of school, and that any students in grades above the third who are manifesting signs of reading difficulty be given diagnostic assessment as well. These signs may include:

- slow and labored oral reading
- homework not completed
- poor participation in class work
- poor grades
- limited comprehension

IN LATE KINDERGARTEN, AND THE FIRST HALF OF FIRST GRADE

Students in late kindergarten and early first grade are usually in the **emergent stage of reading.** Most of them have some measurable set of concepts about the purposes of reading and the nature of print, along with some awareness of language at the word, syllable, and perhaps even the phoneme level. But, except for the precocious children who have already begun to read, most children this age have not quite "put it all together" to read connected text without a great deal of support. The assessments of emergent literacy on the *DLI* are done in two phases, the first for more advanced emergent readers and the second for those who are less advanced.

WHAT TO LOOK FOR. Diagnostic assessment of early readers focuses on several key elements of emergent literacy. The first group of assessments examines children's **knowledge of the alphabet,** naming alphabet letters, recognizing upper and lower case letters, and being able to write alphabet letters. This part of the assessment was adapted with permission from Professor Darrell Morris's *Early Reading Screening Inventory* (Morris, 2005). It also tests the **concept of word:** that is, whether or not children have enough metalinguistic awareness, or consciousness of language, to recognize that spoken language is produced in units of words, and that printed language represents words as clusters of letters bounded by spaces. It tests another form of metalingusitic awareness, as well: the ability to segment spoken words into phonemes, the smallest sound units of speech. **Phonemic segmentation** is a kind of phonological awareness, considered a prerequisite for children to learn phonics, the relations between letters and sounds. The first level of emergent literacy assessment concludes with a short test of children's **early word recognition**. Students are first asked to identify a set of familiar words that are considered **environmental print**—examples of words children often see around them. The second set contains **decodable words** that have common letter-to-sound relationships. That concludes the first level of emergent literacy assessment.

For children who find the first level of emergent literacy assessments very challenging (that is, they score below 50% on an average of all of the measures), the second level emergent literacy inventory should be used. The second level of emergent literacy assessment was modeled on the late Professor Marie Clay's *Concepts About Print Test* (Clay, 2000). This level tests the child's awareness of the most fundamental aspects of written language, including the fact that readers read print and not pictures, the arrangement of print on the page, the relations between upper and lower case versions of the same letters, and the purpose of punctuation.

If children score above 60% on the first level emergent literacy assessment, assessing the second level of the *DLI* is optional. It is fairly safe to assume that an adequate score on the first set of measures indicates that the children have had enough exposure to print to enable them to score well on the print concepts measure.

IN EARLY TO MID-FIRST GRADE

Students at the early to mid-first grade level are advancing through the Primer level and on to the first grade level passages (although some will be more advanced, and some less). Students in mid- to late first grade should be tested first on the Pre-Primer level, beginning with the word lists. Depending on how they respond, they should either advance to higher word lists and on to the appropriate text passage, or they should go back to the emergent literacy assessments. (Instructions follow in the next section.)

WHAT TO LOOK FOR. When you test the children with the Pre-Primer and Primer word lists, you are observing to see how many words they recognize "at sight" (or instantly), and how many more words they recognize when they are allowed to study and decode them. The difference between the two measures is an indication of their phonics knowledge.

When the students read the Pre-Primer and Primer levels of text with your support, you can observe them orchestrating some aspects of reading: word recognition, using the pictures to establish the context of the passage and self-correcting miscued words to make sense within that context, and showing some perseverance in the face of a difficult task.

LATE FIRST GRADE AND UP

From late first grade and up, the sequence of steps in doing a diagnostic assessment remain essentially the same. Begin testing with the word lists, and establish the independent, instructional, and frustration levels of word recognition. Take separate measures of flashed and untimed word recognition. Then, proceed to the text passages and assess the student's reading rate, oral reading accuracy (or word recognition in context), reading comprehension (including recall, making inferences, and vocabulary), and listening comprehension.

WHAT TO LOOK FOR. The information revealed by all of these measures gives a fairly thorough profile of a student's reading abilities, showing both areas of strength and areas of need.

- From the three **word recognition measures** (flashed, untimed, and in context), you can determine if the student has a well-developed sight vocabulary, is able to use phonics to decode unknown words, and is able to use context to improve word recognition.
- From timing the student's oral and silent reading, you can determine reading rates.
- From asking comprehension questions and scoring responses to them, you can measure the student's understanding of main important ideas, ability to make inferences, and knowledge of vocabulary.
- From comparing reading fluency and comprehension in different kinds of passages, you can assess the student's ability to adjust her reading to the demands of different genres.
- From asking the student different questions after he has read a text passage, you can assess his comprehension.
- From reading aloud the passages to the student and asking the questions orally, you can compare the student's listening comprehension and reading comprehension.
- From reading passages written in different genres at the same level, you can get a window into how the student handles these different text types.

Using a combination of indicators—word recognition in isolation, word recognition in context, comprehension, and listening comprehension—can help you determine a student's reading levels. When the indicators are in agreement, assignments to reading texts at various levels can be made with a fair amount of confidence. When they are out of agreement, as they often are, more judgment is called for on the part of the examiner. For example, if a student scores higher on comprehension than on word recognition and higher still on listening comprehension, the examiner can provisionally conclude that the student can be placed for instruction in material that matches her comprehension scores, provided she is given a lot of support in word recognition. When she is provided with material to read independently, however, that material would normally be chosen closer to the word recognition score, because reading independently when word recognition is laborious depresses student motivation.

The different ways the *Developmental Literacy Inventory* indicates reading levels and the scores that are used to determine them are summarized in Table 2 on page 419 in the Appendix.

These criteria are taken from Betts (1946) and have been widely accepted for over sixty years.

Note that when administering the *Developmental Literacy Inventory*, it is not necessary to calculate these percentages, as a scoring chart is provided for each word list and text passage.

▶ Using the *DLI* for Monitoring Assessment

Once teachers have begun a course of instruction for groups of students and individual students, they need to make sure that the instruction is working. For this reason, teachers use **monitoring assessment**—periodic checks to see how well their students are progressing in key areas of literacy. Like the screening assessments, monitoring assessments are meant to be completed in limited amounts of time, so they usually measure only a sampling of literacy behaviors. Our recommendation is that you use one measure from the *DLI* that can be given repeatedly across the year. Because there is a significant correlation between reading fluency and comprehension (Deno, et al., 2001), **reading fluency** (measured as reading rate and accuracy of word reading) is often used as an all-around indicator for monitoring students' progress as readers. That may be because, as Charles Perfetti (1985) asserted over twenty years ago, the more efficiently readers process print, the more mental concentration they have available to them for getting the meaning of what they read.

MONITORING READING FLUENCY

Reading fluency is most simply measured by counting the number of words children read per minute, minus the errors. This yields a measure called **Words Correctly read Per Minute (WCPM)**, which is calculated using this formula:

$$\frac{(\text{Total words read, minus words read incorrectly}) \times 60}{\text{Reading time in seconds}} = \text{WCPM}$$

Thus, for example, if a third grade student reads 125 words in one minute, but makes five reading errors, we would calculate her fluency rate of Words Correctly read Per Minute:

$$\frac{(125 - 5) \times 60}{60} = \frac{120 \times 60}{60} = 120 \text{ WCPM.}$$

Normally, reading fluency is monitored six times per year, or every six weeks.

Typical reading rates for students reading grade level material look like those in Figure 1.1 on page 15.

These scores, and scores for other grades, have been built into the scoring rubrics included in the examiner's version of each text passage in the *DLI*.

FIGURE 1.1 Reading Rates, Grades 2–5

Grade	Percentile	Fall WCPM	Winter WCPM	Spring WCPM
2	75	82	106	124
	50	53	78	94
	25	23	46	65
3	75	107	123	142
	50	79	93	114
	25	65	70	87
4	75	125	133	143
	50	99	112	118
	25	72	89	92
5	75	126	143	151
	50	105	118	128
	25	77	93	100

(50th percentile for upper grades: 125–150 WCPM)

Source: From *Curriculum-Based Oral Reading Fluency Norms for Students in Grades 2 Through 5*, by J. Hasbrouck and G. Tindal, 1992, *Teaching Exceptional Children, 24*, p. 42. Copyright 1992 by The Council for Exceptional Children. Reprinted with permission.

To monitor a student's progress during the year, it is suggested that you first administer the entire *DLI* as described for diagnostic purposes. After an interval (usually six weeks), test the student again for reading fluency (WCPM) on the same passage at which she or he scored at the instructional level. Once the student has reached the grade level average as indicated on the rubric contained on the examiner's version of the text passage, you can move to the next highest level of text passage and test again until the student reaches the fluency score that is average for that for level. If possible, you should test the student with the same genre of passage—staying consistently with narrative, social studies, or science passages.

MONITORING OTHER ASPECTS OF READING

Teachers may have reasons to monitor other aspects of reading besides fluency. Any aspect of reading on which a student shows weakness can be tracked through the year. For example, to test a student's progress in word recognition, word lists can be used; and, assuming the student will make some progress up through the levels of word lists, she may be tested every six weeks during the year and peak at the instructional and frustration levels in a different list.

▶ Using the *DLI* for Assessment of Outcomes

Toward the end of the school year, many schools mandate testing to ensure that students have met grade level expectations for a year's instruction in literacy. Under the federal *No Child Left Behind* legislation, states have been required to develop group-administered tests that are given to every child in each grade across the entire state. In these circumstances, teachers normally will not use the *Developmental Literacy Inventory* for the end-of-year assessment of outcomes. However, teachers are still advised to study the state-mandated tests carefully, and to decide which measures on the *Developmental Literacy Inventory* correspond with the state-mandated tests. Those measures should be included in the ones chosen for the monitoring assessments so that teachers will ensure that students are making progress in the aspects of literacy for which they will be held accountable later in the year.

▶ ▶ ▶ Administering the *Developmental Literacy Inventory*

In this section, we explain how to administer the *Developmental Literacy Inventory*. You can use the *DLI* to determine a student's reading level and measure the student's progress in learning to read. You can also use the instrument to examine a student's strengths and weaknesses in reading.

▶ Getting Ready to Test

FIND A QUIET PLACE AND PLAN FOR THE TIME NEEDED

Testing for the purpose of determining a student's reading levels, reading rate, and main areas of strength and weakness can take thirty to forty minutes. Older students' reading levels are spread across more grade levels, and they will take proportionately longer to test. If the *Demtup Word Knowledge Inventory* is administered, it will take an additional fifteen minutes. It is best to conduct this test in a separate sitting, so as not to tire the student.

ARRANGE THE SPACE AND ASSEMBLE THE MATERIALS

Before you begin, assemble all of the materials you will need:

- the student section of the *DLI*
- a photocopy of the examiner's pages for recording the student's responses
- two index cards
- blank paper and pencils
- a watch with a second hand
- a tape recorder (optional)

REASSURE THE STUDENT

Before beginning, tell the student that you want to know how she or he reads and writes. (Avoid using the word "test.") There will be no grade. It is important for the student to do her or his best, although there will be some activities she or he will not be sure about.

SIT BESIDE THE STUDENT

If you are right-handed, place the student to your left, with your materials for recording placed off to the right and out of the student's view. If you are left-handed, do the reverse.

▶ Where to Begin Testing

IF THE STUDENT IS IN LATE KINDERGARTEN, OR THE FIRST HALF OF FIRST GRADE

It is likely that you will be assessing this child's emergent literacy. Some children may already have begun reading text at this age, so you have to be flexible in your approach. It is best to begin testing with the Emergent Literacy Assessments, Part I. If the student scores below 50% on the total of the assessments, proceed to the Emergent Literacy Assessments, Part II. If the child scores above 50% on the total of all the assessments, proceed to the Pre-Primer Assessments.

IF THE STUDENT IS IN THE SECOND HALF OF FIRST GRADE

Bear in mind that some children will have begun reading very simple text, supported with pictures, a few might be able to read text with several lines on a page, and some will be unable to do either. Again, you will want to be prepared for whatever reading ability the child brings to the task. It is best to begin testing with the Pre-Primer word list. It's found on page 60. Keep testing the child on harder word lists as long as she can read the words successfully—that is, until the child makes six or more word reading errors on a single list. Then, look back over her scores on the word lists.

- If the child reads any list with two errors or fewer, go to the reading passage that corresponds to the grade level of that list. Test the child on that passage, according to the instructions given on pages 25–28 (for the child who placed on the Pre-Primer or Primer level) or on pages 28–29 (for the child who placed at the level of grade 1 or higher).
- If the child reads ten or more words incorrectly on the Pre-Primer word list, test the child on the Emergent Literacy Assessments, Part I. Continue to Emergent Literacy Assessments, Part II, if the child scores below 50% on an average of the assessments.

IF THE STUDENT IS IN SECOND GRADE OR HIGHER

You can assume that this student will have progressed beyond the emergent level, although a few may not have. Start by testing with the word lists, and, as a rule of thumb, begin with the list that is one year below the student's grade placement. For a second grader, that would be the list for grade 1, for a third grader, the list for 2.1; for a fourth grader, the list for grade 3, and so on.

Remember your objective! If you are assessing for screening purposes, you merely want to use the word lists to find the appropriate level of text passage to administer—so you will be looking for the highest level list the child can read at the independent level (that is, with two errors or fewer). On the other hand, if you are testing for diagnostic purposes, you will want to test with both harder and easier word lists until you have established the student's independent, instructional, and frustration reading levels (see the "Suggestions for the Examiner" box).

Follow the testing of the word lists with the reading passages, as explained in the following sections.

▶ Emergent Literacy Assessment

When a child cannot yet read many words or understand written texts, there are still questions to be answered about his or her **emergent literacy**. In the *Developmental Literacy Inventory*, two groups of emergent literacy assessments are provided. The first group, called Emergent Literacy I, tests literacy knowledge that is immediately necessary to be successful in reading instruction. The second group, called Emergent Literacy II, is used for children who are less developed as emergent readers. It tests concepts about print.

EMERGENT LITERACY I: CORE LITERACY KNOWLEDGE

The assessment of core literacy knowledge focuses on alphabet knowledge, the concept of word, phonemic segmentation, and word recognition.

To administer Emergent Literacy I: Core Literacy Knowledge, you will need a **student form** and an **examiner's form**. Be sure to duplicate in advance a copy of the examiner's form for each student you will be testing.

ALPHABET INVENTORY. The alphabet inventory (after Morris, 1998) tests students' **recognition** of letters of the alphabet, both upper and lower case. It also tests their **production** of letters, without regard to their case. To assess a student's knowledge of the alphabet, you will need a student's form of the Alphabet Inventory, a blank sheet of paper and a pencil for the student to use in writing the letters, and a copy of the examiner's form.

1. *Ask the student to identify the letters of the alphabet.* Put the student's version of the alphabet inventory in front of the student and use the examiner's version for recording responses. Point to each letter and ask the student to name it. Record the answer on the examiner's version. Circle any letters the student cannot identify, and write in what the student says when he or she misidentifies any letter. Test the student on both the lower case and the upper case letters.
2. *Ask the student to write the letters as you call them out.* Call out the letters of the alphabet and ask the student to write them in order, next to the letters on the response sheet. (The numbers will help you identify which letters the student was writing, later, when you score the inventory.) Accept correctly written letters whether the student writes them in upper case or lower case.

THE CONCEPT OF WORD. The concept of word is an important means by which students make accurate matches between speech and print. To assess a student's concept of word, follow this procedure designed by Morris (1998).

Teach the student to memorize the poem "My Little Dog Petunia" orally, *without showing her the written version.* You may point to the pictures in the sheet on page 42 to support the student's memorizing.

Once the student can say the words from memory, show him or her the written poem, and explain that those written words say the poem just learned.

Now, read through the poem yourself at a slow, natural rate, pointing to each word with your finger as you read it. Then, explain that you want the student to read the poem the way you did, but one line at a time.

Ask the student to say or read the first line, pointing to each word as she says it. Enter a score of "1" under Voice-pointing on the Examiner's Form if she points to every word in that line correctly, and a score of "0" if she incorrectly points to any word in that line. Next, ask the student to point to the word "little." Enter a score of "1" under Word Identification on the Examiner's Form if she points to it and "0" if she does not. Now ask her to point to the word "Petunia." Enter a score of "1" under Word Identification if she points to it and "0" if she does not.

Now, go to the second line and repeat the process, testing first the student's voice pointing and then the student's word identification. Award 1 point if the student points to every word in the line just as she says it, and a 0 if the student makes any errors. Then, ask her to point to "very," and then to "strange." Award 1 point for each word the student correctly points to, and 0 for each error. Repeat these instructions for lines three and four.

ASSESSMENT OF PHONEME SEGMENTATION: THE *YOPP-SINGER TEST*. You can test the student's ability to segment words into their constituent sounds, called **phonemes**, by using the Yopp-Singer Test of Phoneme Segmentation. You will need only the Examiner's version of the assessment (page 48), since the test is read aloud to students and they respond orally.

The originator of this test, Hallie Kay Yopp,* offers the following instructions:

> Begin by saying "Today we're going to play a word game. I'm going to say a word and I want you to break the word apart. You are going to tell me each sound in the word in order. For example, if I say 'old,' you should say 'o' 'ul' 'duh.' Let's try a few together."
>
> For the practice round, say these words one at a time: *ride, go, man.* Ask the student to say each word, pronouncing each sound, the way you said "old" as "o" "ul" "duh." If she doesn't segment a word correctly, say, "Listen to me as I do it, and watch my mouth." Segment the word properly, and ask the student to segment it again.
>
> Now, go on to the test. Say each word slowly and ask the student to repeat the word, saying each sound separately. On your answer sheet, circle the words that the student segments correctly. Incorrect responses may be recorded on the blank line following the item. Note that some words have more letters than sounds. The number of sounds is written in parentheses to the right of each word. . . .
>
> Feedback is given to the student as he or she progresses through the list. If the student responds correctly, the examiner nods, or says, "That's right." If the student gives an incorrect response, he or she is corrected. The examiner provides the appropriate response.
>
> A student's score is the number of items correctly segmented into all constituent phonemes. No partial credit is given. For the response /c/-/at/ instead of /c/-/a/-/t/, the response may be noted on the blank line following the item, but is considered incorrect for purposes of scoring. Correct responses are only those that involve articulation of each

*The author, Hallie Kay Yopp, California State University, Fullerton, grants permission for this test to be reproduced. The author acknowledges the contribution of the late Harry Singer to the development of this test.

phoneme in the target word. Blends, like *bl* should have two sounds /b/-/l/, whereas diagraphs, like *sh* and *th* only have one sound each.

Teachers of young children should expect a wide range of performance on this test. Students who obtain high scores may be considered phonemically aware. Students who correctly segment some items are displaying emerging phonemic awareness. Students who are able to segment only a few items or none at all lack appropriate levels of phonemic awareness.

WORD RECOGNITION. Emergent readers can often recognize a few words. The assessment of word identification (after Morris, 1998) tests both high frequency words and decodable words.

Show the student the list of words on page 44 and ask him to identify them. Mark the student's responses on the Assessment of Word Identification Response Sheet on page 49. Award the student 1 point for each correctly identified word.

EMERGENT LITERACY II: PRINT CONCEPTS

Young would-be readers need orienting concepts about print so that they can focus their attention properly during acts of reading, including classroom instruction. The Print Concepts Assessment (after Marie Clay, 1975) reveals whether a young reader knows the units, layout, and terminology of print. This measure can be administered to children who are not yet reading.

MATERIALS NEEDED. You will need a simple book to read with the student as you ask him or her to do a series of tasks. A booklet developed for this purpose is provided for you (see pages 52–55), but you may use a children's book of your own, as long as it has these features:

- a double-page spread with print on one page and a picture on the other page
- a page with two or more lines of print
- a page with a single line of print
- a page that has both upper case and lower case versions of two different letters
- a page that has several punctuation marks, including periods, a question mark, an exclamation point, and quotation marks

You will also need two index cards. A master copy of the Assessment of Print Concepts Response Sheet is provided for you (see page 58). You should make a photocopy of that response sheet for each student you will be testing.

Knowledge of the layout of books Hold the book out to the student, with the spine facing toward the student. Say, "We're going to read this book. Show me the front of the book." Award 1 point if the student holds the book so that the front is properly facing up. Then, read the title of the book.

Knowledge that the print, not the pictures, is what we read   Show the student a double spread with text on one page and a picture on the other. Say, "Show me where we read. Point to the spot where we begin reading." Award 1 point if the student points to the text and not to the picture. Then, read the text on that page.

Directional orientation of print on the page   Show the student a page with at least two lines of print. Say, "We're going to read this page. Show me where we begin reading. Point to the place where we begin. Show me where we go after that. Now, show me where we go after that." Award 1 point if the student points to the upper left-hand word, then sweeps across to the right, then goes the whole way back to the left and down one line, then across to the right. Then, read the text on that page.

Understanding of the term "word"   Turn to a page that has one line of print. First, take an index card in each hand and say, "Look. I can hold these cards so you can only see one or two words. Here. You try it." Hand the cards to the student. "Show me *one word*. Now, show me *two words*." Award 1 point if the student brackets one word and two words. Then, read the text on that page.

Understanding of the term "letter"   Next, take the index cards in each hand and say, "Look. I can hold these cards so you can only see one or two letters. Here. You try it." Hand the cards to the student. "Show me *one letter*. Now show me *two letters*." Award 1 point if the student brackets one letter and two letters. Then, read the text on that page.

Knowledge of punctuation   Find a page with a period on it. Say, "What is this? What are we supposed to do when we get to it?" Then, find quotation marks, a question mark, and an exclamation point. As you point to each one, say, "What is this? What does it tell us?" Award 1 point if the student correctly explains the purposes of *all three*. Then, read the text on that page.

▶ Assessment of Word Recognition, Comprehension, and Fluency

ASSESSING WORD RECOGNITION IN ISOLATION

The *Developmental Literacy Inventory* contains lists of twenty words, each calibrated to present a different level of challenge to a reader. The word lists can be administered in two ways. In the *flashed* condition, students are shown the words so quickly that they do not have time to study their parts and decode or sound out the words. The flashed condition is meant to show how many words at a particular grade level students recognize instantaneously. The students are also shown the words in an *untimed* presentation. The untimed presentation allows you to observe the students' ability to decode unknown words. Observing the students' performance on both the flashed and untimed presentations, and comparing those scores will give you useful insights into students' sight word recognition (the words students have stored in memory) and their decoding ability (their ability to recognize words by studying their parts). Here are the instructions for administering the word lists.

FLASH THE WORDS FIRST. THEN, SHOW THEM UNTIMED, AS NECESSARY. With the student's version of the word list in front of student, prepare to "flash" the words for the student. Our preferred way to do this is to use two index cards to mask each word so that it can be exposed very briefly—about a quarter of a second of exposure. First, cover the word with the edges of the two cards touching just above the word. Then, pull down the lower card to expose the word, and quickly pull down the upper card to mask it again. (See Figure 2 on page 425 in the Appendix.)

Suggestion for the Examiner

Before you test a student, it is important to practice "flashing" words until you can do it flawlessly. You will want to be sure that the student's reading errors were not caused by inexact presentations.

Before flashing the first word, show the student where the word will appear between the cards.

If the student correctly recognizes the word in the "flashed" condition, continue to the next word. Put a check mark in the space beside the target word in the "Flashed" column if the student reads it correctly.

If the student misses the word, write what the student says in the space by the word in the "Flashed" column on the Word Recognition Response Sheet. Then, take the cards away and ask the student to read the word again. If the student now identifies the word correctly, place a check mark in the space by the word in the "Untimed" column. If the student misses the word again in the untimed condition, write what the student says in the space by the word in the "Untimed" column. If the student says nothing, put a "0" in the "Untimed" column.

Now, flash the next word down in the column, and proceed as explained above. When you complete a list of words, enter the number of the student's errors in the space at the bottom of each Word Recognition Response Sheet. The chart at the bottom of the sheet will tell you if the number of errors indicates an independent, instructional, or frustration level.

Continue testing until the student misses seven or more words on a single word list. Note, though, that if a child misses the first eight or ten words on a list, you should stop testing with that list and drop back to a lower level list.

Remember your purpose for testing with the word lists. If you are **screening** the student, you can administer word lists only until you reach the highest level word list on which the student makes no more than two errors. That will be the level at which you will begin reading and testing the text passages. If you are doing **diagnostic testing**, you will want to keep testing the student on more difficult word lists until the point of frustration is reached—seven or more errors on a single list.

▶ Administering the Text Passages

The text passages yield the most important data in the *DLI*. They enable you to observe many different aspects of students' reading behavior, and in nearly authentic contexts. For the least mature readers, the *DLI* has Pre-Primer and Primer texts that resemble "little books" for emergent readers: short, highly patterned, with repeated words. For late first graders and up, the *DLI*'s narrative texts resemble literature read at each grade level, and the social studies and science passages are modeled after textbooks at those levels.

The assessment tasks that accompany each passage offer you a window into students' **reading fluency** (their reading rate and accuracy), their **word recognition in context**, their **comprehension**, their **vocabulary**, and their **listening comprehension**.

ADMINISTERING THE PRE-PRIMER AND PRIMER PASSAGES

If the student's score comes out as independent at the Pre-Primer level (that is to say, the student missed no more than two words on the Pre-Primer word list), proceed to the Pre-Primer passages and begin testing the student on them.

The Pre-Primer and Primer passages are intended for the earliest beginning readers, those who have some sight vocabulary as indicated by an instructional level score on the flashed administration of at least the Primer word list in the Word Recognition Inventory. Pre-Primer level text is typical of material read in the later months of kindergarten and the first weeks of first grade. Primer material is typical of the first semester of first grade. You will begin by administering the Pre-Primer A passage, followed by Pre-Primer B and C if the student's scores are at or above the instructional level.

To determine if the Pre-Primer or Primer passages are appropriate in difficulty for the student you are assessing, first administer the Primer level word list from the Word Recognition Inventory. If a student achieves a score of 70% or higher on the flashed administration of the list, she recognizes enough sight words to read the Pre-Primer and Primer passages. If a student achieves a flashed score of less than 70%, use the Emergent Literacy Inventory instead. This part of the *Developmental Literacy Inventory* is designed for use in assessing emergent readers who are not yet ready for the reading passages.

Before asking a student to read the Pre-Primer A passage, you will "walk through" the text with the student, preparing the way for the student to read the text successfully. This includes reading the title to the student and demonstrating how to point to each word while reading, looking at the illustration on each page, and having the student find and point to key words on each page.

INTRODUCING THE PASSAGE

Place the little book containing the passage, closed, in front of the student. Say, "Let's look at this book together before you read it to me. The title of this book is (*Title: for example, "What Is Red?"*). Watch what I do. (*Read the title aloud, pointing underneath each word as you say it.*) Now you read the title just like I did." (*Observe as the student says the words and points. Correct any pointing errors by saying, "Watch me again. Then you do just what I do."*)

Open the book to the first page. Do not read the page to the student. Point to the picture and say, "What do you see in this picture? That's right (*for example, apples*). Show me where it says *apples* on this page. (*Observe the child's attempt. Do not point out the word yourself.*) Repeat this procedure with each page, having the student name the key items in the illustration and point to one or more key words on each page (depending on how many words are on the page).

When you have walked through the book, return to the cover and say, "Now you read it to me. Start with the title. Point to each word as you read it." Follow along on the examiner's page for the passage as the student reads the little book. Write errors above the line of text, and write the number of errors occurring for each line under "Errors by Line." Use the Scoring Guide for Oral Reading at the bottom of the page to determine if the passage represents the student's independent, instructional, or frustration reading level.

If the Pre-Primer A passage represents the student's independent or instructional level, proceed to the Pre-Primer B passage. Repeat the procedure described above, looking at each picture with the student and having him or her find and point to a key word on each page prior to having the student read the text independently. If the student's score on Pre-Primer B is in the independent or instructional range, proceed to Pre-Primer C. If the student's score on Pre-Primer C is in the independent or instructional range, proceed to the Primer passage. If the student's score on the Primer passage is in the independent or instructional range, proceed to the first grade passage. Follow the directions for introducing the Primer and first grade passages that are found at the top of the corresponding examiner's page for the passage. At and beyond the Primer level passage, you will not be providing the structured support to the reader in the form of a preliminary walk-through that you provided with the pre-first grade passages. If at any point the student's score represents the frustration level, stop.

EXAMPLE WALK-THROUGH DIALOGS WITH A STUDENT READING PRE-PRIMER PASSAGES

Example 1: The Selected Passage is Pre-Primer A, "What Is Red?"

EXAMINER: The title of this book is "What Is Red?" Watch what I do. (*Reads the title while pointing under each word.*) Now, you read the title just like I did.

STUDENT: What Is Red? (*Points to each word.*)

EXAMINER: Good. Let's look at the first page. What do you see in the picture?

STUDENT: Apples and a bowl.

EXAMINER: Good. Show me where it says *apples*.

STUDENT: (*Points to the word correctly. If the student points to the picture, say, "Show me the word 'apples.'"*)

EXAMINER: Good job. Let's look at the next page. What do you see in the picture?

STUDENT: Some flowers.

EXAMINER: That's right. Can you show me where it says *"flowers"*?

STUDENT: (*Points to another word.*)

EXAMINER: Good try; look again. Where does it say *"flowers"*? (*May emphasize the /f/ sound.*)

EXAMINER: Good job. Let's look at the next page. What do you see in the picture? (*Examiner continues through each page, as the student points to birds and cars.*)

EXAMINER: Let's look at the last page. Can you show me where it says *"love"*?

STUDENT: (*Points to the word correctly.*)

EXAMINER: Great job! Now, you read the book to me. Start with the title. Point to each word as you read it. (*Closes the book so that the student is looking at the cover page.*)

Example 2: The selected passage is Pre-Primer C, "Sandy Helps Out"

Examiner: The title of this book is "Sandy Helps Out." Watch what I do. (*Reads the title while pointing under each word.*) Now, you read the title just like I did.

STUDENT: Sandy Helps Out. (*Points to each word.*)

EXAMINER: Good. Let's look at the first page. What is Sandy doing in the picture?

STUDENT: Making the bed.

EXAMINER: Show me where it says "*helps.*" Now, show me where it says "*bed.*"

STUDENT: (*Points to the words correctly.*)

EXAMINER: Good! What's Sandy doing in this picture?

STUDENT: Putting on the plates and forks.

EXAMINER: Where is Sandy putting the plates and forks?

STUDENT: On the table.

EXAMINER: Do you know what that's called, when you help get the table ready for dinner by putting the dishes, silverware, and napkins at each place? (*If student can't produce "setting the table," say, "That's called setting the table."*) Can you show me where it says *set*? Can you show me where it says "*table*"?

STUDENT: (*Points to one or both incorrectly.*)

EXAMINER: Good try; look again. Where does it say *set*? (*May emphasize the /s/ sound.*) Where does it say *table*? (*May emphasize the /t/ sound.*)

STUDENT: (*Points to the words correctly.*)

EXAMINER: Good! (*Examiner continues through each page, as the student points to "pick," "toys," "fold," "clothes," "feed," and "dog."*) Look at the last picture. What do you think Mom is saying to Sandy after she has been such a good helper?

STUDENT: Umm, thanks?

EXAMINER: Good! Where does it say "*Thank you*"?

STUDENT: (*Points to the words correctly.*)

EXAMINER: Great job! Now, you read the book to me. Start with the title. Point to each word as you read it. (*Closes the book so that the student is looking at the cover page.*)

READING TEXT PASSAGES FOR GRADE 1 AND ABOVE

Beyond the emergent (Pre-Primer and Primer) level, the *DLI* contains text passages written on levels 1 (second half of grade one), 2.1 and 2.2 (first and second halves of second grade), 3–6, and middle school and high school levels.

CHOOSE THE GENRE OF TEXT PASSAGES. You have three genres of text passages from which to choose. The narrative passages come first, followed by the social studies passages, and then the science passages. Normally, you test students using the narrative passages first. But remember your purpose for assessing. Do you want to know how well the student performs in passages that present information, as opposed to telling stories? If so, after the instructional and the independent reading levels have been identified using the narrative passage, you may test the student at one or both of those levels using the corresponding science or social studies passage.

TURN TO THE TEXT PASSAGE THAT CORRESPONDS TO THE STUDENT'S INDEPENDENT LEVEL ON THE WORD RECOGNITION ASSESSMENT. This will be the level at which the student made no more than two errors in the flashed presentation. Find the Response Sheets that correspond to that text. You will be prompted to explain to the student that she or he will read the text orally and then answer questions about it.

READ THE INTRODUCTION TO THE PASSAGE. The introductory statement is intended to prepare the student to read or attend to the passage that follows. It includes the title of the passage, and provides you a chance to pronounce for the student any proper names in it.

ASK THE STUDENT TO READ THE PASSAGE ALOUD. Using a watch with a second hand, mark the time when the student begins to read. Also, be sure to record the time when the student finishes reading.

As the student reads the passage, mark the student's reading errors on the response sheet, as explained in Figure 1.2 on page 30. While the student is reading aloud, you will follow along on your copy of the text and mark all of the oral divergences from the text, or miscues, on your copy of the passage. This is also known as taking a *running record*. Errors are important reading behaviors that are counted to determine the reader's degree of oral reading accuracy. Errors can be examined to determine the student's word analysis strategies during the oral reading. Oral reading errors or miscues are marked in Figure 1.2.

Suggestion for the Examiner

At least until you become proficient at marking the errors, you may want to tape record the session. If you do, put the tape recorder in an inconspicuous place, and use a long-playing tape so you won't have to change it while you are testing. You will still need to mark the errors while you test, however, in order to know when to advance to another level passage and when to finish testing. The tape recording will serve as a backup to reinforce your accuracy in scoring the child's reading.

SCORING ORAL READING ACCURACY

For each passage that the student read orally, score his or her oral reading accuracy by counting the uncorrected miscues listed in Figure 1.2. Write the number of uncorrected miscues occurring in each line of text at the end of each line. Add to get the total number of miscues for each

FIGURE 1.2 Marking Oral Reading Miscues

- **Substitution**: The reader substitutes a different word for a word in the text. Write the substitution over the intended word and draw a line through that word.

  Example: A rabbit can ~~hop.~~ *hope*

  A substitution counts as an error for scoring purposes.

- **Insertion**: The reader inserts a word that is not in the text. Use a caret to show where the insertion occurred and write the inserted word above the text.

  Example: Tomorrow will be a ^*nice* sunny day.

  An insertion counts as an error for scoring purposes.

- **Word omission**: The reader omits a word or phrase. Circle the omitted word or phrase.

  Example: It was not a (very) good idea.

  A word omission counts as an error for scoring purposes.

- **Words given by the examiner**: After giving the reader time and encouragement to try the word, the examiner supplied the word. Put parentheses around the supplied word.

  Example: The pirates sailed for the (Tortugas).

  A word given by the examiner counts as an error for scoring purposes.

Self-corrections made by the reader without help from the examiner are recorded by entering a check mark over the original word that was misread, with an arrow extending back from the place in the sentence where the correction was made.

  Example: It was not a (very) good idea.

Self-corrections are not counted as reading errors for scoring purposes, but they do give important indicators that students are monitoring their own comprehension, that is, they can tell when they have read a sentence or phrase incorrectly.

Very long **pauses** between words or phrases may be marked with slashes where the pauses occur—at the rate of one slash per second.

  Example: The pirates sailed for the ||Tortugas.

While pauses are not counted as errors, recording them enables you to go back and recreate the student's reading of the passage, and to ask why she or he made the pause. (Often, students pause before they read a difficult word, and sometimes they pause after they realize they have read the preceding words incorrectly.)

Repetitions are marked with a wavy line under the words that the child repeated.

  Example: The pirates sailed for the Tortugas.

They are not counted as errors.

---

passage. To determine the reader's functional reading level for each passage, use the Oral Reading Accuracy scoring guide on the examiner's page for each passage.

Count the number of oral reading errors and record them in the space provided toward the bottom of the response sheet, and determine if the score equates to an independent, instructional, or frustration reading level.

Ask the student the comprehension questions and score the answers. Write the number of correct responses in the space provided on the response sheet. Tally up the correct responses and also enter their number on the space provided. Determine if that score also equates to an independent, instructional, or frustration reading level.

Drop back to a lower level passage if necessary. Before moving to the higher level passages, you should first find a text passage on which the student scores at his or her independent level on both word recognition in context and comprehension. If the student scores below the independent level in either area in the first passage tested, you should drop back one or more passages and test those until the independent level is reached on both word recognition and comprehension.

Test higher level passages until the frustration level is reached. Continue to have the student read passages aloud, mark the student's oral reading errors, ask comprehension questions, and then, score those results. Enter the scores in the spaces at the bottom of each response sheet. When the level is reached at which the student scores at the frustration level on both word recognition in context and comprehension, this part of the testing is complete.

Please note: If the student's scores on the word recognition test in isolation (that is, the lists of words that are flashed and untimed) indicates that she or he should now be tested in text passages at the Pre-Primer or Primer level (late kindergarten and early first grade), please refer to special instructions for testing in the passages on those levels. Special instructions for administering the Pre-Primer and Primer passages are found on pages 25–28.

SCORING ORAL READING ACCURACY FOR ENGLISH LANGUAGE LEARNERS AND SPEAKERS OF OTHER DIALECTS OF ENGLISH

The *DLI* informal reading inventory process will function well in English with English language learners, but some adaptations are indicated. For example, mispronunciation is one element of evaluating oral reading accuracy in the informal reading inventory, and each occurrence is counted as an oral reading error or miscue. When a mispronunciation error can be attributed to a conflict point with the mother tongue or dialect of English, *and when it does not interfere with comprehension*, a short /i/ pronounced as a long /e/, for example, then an error would *not* be counted (Gillet, Temple, & Crawford, 2008; Temple, Ogle, Crawford, & Freppon, 2008). In other words, we would not penalize a student for having an accent, Spanish, Brooklyn, Australian, or otherwise. In an investigation of teachers who administered IRIs to Spanish-speaking children, Lamberg, Rodriguez, and Tomas (1978) concluded that to avoid such problems, teachers need special training to use IRIs with English language learners.

Kenneth Johnson (personal communication, 1977) provides a test sentence to illustrate this principle for the African American child whose mother tongue is African American Vernacular English. The sentence often elicits a mispronunciation that has the potential to interfere with comprehension. The child is asked to read the following sentence aloud: "As I passed the sign, I read it." In conformance with African American Vernacular English, the African American child sometimes pronounces *passed* as *pass*, dropping the *-ed* suffix that is also a past tense marker. If the child comprehends the marker, that is, understands that *passed* is in the past tense even though he pronounced it as in the present tense, then the child will pronounce the word *read* in the past tense. If not, the child will pronounce *read* in the present tense. According to Johnson, these children almost always pronounce *read* correctly in the past tense.

FIND THE STUDENT'S READING RATE

It is useful to determine students' reading rates at their instructional level and their independent reading level, and also at their grade placement level.

To calculate a student's reading rate, subtract the starting time from the ending time and plot the results according to the scoring guide. Follow the procedures given after each passage for computing the student's reading rate as WCPM (words correctly read per minute). The scoring guide will indicate if the student's reading rate is on, above, or below average for reading at that grade level.

If you wish to assess the student's reading fluency beyond the reading rate—that is, taking into account phrasing, honoring syntax, and expression—you may use the NASEP Oral Reading Fluency Scale found in Table 6 in the Appendix, page 423.

TEST THE STUDENT'S LISTENING COMPREHENSION

Once the student reaches the frustration level at both word recognition in context and comprehension, you may invite the student to stop reading and listen to you as you read. Explain that you will read a passage aloud and ask the student questions about the passage later.

Read the passage at a moderate pace, with expression. When you have finished reading, ask the student the comprehension questions and score the responses as you would if the student had read the passage. You may continue reading and questioning until you reach a level at which the student's responses to comprehension questions fall below 70% accuracy.

The level at which the student's responses are closest to 75% accuracy is considered to be that student's level of listening comprehension.

TEST THE STUDENT'S SILENT READING

Once you have determined the student's instructional and independent levels of oral reading, you should test for the student's instructional and independent levels of silent reading. To achieve the best comparison, test the student's comprehension and reading rate in the same-genre passage (narrative and narrative, social studies and social studies, or science and science).

ADMINISTER THE *DEMTUP NAMES TEST*

The *Demtup Names Test* shows a student's ability to use phonics cues alone (without the support of context or meaning) in order to read words. The *Demtup Names Test* is usually administered in a separate sitting. Procedures for administering the *Demtup Names Test* are provided with the test on page 397.

TEST THE STUDENT ON THE SOCIAL STUDIES OR SCIENCE PASSAGES

Once the instructional level and independent level have been identified in the narrative passages, you may choose to test the student at those levels using the corresponding text passages from social studies or science, or both.

ENTER THE RESULTS ON THE SCORE SUMMARY SHEET

Enter the requested scores in each of the boxes of the Score Summary Sheet. The scores for word recognition in isolation/flashed, word recognition in isolation/untimed, word recognition in context, and comprehension may be entered as "IND," "INSTR," and "FR" for "independent," "instructional," and "frustration." Reading rates will be entered as WCPM.

Note that some teachers prefer the more detailed procedure of converting all scores (except reading rates) to percentage scores to make it easier to compare different aspects of a student's performance. Percentage scores can be calculated by dividing the number of accurate responses by the total number of possible responses (use a calculator!).

To compute word recognition in isolation scores, for example, if a student makes 17 correct responses in the "Flashed" condition on the list of words for grade 3, divide 17 by 20 (the total number of words on each list) to get the answer, 85%.

$$17 \div 20 = 85\%$$

85% is the number you would enter in the score summary sheet, in the column labeled "Flashed" on the "Word Recognition" part of the chart, in the row for grade 3. All of the word recognition in isolation lists contain 20 words, so you will always divide the number of correct responses by 20.

To compute word recognition in context scores, you must find the number of words in the text passage. That number is provided right after the passage on the examiner's version of the test, the version on which you record the child's responses. In the case of the third grade narrative passage, Form A, for instance, the number of words is 233. If a student makes 13 word recognition errors in context (that is, he reads 13 words incorrectly), according to the criteria given for word reading errors, you subtract the errors from the total number of words to get the number of words read correctly:

$$233-13 = 220$$

Next, you divide the number of words read correctly by the total number of words in the passage to calculate the percentage of words that were read correctly:

$$220 \div 233 = 94\%.$$

The number 94% will be entered in the score summary sheet, in the column labeled "In Context" on the "Word Recognition" part of the chart, in the row for grade 3. Now we can compare the two figures—and in this case it turns out the child is reading words in context about as well as we would expect him to, since both the word recognition in isolation flashed score and the word recognition in context score fall at the higher end of the range of scores for the instructional reading level.

To calculate reading comprehension scores as percentages, again divide the number of correct responses by the total number of questions. Note that at level Primer, there are four questions; at level 1, there are six questions, and at all other levels, there are eight questions. To continue with our example, suppose a child answers five questions correctly in the third grade narrative passage. You would divide 5 by 8:

$$5 \div 8 = 62.5\%.$$

This figure will be entered in the score summary sheet, in the column labeled "Reading Passages," "Narrative" on the "Comprehension" part of the chart, in the row for grade 3. Now, we can compare two kinds of word recognition scores with the child's reading comprehension score and we see there is a problem. The chart on page 419 tells us that 62.5% is a frustration level score for reading comprehension, and it falls considerably below the child's word recognition scores. Comprehension may be an area of concern with this child's reading.

Once the scores have been entered in the score summary sheet, the pattern of scores can be examined for overall reading levels, and also for indications of the student's strengths and weaknesses in the different aspects of his or her reading ability.

Computing Word Recognition and Comprehension Scores as Percentages

Word Recognition in Isolation

Here's a shortcut. There are 20 words on each list, so each word is worth 5 percentage points. Multiply the number of errors times 5 and subtract that figure from 100 to obtain a percentage score for word recognition in isolation. Assume that if a word is read correctly when it is flashed, it is also read correctly untimed. Use the flashed word recognition score as the baseline score for the untimed condition, and add 5 percentage points for every additional word that the student recognized when it was presented untimed.

$$\text{Word rec. in isolation score} = \frac{\text{Total number of correctly read words}}{\text{Total number of words in list}}$$

Word Recognition in Context

There are different numbers of words in each passage, so calculate the word recognition in context score by first subtracting the number of errors from the total number of words to yield the number of words correctly identified. Then, divide the words correctly identified by the total number of words in the passage.

$$\text{Word rec. in context score} = \frac{\text{Total number of correctly read words in passage}}{\text{Total number of words in passage}}$$

Comprehension Scores

To calculate the scores for comprehension, divide the number of correctly answered questions by the total number of questions.

$$\text{Comprehension score} = \frac{\text{Total number of correctly answered questions}}{\text{Total number of questions}}$$

▶ Quick Instructions

- Begin by testing word recognition in isolation, one year below grade placement.

- Record both scores, but count the flashed presentation for determining reading levels.

- Drop back, if necessary, until you reach the independent level (0–2 errors flashed).

- Move ahead until you reach the frustration level (7 or more errors flashed).

- Go to the text passages, Narrative Form.

- Begin at the level passage that corresponds to the student's independent reading level on the word recognition test.

- Drop back if necessary to find the independent level on both word recognition in context and comprehension.

- Read the introductory statement.

- Record the time the student begins reading.

- Mark the student's reading errors.

- Record the time the student finishes reading.

- Ask the comprehension questions and score the responses.

- Enter oral reading and comprehension scores on the bottom of the response sheet.

- Continue administering passages until you reach the frustration level on both word recognition in context and comprehension.

- Test for listening comprehension: Read aloud the frustration level passage and ask and score the questions. Proceed until you find a passage where the comprehension score is close to 75% (4–5 questions correctly answered).

Later, go back and compute the reading rates for texts that the student read at the instructional and independent levels.

▶ *Developmental Literacy Inventory* Score Summary Sheet

Student: _____   Grade/Class: _____

Examiner: _____   Date: _____

	Word Recognition				Comprehension						Reading Rate		
	Flashed	Untimed	In Context		Reading Passages			Listening Comprehension					
					Narrative	Soc. Studies	Science	Narrative	Soc. Studies	Science	Narrative	Soc. Studies	Science
PP					✕	✕	✕	✕	✕	✕	✕	✕	✕
P					✕	✕	✕	✕	✕	✕	✕	✕	✕
1													
2.1													
2.2													
3													
4													
5													
6													
MS													
HS													

Independent Level _____

Instructional Level _____

Frustration Level _____

▶ Summary of Assessment of Emergent Literacy

Student: _____ School: _____ Date: _____

Examiner: _____

EMERGENT LITERACY ASSESSMENT I: KEY COMPONENTS

A. Alphabet Knowledge

_____ Upper Case Recognition
_____ Lower Case Recognition
_____ Production

Observations:

Total for Alphabet Knowledge: _____/ 78.**Percentage score:** _____

B. Concept of Word

Voice-Pointing: _____ (of 4)
Word Identification: _____ (of 8)

Observations:

Total for Concept of Word: _____/ 12**Percentage score:** _____

C. Phoneme Segmentation

Observations:

Total for Segmentation: _____/ 22   **Percentage score:** _____

D. Word Identification

Decodable Words_____/10
Sight Words _____/10

Observations:

Total for Word Identification: _____/20   **Percentage score:** _____

Total Score for Emergent Literacy Assessment I: _____/138

Percentage score: _____

EMERGENT LITERACY ASSESSMENT II: PRINT CONCEPTS

1. Knowledge of the layout of books   _____/1 point

2. Knowledge that the print, not the pictures, is what we read   _____/1 point

3. Directional orientation of print on the page   _____/1 point

4. Understanding of the term "word"   _____/1 point

5. Understanding of the term "letter"   _____/1 point

6. Knowledge of punctuation   _____/1 point

Observations:

Total for Print Concepts: _____/ 6   **Percentage score:** _____

EMERGENT LITERACY I: CORE LITERACY KNOWLEDGE

STUDENT'S VERSION

R M P G F A Z S T

N B I W Q O K X C

U L V J D Y E H

r m p g f a z s t

n b i w q o k x c

u l v j d y e h

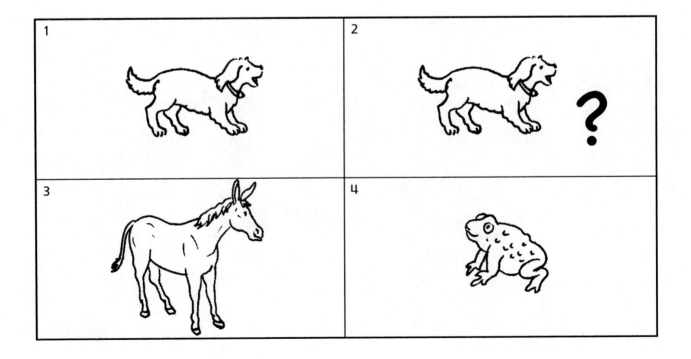

My little dog Petunia

is a very strange dog.

She bellows like a mule

But she leaps like a frog.

First List	Second List
bed	and
sad	good
ride	you
pin	the
pole	one
tub	come
got	is
duck	said
ball	play
rule	look

EMERGENT LITERACY I: CORE LITERACY KNOWLEDGE

EXAMINER'S VERSION

► Assessment of Alphabet Knowledge

Student: _____ School: _____ Date: _____

Examiner: _____

(See page 20 for instructions)

R M P G F A Z S T

N B I W Q O K X C

U L V J D Y E H

r m p g f a z s t

n b i w q o k x c

u l v j d y e h

Total alphabet recognition:_____/52

Total alphabet production: _____/26

Student: _____ School: _____ Date: _____

Examiner: _____

(See pages 20–21 for instructions)

	Voice-Pointing	**Word Identification**
My little <u>dog</u> <u>Petunia</u> 1 2	_____	_____
Is a <u>very</u> <u>strange</u> dog. 1 2	_____	_____
She <u>bellows</u> <u>like</u> a mule 1 2	_____	_____
But <u>she</u> leaps like a <u>frog.</u> 1 2	_____	_____

Voice-Pointing: _____ (of 4)

Word Identification: _____ (of 8)

Total Concept of Word (voice-pointing + word identification): _____ (of 12)

EXAMINER PAGES

▶ Assessment of Phoneme Segmentation (*The Yopp-Singer Test*)

Student: _____ School: _____ Date: _____

Examiner: _____

1. dog (3) _____

2. keep (3) _____

3. fine (3) _____

4. no (2) _____

5. she (2) _____

6. wave (3) _____

7. grew (3) _____

8. that (3) _____

9. red (3) _____

10. me (2) _____

11. sat (3) _____

12. lay (2) _____

13. race (3) _____

14. zoo (2) _____

15. three (3) _____

16. job (3) _____

17. in (2) _____

18. ice (2) _____

19. at (2) _____

20. top (3) _____

21. by (2) _____

22. do (2) _____

Score (number correct) _____ / 22 Percentage score: _____

▶ Assessment of Word Identification

Student: _____ School: _____ Date: _____

Examiner: _____

Decodable Words		High Frequency Words	
bed	_____	and	_____
sad	_____	good	_____
ride	_____	you	_____
pin	_____	the	_____
pole	_____	one	_____
tub	_____	come	_____
got	_____	is	_____
duck	_____	said	_____
ball	_____	play	_____
rule	_____	look	_____

Total: _____/10   Total_____/10

EMERGENT LITERACY II: ASSESSMENT OF PRINT CONCEPTS

STUDENT'S VERSION

See instructions for creating these books on page 424.

Bill's Beast

Bill's Beast

Bill likes to go fishing

all by himself.

He fishes in a lake.

The lake is far from town.

2

Something big bit his bait.

Bill told a big farmer.

The farmer told him to

forget it.

5
6

"What was that?" Bill said.

"It is a beast!" he shouted.

Bill went to tell someone.

Now Bill keeps his
problems to himself.

EMERGENT LITERACY II: ASSESSMENT OF PRINT CONCEPTS

EXAMINER'S VERSION

▶ Assessment of Print Concepts

Student: _____ School: _____ Date: _____

Examiner: _____

A. Print Concepts

1. **Knowledge of the layout of books** _____/1 point

   Observations:

2. **Knowledge that the print, not the pictures, is what we read** _____/1 point

   Observations:

3. **Directional orientation of print on the page** _____/1 point

   Observations:

4. **Understanding of the term "word"** _____/1 point

   Observations:

5. **Understanding of the term "letter"** _____/1 point

   Observations:

6. **Knowledge of punctuation** _____/1 point

   Observations:

Total for Print Concepts: _____/ 6   Percentage score: _____

WORD RECOGNITION LISTS

FORM A

ran	had
said	keep
time	leg
see	no
you	walk
bad	from
can	one
end	but
up	red
get	yes

pp

class	want
each	know
face	back
grew	first
jump	just
blue	snow
your	three
last	lake
soon	must
thing	snake

p

plant	light
right	ready
winter	clean
inside	doctor
happy	father
rabbit	round
lunch	kitten
some	leave
because	morning
children	night

smile	feather
above	become
library	grandfather
brave	hair
instead	people
dear	kept
ditch	mountain
popcorn	patch
pretty	snail
monkey	anyway

orange	question
scare	enough
young	kitchen
learn	idea
charge	known
dragon	market
empty	number
rocket	ocean
garden	queen
huge	touch

station

ought

doesn't

coach

type

damp

elbow

mystery

yourselves

midnight

motorcycle

insect

study

easier

headache

snatched

quieter

alive

moment

range

walnut	swerve
valuable	passenger
capture	original
foreign	shovel
mechanical	wreck
hurricane	broad
lettuce	habit
knives	uncover
lobster	witness
mitten	mosquito

iv

buyer	victim
vibration	universe
critical	frightened
diary	gravity
environment	interview
observation	kilogram
landscape	explanation
network	meaningful
wallpaper	naturally
strengthen	pursued

v

appreciation

thorough

propose

kennel

thermometer

nourish

luggage

upstream

manual

stargazer

greenhouse

hesitation

insurance

volcanic

sheriff

drought

straighten

resource

zookeeper

existence

condemn

equivalent

hibernation

luxurious

manufacture

inspection

omitted

hemisphere

universal

dependent

scientifically

kindergarten

continental

colonel

variation

youthful

provision

courteous

exaggerate

molecule

lackadaisical	Machiavellian
parliamentarian	circumlocution
utopian	erroneous
equilibrium	abomination
aerialist	archeology
regulatory	voracious
troubadour	quixotic
prestigious	peregrination
inconclusive	oligarchy
epitome	tantamount

WORD RECOGNITION RESPONSE SHEETS

FORM A

EXAMINER PAGES

	Flashed	Untimed
ran		
said		
time		
see		
you		
bad		
can		
end		
up		
get		
had		
keep		
leg		
no		
walk		
from		
one		
but		
red		
yes		
Total Errors:		

0–2 errors = Independent Level

3–6 errors = Instructional Level

7⁺ errors = Frustration Level

	Flashed	Untimed
class		
each		
face		
grew		
jump		
blue		
your		
last		
soon		
thing		
want		
know		
back		
first		
just		
snow		
three		
lake		
must		
snake		
Total Errors:		

0–2 errors = Independent Level

3–6 errors = Instructional Level

7+ errors = Frustration Level

EXAMINER PAGES

	Flashed	Untimed
plant		
right		
winter		
inside		
happy		
rabbit		
lunch		
some		
because		
children		
light		
ready		
clean		
doctor		
father		
round		
kitten		
leave		
morning		
night		
Total Errors:		

0–2 errors = Independent Level

3–6 errors = Instructional Level

7 + errors = Frustration Level

	Flashed	Untimed
smile		
above		
library		
brave		
instead		
dear		
ditch		
popcorn		
pretty		
monkey		
feather		
become		
grandfather		
hair		
people		
kept		
mountain		
patch		
snail		
anyway		
Total Errors:		

0–2 errors = Independent Level

3–6 errors = Instructional Level

7+ errors = Frustration Level

	Flashed	Untimed
orange		
scare		
young		
learn		
charge		
dragon		
empty		
rocket		
garden		
huge		
question		
enough		
kitchen		
idea		
known		
market		
number		
ocean		
queen		
touch		
Total Errors:		

0–2 errors = Independent Level

3–6 errors = Instructional Level

7+ errors = Frustration Level

	Flashed	Untimed
station		
ought		
doesn't		
coach		
type		
damp		
elbow		
mystery		
yourselves		
midnight		
motorcycle		
insect		
study		
easier		
headache		
snatched		
quieter		
alive		
moment		
range		
Total Errors:		

0–2 errors = Independent Level

3–6 errors = Instructional Level

7⁺ errors = Frustration Level

	Flashed	Untimed
walnut		
valuable		
capture		
foreign		
mechanical		
hurricane		
lettuce		
knives		
lobster		
mitten		
swerve		
passenger		
original		
shovel		
wreck		
broad		
habit		
uncover		
witness		
mosquito		
Total Errors:		

0–2 errors = Independent Level

3–6 errors = Instructional Level

7⁺ errors = Frustration Level

	Flashed	Untimed
buyer		
vibration		
critical		
diary		
environment		
observation		
landscape		
network		
wallpaper		
strengthen		
victim		
universe		
frightened		
gravity		
interview		
kilogram		
explanation		
meaningful		
naturally		
pursued		
Total Errors:		

0–2 errors = Independent Level

3–6 errors = Instructional Level

7+ errors = Frustration Level

	Flashed	Untimed
appreciation		
thorough		
propose		
kennel		
thermometer		
nourish		
luggage		
upstream		
manual		
stargazer		
greenhouse		
hesitation		
insurance		
volcanic		
sheriff		
drought		
straighten		
resource		
zookeeper		
existence		
Total Errors:		

0–2 errors = Independent Level

3–6 errors = Instructional Level

7+ errors = Frustration Level

	Flashed	Untimed
condemn		
equivalent		
hibernation		
luxurious		
manufacture		
inspection		
omitted		
hemisphere		
universal		
dependent		
scientifically		
kindergarten		
continental		
colonel		
variation		
youthful		
provision		
courteous		
exaggerate		
molecule		
Total Errors:		

0–2 errors = Independent Level

3–6 errors = Instructional Level

7⁺ errors = Frustration Level

	Flashed	Untimed
lackadaisical		
parliamentarian		
utopian		
equilibrium		
aerialist		
regulatory		
troubadour		
prestigious		
inconclusive		
epitome		
Machiavellian		
circumlocution		
erroneous		
abomination		
archeology		
voracious		
quixotic		
peregrination		
oligarchy		
tantamount		
Total Errors:		

0–2 errors = **Independent Level**

3–6 errors = **Instructional Level**

7+ errors = **Frustration Level**

WORD RECOGNITION LISTS

FORM B

day	bed
ball	girl
tell	sad
come	beg
road	mother
us	beep
car	hit
boy	bird
mom	dog
look	pet

school	play
gate	far
spot	side
rain	funny
smart	good
pick	ice
drum	show
sister	game
house	sleep
moon	about

p

milk	fight
puppy	spoon
other	path
pool	buy
pull	place
sports	summer
dream	happen
small	spring
soft	land
please	glad

short	least
potato	daughter
quick	donkey
mouth	globe
fence	myself
trade	power
waves	welcome
really	else
poem	person
soak	railroad

pocket	often
dinner	haven't
early	market
large	rough
castle	captain
monkey	mighty
field	possible
nickel	glasses
order	office
return	knob

message	double
obey	electric
figure	memory
engine	kingdom
glance	measure
nervous	moist
disappear	handsome
expert	knuckle
magical	elevator
distance	invited

iii

abroad

accident

monument

microphone

direction

capital

opposite

jewels

notice

disease

connect

garbage

embarrass

poisonous

official

factory

catalog

medicine

listen

accent

dependable	signature
balcony	effective
discouraged	ceremony
macaroni	accurate
orchestra	counselor
migrate	eruption
authority	disaster
hazard	article
constantly	millionaire
available	accompany

v

absence	drowsy
prevention	straightened
variety	revolution
weightless	unconscious
rejection	professional
sensitive	organization
miniature	industrial
saturated	scoreboard
outrageous	reversible
relation	survivor

popularity

extraordinary

foresight

reproduction

inclination

notify

genetic

illustrations

porous

accelerated

extinguish

disposition

lieutenant

testimony

regulation

insistent

promotion

eccentric

insulation

academic

consensual

truculent

aggressor

euphoria

quorum

inscrutable

ombudsman

transcendent

totalitarian

interrogation

ventriloquist

parsimonious

sacrilegious

antique

sovereign

attribute

vestigial

paleontologist

theocracy

palindrome

X

WORD RECOGNITION RESPONSE SHEETS

FORM B

EXAMINER PAGES

	Flashed	Untimed
day		
ball		
tell		
come		
road		
us		
car		
boy		
mom		
look		
bed		
girl		
sad		
beg		
mother		
beep		
hit		
bird		
dog		
pet		
Total Errors:		

0–2 errors = Independent Level

3–6 errors = Instructional Level

7+ errors = Frustration Level

	Flashed	Untimed
school		
gate		
spot		
rain		
smart		
pick		
drum		
sister		
house		
moon		
play		
far		
side		
funny		
good		
ice		
show		
game		
sleep		
about		
Total Errors:		

0–2 errors = Independent Level

3–6 errors = Instructional Level

7⁺ errors = Frustration Level

EXAMINER PAGES

	Flashed	Untimed
milk		
puppy		
other		
pool		
pull		
sports		
dream		
small		
soft		
please		
fight		
spoon		
path		
buy		
place		
summer		
happen		
spring		
land		
glad		
Total Errors:		

0–2 errors = Independent Level

3–6 errors = Instructional Level

7+ errors = Frustration Level

	Flashed	Untimed
short		
potato		
quick		
mouth		
fence		
trade		
waves		
really		
poem		
soak		
least		
daughter		
donkey		
globe		
myself		
power		
welcome		
else		
person		
railroad		
Total Errors:		

0–2 errors = Independent Level

3–6 errors = Instructional Level

7+ errors = Frustration Level

EXAMINER PAGES

	Flashed	Untimed
pocket		
dinner		
early		
large		
castle		
monkey		
field		
nickel		
order		
return		
often		
haven't		
market		
rough		
captain		
mighty		
possible		
glasses		
office		
knob		
Total Errors:		

0–2 errors = Independent Level

3–6 errors = Instructional Level

7⁺ errors = Frustration Level

	Flashed	Untimed
message		
obey		
figure		
engine		
glance		
nervous		
disappear		
expert		
magical		
distance		
double		
electric		
memory		
kingdom		
measure		
moist		
handsome		
knuckle		
elevator		
invited		
Total Errors:		

0–2 errors = Independent Level

3–6 errors = Instructional Level

7+ errors = Frustration Level

	Flashed	Untimed
abroad		
monument		
direction		
opposite		
notice		
connect		
embarrass		
official		
catalog		
listen		
accident		
microphone		
capital		
jewels		
disease		
garbage		
poisonous		
factory		
medicine		
accent		
Total Errors:		

0–2 errors = Independent Level

3–6 errors = Instructional Level

7+ errors = Frustration Level

	Flashed	Untimed
dependable		
balcony		
discouraged		
macaroni		
orchestra		
migrate		
authority		
hazard		
constantly		
available		
signature		
effective		
ceremony		
accurate		
counselor		
eruption		
disaster		
article		
millionaire		
accompany		
Total Errors:		

0–2 errors = Independent Level

3–6 errors = Instructional Level

7+ errors = Frustration Level

	Flashed	Untimed
absence		
prevention		
variety		
weightless		
rejection		
sensitive		
miniature		
saturated		
outrageous		
relation		
drowsy		
straightened		
revolution		
unconscious		
professional		
organization		
industrial		
scoreboard		
reversible		
survivor		
Total Errors:		

0–2 errors = Independent Level

3–6 errors = Instructional Level

7+ errors = Frustration Level

	Flashed	Untimed
popularity		
extraordinary		
foresight		
reproduction		
inclination		
notify		
genetic		
illustrations		
porous		
accelerated		
extinguish		
disposition		
lieutenant		
testimony		
regulation		
insistent		
promotion		
eccentric		
insulation		
academic		
Total Errors:		

0–2 errors = Independent Level

3–6 errors = Instructional Level

7+ errors = Frustration Level

EXAMINER PAGES

	Flashed	Untimed
consensual		
truculent		
aggressor		
euphoria		
quorum		
inscrutable		
ombudsman		
transcendent		
totalitarian		
interrogation		
ventriloquist		
parsimonious		
sacrilegious		
antique		
sovereign		
attribute		
vestigial		
paleontologist		
theocracy		
palindrome		
Total Errors:		

0–2 errors = Independent Level

3–6 errors = Instructional Level

7+ errors = Frustration Level

PRE-PRIMER AND PRIMER PASSAGES

FORM A

See instructions for creating these books on page 424.

Apples are red.

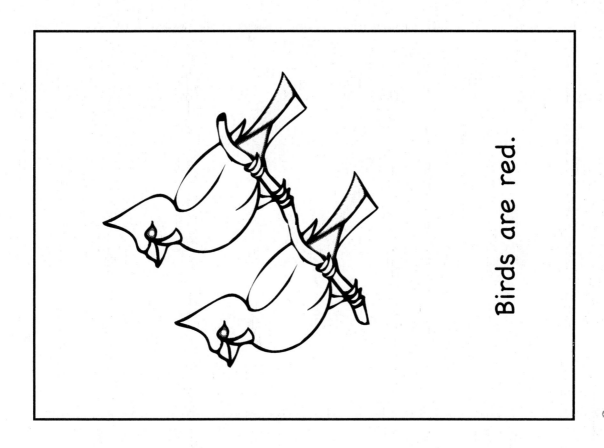

Birds are red.

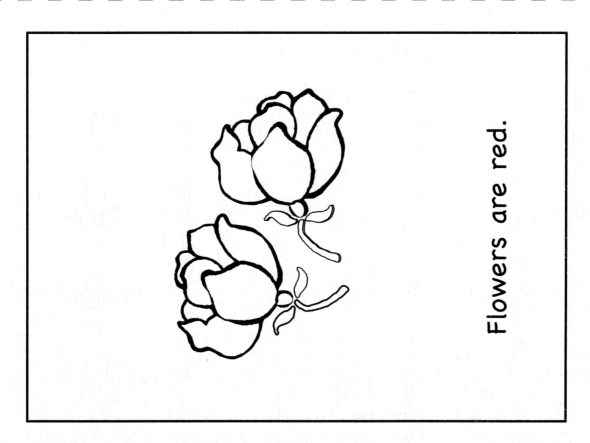

Flowers are red.

I love red!

Cars are red.

110

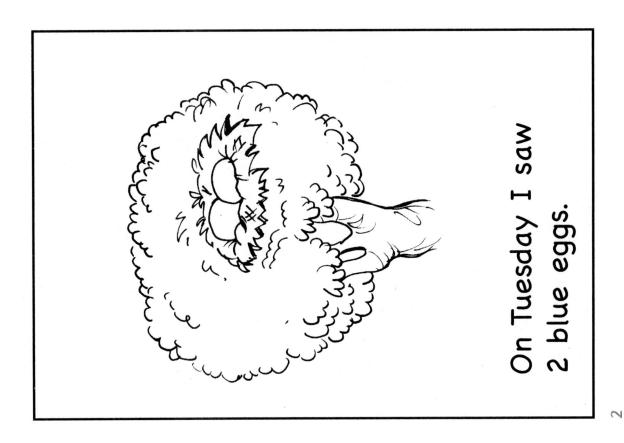

On Tuesday I saw
2 blue eggs.

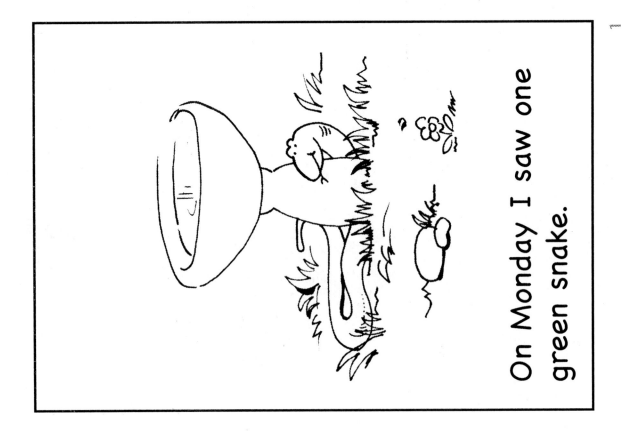

On Monday I saw one
green snake.

112

On Thursday I saw four red bugs.

4

On Wednesday I saw three yellow flowers.

3

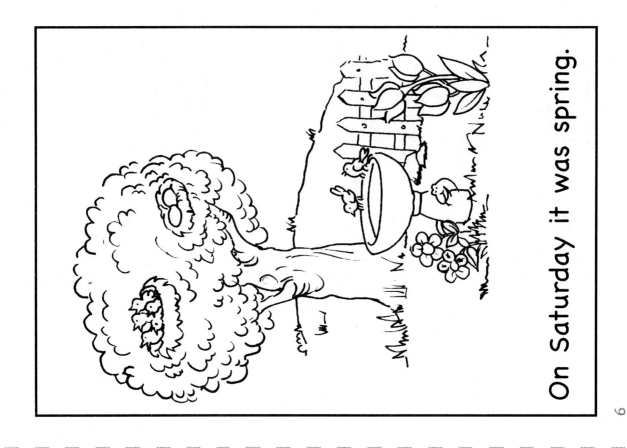

On Saturday it was spring.

On Friday I saw five
baby birds.

Sandy helps set the table.

Sandy helps make her bed.

Sandy helps fold the clothes.

Sandy helps pick up the toys.

"Thank you, Sandy!"

Sandy helps feed the dog.

118

Seeds

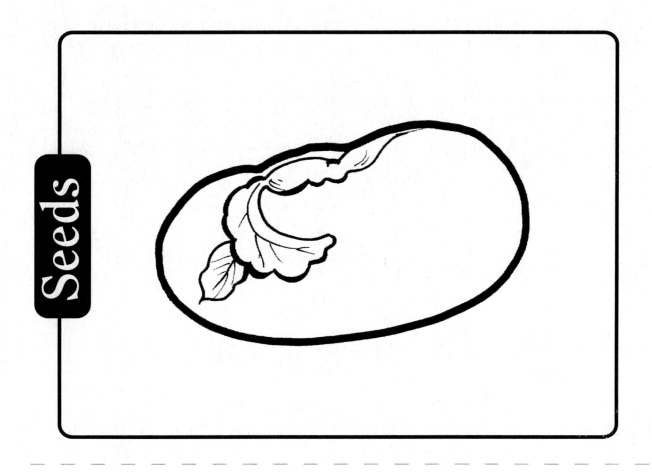

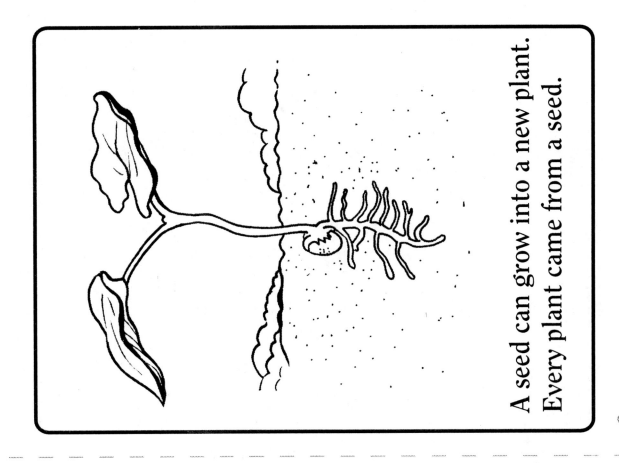

A seed can grow into a new plant.
Every plant came from a seed.

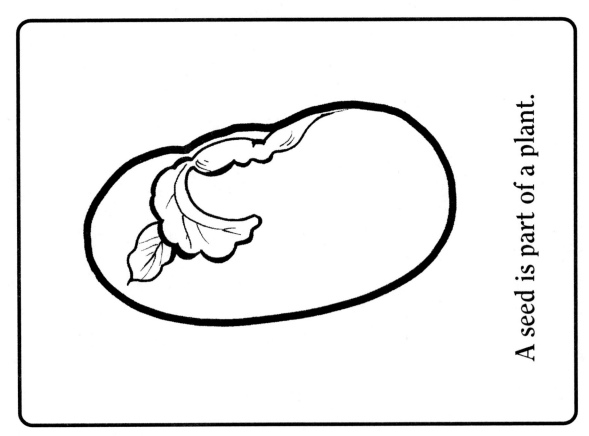

A seed is part of a plant.

A bean seed grows into a bean plant. A corn seed grows into a corn plant.

4

3

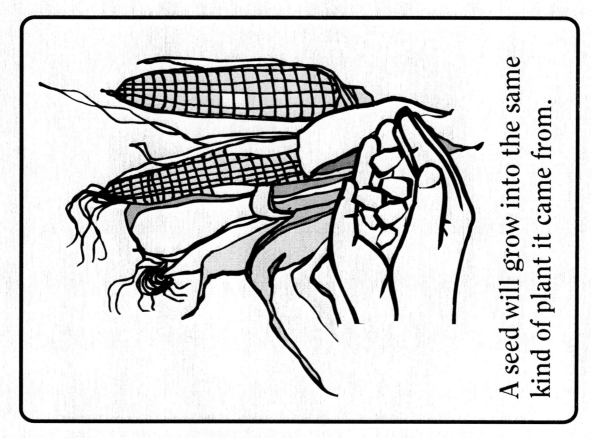

A seed will grow into the same kind of plant it came from.

Sun and rain help seeds to grow.

A seed needs water to grow.
It needs to be warm.

PRE-PRIMER AND PRIMER PASSAGES RESPONSE SHEETS

FORM A

▶ Pre-Primer A: What Is Red?

Teacher Prompts: Say, *"The title of this story is 'What Is Red?' It is about things that are red."* Walk through the pictures in the story. Help the student name the objects in each line. Go back to the beginning and say, *"Please read the story to me. Point to each word as you read."*

	Errors by Line
Apples are red.	_____
Flowers are red.	_____
Birds are red.	_____
Cars are red.	_____
I love red!	_____

Total Errors _____ /15

SCORING GUIDE FOR ORAL READING

(Circle the boxes that correspond to the student's scores)

	Oral Reading Accuracy
Independent Level	0 errors
Instructional Level	1–2 errors
Frustration Level	3 or more errors

▶ Pre-Primer B: Springtime

Teacher Prompts: Say, *"The title of this story is 'Spring Time.' It is about some things you might see in the spring."* Walk through the pictures in the story. Help the student count and name the objects in each line and name the days of the week. Go back to the beginning and say, *"Please read the story to me. Point to each word as you read."*

Errors by Line

On Monday I saw one green snake.   _____

On Tuesday I saw two blue eggs.   _____

On Wednesday I saw three yellow flowers. _____

On Thursday I saw four red ladybugs.   _____

On Friday I saw five baby birds.   _____

On Saturday it was spring.   _____

Total Errors _____ /40

SCORING GUIDE FOR ORAL READING

(Circle the boxes that correspond to the student's scores)

	Oral Reading Accuracy
Independent Level	0–2 errors
Instructional Level	3–5 errors
Frustration Level	6 or more errors

▶ Pre-Primer C: Sandy Helps Out

Teacher Prompts: Say, *"The title of this story is 'Sandy Helps Out.' It is about some ways Sandy helps her family."* Walk through the pictures in the story. Help the student find Sandy's name and tell what she does in each picture. On the last page ask, *"What do you think Mom is saying to Sandy?"* Go back to the beginning and say, *"Please read the story to me. Point to each word as you read."*

Errors by Line

Sandy helps make her bed. _____

Sandy helps set the table. _____

Sandy helps pick up the toys. _____

Sandy helps fold the clothes. _____

Sandy helps feed the dog. _____

"Thank you, Sandy!" _____

Total Errors _____ /29

SCORING GUIDE FOR ORAL READING

(Circle the boxes that correspond to the student's scores)

	Oral Reading Accuracy
Independent Level	0–2 errors
Instructional Level	3–4 errors
Frustration Level	5 or more errors

▶ Primer: Seeds

Teacher Prompts: Say, *"The title of this passage is 'Seeds.' It is about seeds and how they grow."* Walk through the pictures in the passage. Help the student tell what goes on in each picture. Go back to the beginning and say, *"Please read the passage to me. Point to each word as you read."*

Record the time at the beginning: _____.

A seed is part of a plant. A seed has a tiny

plant inside. A seed can grow into a new

plant. Every plant came from a seed.

A seed will grow into the same kind of

plant it came from. A bean seed grows into a

bean plant. A corn seed grows into a corn

plant.

A seed needs water to grow. It needs to

be warm. Sun and rain help seeds grow.

Record the time at the end: _____.

(74 words)

QUESTIONS

1. Where do new plants come from? (*seeds*)
   Recall

2. Can an apple tree grow from an orange seed? Why not? (*No; it must come from an apple seed; a seed grows into the same kind of plant*)
   Inference

3. What does a seed need to grow? (*sun/warmth; rain/water*) [*must name two*] **Recall**

4. Where did the passage say that seeds get water? (*rain*) **Recall**9

SCORING GUIDE FOR ORAL READING AND COMPREHENSION

(Circle the boxes that correspond to the student's scores)

	Oral Reading Accuracy	Reading Comprehension	Listening Comprehension
Independent Level	3 or fewer errors	4 correct responses	
Instructional Level	4–7 errors	3 correct responses	3 correct responses
Frustration Level	8 or more errors	2 or fewer correct responses	

NARRATIVE PASSAGES

FORM A

"Come to dinner," said Jack's mother.

But Jack didn't want to come because he was busy.

He was bending wire, pounding nails, and mixing paint. He was making a toy.

"I don't care if you're busy. Come now." Jack's mother sounded cross.

"Just one more minute," said Jack. He bent wire, pounded nails, and painted the toy.

"Now, Jack," said Mother. "Your dinner will be cold."

Jack came to dinner and showed Mother his toy truck.

"That's so cool!" said Mother. "I didn't know you could make a truck."

▶ ▶ ▶

Last Sunday Hank sat on his porch. "What a good afternoon to do nothing," he said. Just then he saw a red car speed down the street. The car hit the curb! Then the car ran the stop sign! "Yippee!" yelled the driver, and the car sped on.

"Hey!" said Hank, "That was old Mr. Jolly. That man cannot drive."

Just then Sue came outside. "Hank, we need some milk for the baby. Please go to the store for some." Hank drove to the store, bought the milk and started home. He almost got home, but as he was crossing Fourth Street, he heard something.

"Oh, no!" said Hank.

"Yippee!" yelled the driver. A red car ran through the stop sign.

"Wham!" The red car smashed into Hank's car.

Hank climbed out of the window. He still held the bottle of milk.

"Are you hurt?" asked Mr. Jolly.

"No," said Hank. "I'm all right."

"It was all my fault," said Mr. Jolly.

"No, it was all my fault," said Hank. "I saw you out there driving. I should have stayed home."

▶ ▶ ▶

Anita's Uncle Albert had his own airplane. "Why don't you come flying with me, Anita?" he asked.

"OK," she said. Little did she know what she was getting in for!

When they were sitting inside the tight cockpit, Uncle Albert looked at some dials and pulled some knobs. He spoke into the radio, and a voice answered "You're clear for take-off." The airplane's engine roared, and soon they were speeding down the runway. Suddenly, trees looked like bushes, and people looked like ants.

When they were high in the air, Uncle Albert showed Anita how to steer the plane. He showed her how to make it climb and dip. He let Anita hold the steering wheel. She was flying!

Uncle Albert nodded, then nodded again, and then snored. Her uncle went to sleep!

"Wake up," said Anita. But Uncle Albert just snored, so Anita flew the plane.

Uncle Albert suddenly opened his eyes. "Oh, my goodness. I went to sleep," he said. "I shouldn't have done that."

Anita was glad he was awake. Uncle Albert saw the runway and made the plane go down. "Hold on tight," he said. They landed, and do you know what? It was the wrong airport!

▶ ▶ ▶

The West Street School Talent Show was about to start. James stood behind the curtain in the school auditorium. He was going to tell jokes, but right now he didn't feel funny, he felt anxious. A wave of heat was building under his shirt buttons. He peeked around the curtain and saw his good friend Kevin yawning and swinging his legs. There next to him was his friend Juana. She was scratching her arm and frowning. James wished he were down there with them, and not up here on the stage.

James felt something cold tickle his forehead. A thin stream of sweat ran down his face and dripped off his nose. James watched in wonder as it splashed onto his necktie. His mouth felt dry, and he couldn't swallow.

"Ah, Mrs. Mora?" he said as his teacher walked up.

"James, you're on!" she said. Then she pushed him out into the lights. The stage looked wide as a football field. As he started the long march out to the microphone, the audience hushed.

When he reached the microphone, James stuck his hands backwards into his pockets. Then he cocked his head sideways and said in a loud voice, "You know? A funny thing happened to me on the way to the show this morning." Juana stopped scratching and smiled up at him. So did Kevin.

Suddenly James was having fun up there!

▶ ▶ ▶

Rachel lived in a red brick apartment building where the landlady didn't allow dogs. The landlady, Mrs. Benson, had even put up a sign that said, "No Dogs Allowed!"

But Rachel really wanted a dog. One day when the landlady was upset because a squirrel had scared away her birds, Rachel saw her chance. "You know, Mrs. Benson? I think I know what will help," said Rachel. But the landlady shrugged and kept frowning, so Rachel couldn't share her idea.

Another day the landlady was crying and fussing, because stray cats had torn up her potted plants, and she didn't know what to do. "Mrs. Benson, I know what will help," said Rachel. But the landlady just frowned and walked away.

A week later Rachel saw the landlady standing in her door, and wringing her hands with worry. The landlady said she had heard on the radio that there was a burglar loose in the neighborhood, so Rachel said, "Mrs. Benson, this time I'm sure I know what will help."

"Rachel," said the landlady, "You keep saying that, so now I've got to know. What in the world do you think could help?"

"Well, you need something to keep squirrels away from your birds, right?"

"Right," said the landlady.

"And keep cats away from your plants, right?"

"Right," said the landlady.

"And keep burglars away from you, right?"

"Right!" said the landlady. "Now tell me what it is!" said the exasperated landlady.

"Well," said Rachel, scratching her chin. "There is only one thing that can do all that," said Rachel.

"I want it. I'll take it. Bring it to me now!" said the landlady.

Rachel promised to bring it that afternoon. And do you know what it was?

"Mrs. Benson, meet Fluffy!" said Rachel, as she led a puppy up the sidewalk.

"Hello!" said the landlady. "I didn't know you were what we needed." She scratched the puppy behind the ears. "Welcome to our apartments."

Fluffy licked the landlady's palm. Rachel grinned.

▶ ▶ ▶

iv

Mrs. Fidget got a sweepstakes ticket with her change for the diet soda, small size. She scratched off the paint and read the message, twice. "You have won the car!" it said. "The brand new Zoomer Z-3000 is yours!" Right away she drove her rusty brown station wagon with the one yellow fender to the Zoomer dealership, where the salesman frowned at her decrepit vehicle, her baggy sweater, and her falling-down socks. He eyed the sweepstakes ticket at arm's length.

"Have you ever owned a Zoomer, Mrs. Fidget?"

"No, sir," said Mrs. Fidget, and her grin was a mile wide. "It's a short little thing, isn't it?"

"We'll have to put you through our new owners' training course, then." The salesman guided her inside. He said, "Step one: All Zoomer drivers must look the part." Then he pushed a long, shiny black leather coat and a pair of wrap-around sunglasses onto Mrs. Fidget.

"But I can hardly see through these!" Mrs. Fidget shouted.

"You must look like a Zoomer driver, Mrs. Fidget! Now on to Step Two: Parking the Zoomer." The salesman pointed to two large pictures on the wall. One showed a Zoomer parked on a busy sidewalk, forcing the pedestrians into the street. The other showed a bright red Zoomer using two handicapped parking spaces near a large, bustling department store.

"My word, that's not nice!" Mrs. Fidget protested.

"As we say, Mrs. Fidget, 'The Zoomer driver owns the entire road.' But now let's go on to Step Three: Public relations." The serious salesman pointed to a picture of a driver with his head tipped back, a snooty expression on his face. "The angle of the head is so important, Mrs. Fidget. This man has no time for ordinary people. The road is his! Can you hold your head like that and sneer at people?"

"Of course I can't," said Mrs. Fidget.

"You'll get the idea with practice. But now let's proceed to Step Four."

"No, let's not," said Mrs. Fidget, shaking off the leather coat and yanking off the dark sunglasses. "Show me that lottery ticket again. Wasn't there a second prize? Yes, you keep your sports car. I'll settle for the little bird feeder."

▶ ▶ ▶

Paco awoke to his father's voice saying "Up and at 'em." He opened his eyes and saw the sun between the spruce trees on the other side of the lake. "Come on, the fish won't wait," said his father, from the other room now. Paco was still getting accustomed to that voice, as this was the first vacation Paco had spent with his father since his parents had divorced two summers ago.

Paco splashed water on his face and stepped out into the morning. He saw that his father had slid the canoe into the water and was waiting in the stern. "Remember to step to the middle," his father said as Paco stepped lightly into the canoe and swung onto the cool metal front seat. His father paddled the canoe away from the shore. Soon they were coasting to a stop near a dead tree floating just above the surface, like a crocodile.

"Cast near the trunk, but not too close."

"I know, Dad," said Paco. But his first cast arched neatly and plopped on top of the trunk. Without commenting, his father paddled the canoe to the other side of the dead tree, extricated the lure from the bark, and gently tossed it into the water.

"Now you can reel it in, but let's go to another spot," he said, and if he was annoyed at ruining this spot for further fishing, he kept it to himself. Together they paddled further down the shore, feathered their paddles, and coasted to a stop beside a dead sycamore tree rising from the water. The water was sprinkled with cottonwood fuzz, and it made Paco's reflection look hazy and distant. Paco smelled fish.

"Cast over by the trunk, but go easy," said his father. Paco looped the lure out in a perfect arc. It made a small splash in the water, and he reeled it back toward the canoe, jerking occasionally. With a jolt something pulled the lure straight down, then trembled on the line as Paco reeled and the rod bent.

As Paco lifted the gasping bass into the canoe, he felt his father's hand on his shoulder. "You know how to fish," his father said.

▶ ▶ ▶

"I wonder if she'll be there again tonight," said Inez, with a thoughtful expression coming to her face.

"Who?" asked Julio, looking goofy as always as his sneakers slapped the sidewalk between the darkened buildings.

"The old lady, the one who looked so cold sitting there. Don't you remember how she was shivering, and how you could hear her teeth chattering?"

Julio suddenly remembered then, and shuddered without making a comment. Yesterday on their way home from late play practice the two friends had seen the shabby profile of a woman huddled in the entrance of an out-of-business jewelry store. The lone streetlight illuminated just the woman's legs, enveloped in a greasy, thread-bare blanket with old newspapers spread over it. As the two friends had hurried past, they saw the gleaming reflection of the streetlight in the old derelict's open eyes. Inez had gasped, but Julio had pulled her quickly on.

Now it was another night, and she asked, out of sympathy mixed with curiosity, "What do you suppose she was doing there?"

"She's homeless, silly."

"I know that. But how would she occupy herself, alone in the cold and dark like an old hibernating bear? I wonder what she was thinking about. What she was feeling."

"She was probably feeling cold and thinking about getting warm," said Julio in a matter-of-fact manner. "Why do you worry about this stuff?"

"Because she's a human being. Suppose it was you sitting there?" said Inez.

"I wouldn't be sitting there, because when it's cold, I go inside. Duh."

The two of them continued along in silence, and when they were still three blocks from the out-of-business jewelry store Julio said, "You're right. Suppose there wasn't any place inside you could go."

"Wouldn't you have kids who could take care of you?" said Inez.

"Or friends to welcome you out of the cold?" said Julio.

"Maybe she tried those, but maybe she didn't have anywhere else to go," said Inez.

"We could ask her," said Julio.

"No," said Inez. They were in front of the out-of-business jewelry store now and in the doorway lay the stained blanket and one yellow rose.

▶ ▶ ▶

When Liliana's family immigrated to New York City from the Spanish-speaking Caribbean, she was selected for the non-academic track in high school, a course of instruction that led directly to work after graduation. This wasn't particularly unusual since in her barrio families generally struggled to accommodate themselves to an unfamiliar language and culture, and to keep their heads above water in an unforgiving urban environment. Students were fortunate merely to finish high school, and only occasionally would an individual consider pursuing further education at a college.

In the fall semester of her senior year, her guidance counselor called her for an interview. Liliana was tall and beautiful, so after a quick perusal of her file, the counselor did what presumably he often did: he suggested a vocation as a beautician. Liliana, however, didn't want to arrange other people's hair, or decorate their faces with cosmetics; she wanted to go to college.

"But you can't," said the counselor, reexamining the file with a sudden stab of uncertainty. "You haven't taken the right courses, and, besides, where would you go to college?"

Liliana had an answer prepared, because as a young girl, she had participated in a program called the Fresh Air Fund that dispatched urban children from New York City to spend the summer with families in the country. Her host family had taken her to investigate the campus of a nearby college.

Eight years later in the counselor's office, Liliana said, "William Smith College." The school was unfamiliar to him, but he reluctantly agreed to help Liliana apply for admission, reminding her that she would require serious financial assistance, of course.

Liliana was accepted to William Smith College and she was offered an unusually generous scholarship. She matriculated, and although she was often home-sick, and frequently she wondered what she was doing among so many students who were wealthier than herself, she worked hard, and managed not only to graduate but to achieve a high grade point average. Then she submitted an application to law school and was accepted.

Years later, her high school guidance counselor happened to encounter an article in the *New York Times* introducing the new legal advisor for the Fresh Air Fund: Liliana. A short while later he read about her again, when she had been appointed to the Board of Trustees of William Smith College.

X

NARRATIVE PASSAGES
RESPONSE SHEETS

FORM A

▶ Narrative 1st Grade Level: Jack's Dinner

Introduction: The title of this story is "Jack's Dinner." Sometimes it's hard to stop what you are doing when you are called to dinner. Read to find out what happened when Jack was busy at dinner time. I will ask you questions about the passage after you finish reading.

Record the time at the beginning: _____.

"Come to dinner," said Jack's mother.

But Jack didn't want to come because he was busy.

He was bending wire, pounding nails, and mixing paint. He was making a toy.

"I don't care if you're busy. Come now." Jack's mother sounded cross.

"Just one more minute," said Jack. He bent wire, pounded nails, and painted the toy.

"Now, Jack," said Mother. "Your dinner will be cold."

Jack came to dinner and showed Mother his toy truck.

"That's so cool!" said Mother. "I didn't know you could make a truck."

Record the time at the end: _____.

This text has been rated at 300L
It has 89 words

QUESTIONS

1. Why didn't Jack want to come to dinner? (*He was busy.*) **Recall**

2. What was Jack making? (*a toy*) **Recall**

3. Why did Mother want Jack to come then? (*because his dinner will get cold*) **Recall**

4. How do we know that his mother's feelings changed? (*The text said she sounded cross; then she said "that's cool!"*). **Inference**

5. In the sentence, "Jack's mother sounded cross," what does *cross* mean? (*irritated, angry*) **Vocabulary**

6. In this passage, how could Jack keep his mother from getting cross with him? (*Explain that he would need more time before dinner; not start a project at dinner time.*) **Inference**

SCORING GUIDE FOR ORAL READING AND COMPREHENSION

(Circle the boxes that correspond to the student's scores)

	Oral Reading Accuracy	Reading Comprehension	Listening Comprehension
Independent Level	3 or fewer errors	6 correct responses	
Instructional Level	4–9 errors	5 correct responses	5 correct responses
Frustration Level	10 or more errors	4 or fewer correct responses	

COMPREHENSION SCORES, BY TYPE

	Recall Questions	Inference Questions	Vocabulary Questions
Student's Correct Answers			
Possible Correct Answers	3	2	1

READING RATE SCORING GUIDE FOR GRADE 1

If the results computed just above show that the student read this passage at his independent level, you may wish to calculate his reading rate and compare that to other readers at his grade level.

1. Here is the number of words in this passage: 89

2. Write the number of words read incorrectly here: _____

3. Subtract #2 from #1 and write the answer here: _____

4. Using a calculator, multiply #3 by 60 seconds and write the answer here: _____

5. Write the student's reading time in seconds here: _____

6. Using a calculator, divide #4 by #5 and write the answer here: _____

The answer in #6 is the reading rate (words read correctly) per minute.

To interpret this number, first, locate the column in the chart below that represents the time of the year when this test was administered. Then, circle the reading rate that most closely matches your student's reading rate for this passage. Read across to the left to find the student's percentile rank— that is, an estimation of where that reading rate falls within those of other students at that grade level at that time of year.

ORAL READING FLUENCY NORMS FOR GRADE 1

Percentile	Fall WCPM	Winter WCPM	Spring WCPM
90		81	111
75		47	82
50		23	53
25		12	28
10		6	15

From Hasbrouck and Tindal, 2004.

▶ Narrative 2nd Grade Level (2.1): Driving on Sunday

Introduction: *The title of this story is "Driving on Sunday." Sometimes adventures can happen when you least expect them. Read about how poor Hank was sent on an adventure. I will ask you questions about the passage after you finish reading.*

Record the time at the beginning: _____.

Last Sunday Hank sat on his porch. "What a good afternoon to do nothing," he said. Just then he saw a red car speed down the street. The car hit the curb! Then the car ran the stop sign! "Yippee!" yelled the driver, and the car sped on.

"Hey!" said Hank, "That was old Mr. Jolly. That man cannot drive."

Just then Sue came outside. "Hank, we need some milk for the baby. Please go to the store for some." Hank drove to the store, bought the milk and started home. He almost got home, but as he was crossing Fourth Street, he heard something.

"Oh, no!" said Hank.

"Yippee!" yelled the driver. A red car ran through the stop sign.

"Wham!" The red car smashed into Hank's car.

Hank climbed out of the window. He still held the bottle of milk.

"Are you hurt?" asked Mr. Jolly.

"No," said Hank. "I'm all right."

"It was all my fault," said Mr. Jolly.

"No, it was all my fault," said Hank. "I saw you out there driving. I should have stayed home."

Record the time at the end: _____.

This text has been rated at 340L
It has 181 words

QUESTIONS

1. What did Hank see as he was sitting on his front porch? (*He saw a red car speeding down the street.*) **Recall**

2. How did Mr. Jolly show that he was a bad driver? (*hitting curbs, swerving side to side, running stop signs*) **Inference**

3. In the phrase " 'Yippee!' yelled the driver, and the car sped on," what does *sped* mean? (*drove fast*) **Vocabulary**

4. How can you tell Mr. Jolly was having fun driving? (*He was yelling "Yippee!"*) **Inference**

5. Why did Hank's wife, Sue, send him to the store? (*to get milk for the baby*) **Recall**

6. What happened as Hank was on his way home from the store? (*Mr. Jolly ran a stop sign and hit his car*) **Recall**

7. Why do you think Hank climbed out the car window? (*His door was smashed.*) **Inference**

8. Why do you think Hank blamed himself for the accident instead of Mr. Jolly? (*He knew Mr. Jolly was a bad driver; he saw Mr. Jolly driving badly.*) **Inference**

Errors in oral reading accuracy: _____

Correct comprehension responses: _____

SCORING GUIDE FOR ORAL READING AND COMPREHENSION

(Circle the boxes that correspond to the student's scores)

	Oral Reading Accuracy	Reading Comprehension	Listening Comprehension
Independent Level	5 or fewer errors	7–8 correct responses	
Instructional Level	6–18 errors	6–7 correct responses	6–7 correct responses
Frustration Level	19 or more errors	5 or fewer correct responses	

COMPREHENSION SCORES, BY TYPE

	Recall Questions	Inference Questions	Vocabulary Questions
Student's Correct Answers			
Possible Correct Answers	3	4	1

READING RATE SCORING GUIDE FOR GRADE 2

If the results computed just above show that the student read this passage at his independent level, you may wish to calculate his reading rate and compare that to other readers at his grade level.

1. Here is the number of words in this passage: 181

2. Write the number of words read incorrectly here: _____

3. Subtract #2 from #1 and write the answer here: _____

4. Using a calculator, multiply #3 by 60 seconds and write the answer here: _____

5. Write the student's reading time in seconds here: _____

6. Using a calculator, divide #4 by #5 and write the answer here: _____

The answer in #6 is the reading rate (words read correctly) per minute.

To interpret this number, first, locate the column in the chart below that represents the time of the year when this test was administered. Then, circle the reading rate that most closely matches your student's reading rate for this passage. Read across to the left to find the student's percentile rank— that is, an estimation of where that reading rate falls within those of other students at that grade level at that time of year.

ORAL READING FLUENCY NORMS FOR GRADE 2

Percentile	Fall WCPM	Winter WCPM	Spring WCPM
90	106	125	142
75	79	100	117
50	51	72	89
25	25	42	61
10	11	18	31

From Hasbrouck and Tindal, 2004.

▶ Narrative 2nd Grade Level (2.2): Anita and the Airplane

Introduction: The title of this story is "Anita and the Airplane." Can you imagine what it would be like to fly in a small airplane? Read to find out what happened when Anita went flying in her Uncle Albert's small airplane. I will ask you questions about the passage after you finish reading.

Record the time at the beginning: _____.

Anita's Uncle Albert had his own airplane. "Why don't you come flying with me, Anita?" he asked.

"OK," she said. Little did she know what she was getting in for!

When they were sitting inside the tight cockpit, Uncle Albert looked at some dials and pulled some knobs. He spoke into the radio, and a voice answered "You're clear for take-off." The airplane's engine roared, and soon they were speeding down the runway. Suddenly, trees looked like bushes, and people looked like ants.

When they were high in the air, Uncle Albert showed Anita how to steer the plane. He showed her how to make it climb and dip. He let Anita hold the steering wheel. She was flying!

Uncle Albert nodded, then nodded again, and then snored. Her uncle went to sleep!

"Wake up," said Anita. But Uncle Albert just snored, so Anita flew the plane.

Uncle Albert suddenly opened his eyes. "Oh, my goodness. I went to sleep," he said. "I shouldn't have done that."

Anita was glad he was awake. Uncle Albert saw the runway and made the plane go down. "Hold on tight," he said. They landed, and do you know what? It was the wrong airport!

Record the time at the end: _____.

This text has been rated at 450L
It has 201 words

QUESTIONS

1. What did Uncle Albert do before the airplane took off? (*looked at dials, pulled knobs, talked on the radio*) **Recall**

2. The voice on the radio said "You're clear for take-off." What does *clear* mean in that sentence? (*everything is okay for you to take off; nothing is in the way*) **Vocabulary**

3. As they were taking off, what did Anita see when she looked down? (*The trees looked like bushes and people looked like ants.*) **Recall**

4. How did the author tell us that Uncle Albert was not a careful person? (*He went to sleep while Anita was flying.*) **Inference**

5. How do we know that Anita did not want to fly the airplane by herself? (*She tried to wake her uncle.*) **Inference**

6. The story says the uncle showed Anita how to make the airplane "climb and dip." What does *dip* mean in that sentence? (*to go lower in the air*) **Vocabulary**

7. What happened after Uncle Albert told Anita to hold on tight? (*The airplane landed.*) **Recall**

8. Why do you think they were at the wrong airport? (*The Uncle didn't know where Anita had flown while he was asleep.*) **Inference**

Errors in oral reading accuracy: _____

Correct comprehension responses: _____

SCORING GUIDE FOR ORAL READING AND COMPREHENSION

(Circle the boxes that correspond to the student's scores)

	Oral Reading Accuracy	Reading Comprehension	Listening Comprehension
Independent Level	6 or fewer errors	7–8 correct responses	
Instructional Level	7–20 errors	6–7 correct responses	6–7 correct responses
Frustration Level	21 or more errors	5 or fewer correct responses	

COMPREHENSIVE SCORES, BY TYPE

	Recall Questions	Inference Questions	Vocabulary Questions
Student's Correct Answers			
Possible Correct Answers	3	3	2

READING RATE SCORING GUIDE FOR GRADE 2

If the results computed just above show that the student read this passage at his independent level, you may wish to calculate his reading rate and compare that to other readers at his grade level.

1. Here is the number of words in this passage: 201

2. Write the number of words read incorrectly here: _____

3. Subtract #2 from #1 and write the answer here: _____

4. Using a calculator, multiply #3 by 60 seconds and write the answer here: _____

5. Write the student's reading time in seconds here: _____

6. Using a calculator, divide #4 by #5 and write the answer here: _____

The answer in #6 is the reading rate (words read correctly) per minute.

To interpret this number, first, locate the column in the chart below that represents the time of the year when this test was administered. Then, circle the reading rate that most closely matches your student's reading rate for this passage. Read across to the left to find the student's percentile rank—that is, an estimation of where that reading rate falls within those of other students at that grade level at that time of year.

ORAL READING FLUENCY NORMS FOR GRADE 2

Percentile	Fall WCPM	Winter WCPM	Spring WCPM
90	106	125	142
75	79	100	117
50	51	72	89
25	25	42	61
10	11	18	31

From Hasbrouck and Tindal, 2004.

▶ Narrative 3rd Grade Level: The Talent Show

Introduction: The title of this story is "The Talent Show." Many people get stage fright, the fear of performing in front of others. But performing on stage can be a lot of fun, too. Read about what happens when James has to perform his comedy show onstage. I will ask you questions about the passage after you finish reading.

Record the time at the beginning: _____.

The West Street School Talent Show was about to start. James stood behind the curtain in the school auditorium. He was going to tell jokes, but right now he didn't feel funny, he felt anxious. A wave of heat was building under his shirt buttons. He peeked around the curtain and saw his good friend Kevin yawning and swinging his legs. There next to him was his friend Juana. She was scratching her arm and frowning. James wished he were down there with them, and not up here on the stage.

James felt something cold tickle his forehead. A thin stream of sweat ran down his face and dripped off his nose. James watched in wonder as it splashed onto his necktie. His mouth felt dry, and he couldn't swallow.

"Ah, Mrs. Mora?" he said as his teacher walked up.

"James, you're on!" she said. Then she pushed him out into the lights. The stage looked wide as a football field. As he started the long march out to the microphone, the audience hushed.

When he reached the microphone, James stuck his hands backwards into his pockets. Then he cocked his head sideways and said in a loud voice, "You know? A funny thing happened to me on the way to the show this morning." Juana stopped scratching and smiled up at him. So did Kevin.

Suddenly James was having fun up there!

Record the time at the end: _____.

This text has been rated at 600L
It has 233 words

QUESTIONS

1. What was James going to do in this story? (*take part in a talent show—tell jokes to students in the school auditorium*) **Recall**

2. Why was James worried? (*He had to perform in front of a large audience of his classmates—he had stage fright.*) **Inference**

3. What did James feel under his shirt buttons? (*a wave of heat*) **Recall**

4. What caused James to feel so hot? (*fear, anxiety*) **Inference**

5. What was the effect on James when Juana and Kevin smiled? (*He felt more confident.*) **Recall**

6. How did the author tell you that the audience was going to pay attention to James? (*When James walked onto the stage, the audience was quiet.*) **Inference**

7. What did James do when he finally got to the microphone? (*stuck his hands backwards in his pockets and spoke loudly*) **Recall**

8. In the phrase, "right now he didn't feel funny, he felt anxious," what does *anxious* mean? (*scared, worried*) **Vocabulary**

Errors in oral reading accuracy: _____

Correct comprehension responses: _____

SCORING GUIDE FOR ORAL READING AND COMPREHENSION

(Circle the boxes that correspond to the student's scores)

	Oral Reading Accuracy	Reading Comprehension	Listening Comprehension
Independent Level	7 or fewer errors	7–8 correct responses	
Instructional Level	8–23 errors	6–7 correct responses	6–7 correct responses
Frustration Level	24 or more errors	5 or fewer correct responses	

COMPREHENSION SCORES, BY TYPE

	Recall Questions	Inference Questions	Vocabulary Questions
Student's Correct Answers			
Possible Correct Answers	4	3	1

READING RATE SCORING GUIDE FOR GRADE 3

If the results computed just above show that the student read this passage at his independent level, you may wish to calculate his reading rate and compare that to other readers at his grade level.

1. Here is the number of words in this passage: 233

2. Write the number of words read incorrectly here: _____

3. Subtract #2 from #1 and write the answer here: _____

4. Using a calculator, multiply #3 by 60 seconds and write the answer here: _____

5. Write the student's reading time in seconds here: _____

6. Using a calculator, divide #4 by #5 and write the answer here: _____

The answer in #6 is the reading rate (words read correctly) per minute.

To interpret this number, first, locate the column in the chart below that represents the time of the year when this test was administered. Then, circle the reading rate that most closely matches your student's reading rate for this passage. Read across to the left to find the student's percentile rank—that is, an estimation of where that reading rate falls within those of other students at that grade level at that time of year.

ORAL READING FLUENCY NORMS FOR GRADE 3

Percentile	Fall WCPM	Winter WCPM	Spring WCPM
90	128	146	162
75	99	120	137
50	71	92	107
25	44	62	78
10	21	36	48

From Hasbrouck and Tindal, 2004.

► Narrative 4th Grade Level: A Dog for Rachel

Introduction: The title of this story is "A Dog for Rachel." In many apartment buildings, pets are not allowed. Rachel lived in an apartment building. Read to find out what happened when she wanted a pet. I will ask you questions about the passage after you finish reading.

Record the time at the beginning: _____.

Rachel lived in a red brick apartment building where the landlady didn't allow dogs. The landlady, Mrs. Benson, had even put up a sign that said, "No Dogs Allowed!"

But Rachel really wanted a dog. One day when the landlady was upset because a squirrel had scared away her birds, Rachel saw her chance. "You know, Mrs. Benson? I think I know what will help," said Rachel. But the landlady shrugged and kept frowning, so Rachel couldn't share her idea.

Another day the landlady was crying and fussing, because stray cats had torn up her potted plants, and she didn't know what to do. "Mrs. Benson, I know what will help," said Rachel. But the landlady just frowned and walked away.

A week later Rachel saw the landlady standing in her door, and wringing her hands with worry. The landlady said she had heard on the radio that there was a burglar loose in the neighborhood, so Rachel said, "Mrs. Benson, this time I'm sure I know what will help."

"Rachel," said the landlady, "You keep saying that, so now I've got to know. What in the world do you think could help?"

"Well, you need something to keep squirrels away from your birds, right?"

"Right," said the landlady.

"And keep cats away from your plants, right?"

"Right," said the landlady.

"And keep burglars away from you, right?"

"Right!" said the landlady. "Now tell me what it is!" said the exasperated landlady.

"Well," said Rachel, scratching her chin. "There is only one thing that can do all that," said Rachel.

"I want it. I'll take it. Bring it to me now!" said the landlady.

Rachel promised to bring it that afternoon. And do you know what it was?

"Mrs. Benson, meet Fluffy!" said Rachel, as she led a puppy up the sidewalk.

"Hello!" said the landlady. "I didn't know you were what we needed." She scratched the puppy behind the ears. "Welcome to our apartments."

Fluffy licked the landlady's palm. Rachel grinned.

Record the time at the end: _____.

This text has been rated at 750L
It has 332 words

QUESTIONS

1. How did Rachel know that pets were not allowed in the apartment building? (*The landlady had put up a sign that said no dogs were allowed.*) **Recall**

2. What was the first problem the landlady had? (*A squirrel frightened away her birds.*) **Recall**

3. In the sentence, "A week later Rachel saw the landlady standing in her door, wringing her hands with worry," what does *wringing* mean? (*rubbing them together*) **Vocabulary**

4. What was the effect on the landlady when she heard that there were burglars in the neighborhood? (*She was really scared; she wanted help—OR this came after two other problems and it made her want help.* [must answer one or the other]) **Recall**

5 Why didn't Rachel just say that the landlady needed a dog? (*She was afraid she might have said no, or she wanted to build more suspense, or she wanted her to be won over by the puppy himself.* [must answer one of the those options]) **Inference**

6. In the sentence, "'Now tell me what it is!' said the exasperated landlady," what does exasperated mean? (*fed up; reaching her emotional limits*) **Vocabulary**

7. How did the dog show the landlady that he liked her? (*licked her palm*) **Recall**

8. How did the landlady show the dog that she liked him? (*scratched behind his ears*) **Recall**

Errors in oral reading accuracy: _____

Correct comprehension responses: _____

SCORING GUIDE FOR ORAL READING AND COMPREHENSION

(Circle the boxes that correspond to the student's scores)

	Oral Reading Accuracy	Reading Comprehension	Listening Comprehension
Independent Level	10 or fewer errors	7–8 correct responses	
Instructional Level	11–33 errors	6–7 correct responses	6–7 correct responses
Frustration Level	34 or more errors	5 or fewer correct responses	

COMPREHENSION SCORES, BY TYPE

	Recall Questions	Inference Questions	Vocabulary Questions
Student's Correct Answers			
Possible Correct Answers	5	2	1

READING RATE SCORING GUIDE FOR GRADE 4

If the results computed just above show that the student read this passage at his independent level, you may wish to calculate his reading rate and compare that to other readers at his grade level.

1. Here is the number of words in this passage: 332

2. Write the number of words read incorrectly here: _____

3. Subtract #2 from #1 and write the answer here: _____

4. Using a calculator, multiply #3 by 60 seconds and write the answer here: _____

5. Write the student's reading time in seconds here: _____

6. Using a calculator, divide #4 by #5 and write the answer here: _____

The answer in #6 is the reading rate (words read correctly) per minute.

To interpret this number, first, locate the column in the chart below that represents the time of the year when this test was administered. Then, circle the reading rate that most closely matches your student's reading rate for this passage. Read across to the left to find the student's percentile rank— that is, an estimation of where that reading rate falls within those of other students at that grade level at that time of year.

ORAL READING FLUENCY NORMS FOR GRADE 4

Percentile	Fall WCPM	Winter WCPM	Spring WCPM
90	145	166	180
75	119	139	152
50	94	112	123
25	68	87	98
10	45	61	72

From Hasbrouck and Tindal, 2004.

Introduction: The title of this story is "Mrs. Fidget and the Sports Car." Have you ever seen the sweepstakes tickets they sometimes give away at fast food restaurants? Here is a story about a woman named Mrs. Fidget who wins a valuable prize in a sweepstakes. I will ask you questions about the passage after you finish reading.

Record the time at the beginning: _____.

Mrs. Fidget got a sweepstakes ticket with her change for the diet soda, small size. She scratched off the paint and read the message, twice. "You have won the car!" it said. "The brand new Zoomer Z-3000 is yours!" Right away she drove her rusty brown station wagon with the one yellow fender to the Zoomer dealership, where the salesman frowned at her decrepit vehicle, her baggy sweater, and her falling-down socks. He eyed the sweepstakes ticket at arm's length.

"Have you ever owned a Zoomer, Mrs. Fidget?"

"No, sir," said Mrs. Fidget, and her grin was a mile wide. "It's a short little thing, isn't it?"

"We'll have to put you through our new owners' training course, then." The sales-

man guided her inside. He said, "Step one: All Zoomer drivers must look the part." Then he pushed a long, shiny black leather coat and a pair of wrap-around sunglasses onto Mrs. Fidget.

"But I can hardly see through these!" Mrs. Fidget shouted.

"You must look like a Zoomer driver, Mrs. Fidget! Now on to Step Two: Parking the Zoomer." The salesman pointed to two large pictures on the wall. One showed a Zoomer parked on a busy sidewalk, forcing the pedestrians into the street. The other showed a bright red Zoomer using two handicapped parking spaces near a large, bustling department store.

"My word, that's not nice!" Mrs. Fidget protested.

"As we say, Mrs. Fidget, 'The Zoomer driver owns the entire road.' But now let's go on to Step Three: Public relations." The serious salesman pointed to a picture of a driver with his head tipped back, a snooty expression on his face. "The angle of the head is so important, Mrs. Fidget. This man has no time for ordinary people. The road is his! Can you hold your head like that and sneer at people?"

"Of course I can't," said Mrs. Fidget.

"You'll get the idea with practice. But now let's proceed to Step Four."

"No, let's not," said Mrs. Fidget, shaking off the leather coat and yanking off the dark sunglasses. "Show me that lottery ticket again. Wasn't there a second prize? Yes, you keep your sports car. I'll settle for the little bird feeder."

Record the time at the end: _____.

This text has been rated at 850L
It has 369 words

QUESTIONS

1. What had Mrs. Fidget bought when she received the sweepstakes ticket with her change? (*a small cup of diet soda*) **Recall**

2. Why do you think she read the ticket twice? (*She was so surprised; she probably hadn't expected to win a valuable prize.*) **Inference**

3. Describe the car Mrs. Fidget already owned. (*a rusty brown station wagon with one yellow fender*) **Recall**

4. What did the car dealer think of Mrs. Fidget? Why do you think so? (*He thought she was sloppy, or someone who didn't care about appearances—certainly not a suitable driver for an expensive sports car, because he frowned at her car, her sweater, and her socks.*) **Inference**

5. What are at least two steps to the training that Mrs. Fidget completed? (*Looking like a Zoomer driver, parking, and "public relations" or how to look toward other people [Must answer two of the three]*) **Recall**

6. In the phrase, "All Zoomer drivers must look the part," what does look *the part* mean? (*look the way they would be expected to look—in this case, like the driver of an expensive sports car*) **Vocabulary**

7. Why did Mrs. Fidget have trouble with the salesman's lessons? (*She didn't want to behave like a self-centered and inconsiderate person, which was what the salesman was trying to teach her.*) **Inference**

8. How would you describe Mrs. Fidget's personality? What kind of a person is she? (*Any of the following will suffice: She is modest, of simple tastes—she doesn't like to put herself forward; and she is unconcerned about money.*) **Inference**

Errors in oral reading accuracy: _____

Correct comprehension responses: _____

SCORING GUIDE FOR ORAL READING AND COMPREHENSION

(Circle the boxes that correspond to the student's scores)

	Oral Reading Accuracy	Reading Comprehension	Listening Comprehension
Independent Level	11 or fewer errors	7–8 correct responses	
Instructional Level	12–37 errors	6–7 correct responses	6–7 correct responses
Frustration Level	38 or more errors	5 or fewer correct responses	

COMPREHENSION SCORES, BY TYPE

	Recall Questions	Inference Questions	Vocabulary Questions
Student's Correct Answers			
Possible Correct Answers	3	4	1

READING RATE SCORING GUIDE FOR GRADE 5

If the results computed just above show that the student read this passage at his independent level, you may wish to calculate his reading rate and compare that to other readers at his grade level.

1. Here is the number of words in this passage: 369

2. Write the number of words read incorrectly here: _____

3. Subtract #2 from #1 and write the answer here: _____

4. Using a calculator, multiply #3 by 60 seconds and write the answer here: _____

5. Write the student's reading time in seconds here: _____

6. Using a calculator, divide #4 by #5 and write the answer here: _____

The answer in line six is the reading rate (words read correctly) per minute.

To interpret this number, first, locate the column in the chart below that represents the time of the year when this test was administered. Then, circle the reading rate that most closely matches your student's reading rate for this passage. Read across to the left to find the student's percentile rank—that is, an estimation of where that reading rate falls within those of other students at that grade level at that time of year.

ORAL READING FLUENCY NORMS FOR GRADE 5

Percentile	Fall WCPM	Winter WCPM	Spring WCPM
90	166	182	194
75	139	156	168
50	110	127	139
25	85	99	109
10	61	74	83

From Hasbrouck and Tindal, 2004.

▶ Narrative 6th Grade Level: Fishing with His Father

Introduction: The title of this story is "Fishing with His Father." Going fishing with a parent can be a lot of fun. But it can also have some problems, too. Read about what happens when Paco goes fishing with his father. I will ask you questions about the passage after you finish reading.

Record the time at the beginning: _____.

Paco awoke to his father's voice saying "Up and at 'em." He opened his eyes and saw the sun between the spruce trees on the other side of the lake. "Come on, the fish won't wait," said his father, from the other room now. Paco was still getting accustomed to that voice, as this was the first vacation Paco had spent with his father since his parents had divorced two summers ago.

Paco splashed water on his face and stepped out into the morning. He saw that his father had slid the canoe into the water, and was waiting in the stern. "Remember to step to the middle," his father said as Paco stepped lightly into the canoe and swung onto the cool metal front seat. His father paddled the canoe away from the shore. Soon they were coasting to a stop near a

dead tree floating just above the surface, like a crocodile.

"Cast near the trunk, but not too close."

"I know, Dad," said Paco. But his first cast arched neatly and plopped on top of the trunk. Without commenting, his father paddled the canoe to the other side of the dead tree, extricated the lure from the bark, and gently tossed it into the water.

"Now you can reel it in, but let's go to another spot," he said, and if he was annoyed at ruining this spot for further fishing, he kept it to himself. Together they paddled further down the shore, feathered their paddles, and coasted to a stop beside a dead sycamore tree rising from the water. The water was sprinkled with cottonwood fuzz, and it made Paco's reflection look hazy and distant. Paco smelled fish.

"Cast over by the trunk, but go easy," said his father. Paco looped the lure out in a perfect arc. It made a small splash in the water, and he reeled it back toward the canoe, jerking occasionally. With a jolt something pulled the lure straight down, then trembled on the line as Paco reeled and the rod bent.

As Paco lifted the gasping bass into the canoe, he felt his father's hand on his shoulder. "You know how to fish," his father said.

Record the time at the end: _____.

This text has been rated at 950L
It has 366 words

QUESTIONS

1. Who woke up first? How do you know? (*Paco's father. He woke Paco up*). **Recall**

2. Why was Paco not used to the sound of his father's voice? (*His parents were divorced and he hadn't had a vacation with his father in two years.*) **Recall**

3. Why do you think that Paco's father said, "Remember to step to the middle?" (*He didn't want him to turn the canoe over—and he wasn't sure if Paco knew how to get into a canoe properly [must answer one or the other].*) **Inference**

4. How much experience did Paco's father have in paddling a canoe? How do you know that? (*He was an expert. He could make the canoe go where he wanted it to, quietly.*) **Inference**

5. How did Paco feel about his father's advice? How do you know? (*He felt he didn't need it. He was irritated by it.*) **Inference**

6. In the phrase, "they paddled further down the shore, feathered their paddles, and coasted to a stop," what does *feathered* mean? (*They turned the paddles parallel to the water so the wind wouldn't blow on them and push the canoe around.*) **Vocabulary**

7. What was the effect on Paco's father when Paco caught a fish? (*relief and pride, maybe he realized he had underestimated the boy*) **Inference**

8. How did the author tell you that the fish was big? (*The fish pulled hard on the line and made the pole bend.*) **Inference**

Errors in oral reading accuracy: _____

Correct comprehension responses: _____

SCORING GUIDE FOR ORAL READING AND COMPREHENSION

(Circle the boxes that correspond to the student's scores)

	Oral Reading Accuracy	Reading Comprehension	Listening Comprehension
Independent Level	11 or fewer errors	7–8 orrect responses	
Instructional Level	12–37 errors	6–7 correct responses	6–7 correct responses
Frustration Level	38 or more errors	5 or fewer correct responses	

COMPREHENSION SCORES, BY TYPE

	Recall Questions	Inference Questions	Vocabulary Questions
Student's Correct Answers			
Possible Correct Answers	2	5	1

READING RATE SCORING GUIDE FOR GRADE 6

If the results computed just above show that the student read this passage at his independent level, you may wish to calculate his reading rate and compare that to other readers at his grade level.

1. Here is the number of words in this passage: 366

2. Write the number of words read incorrectly here: _____

3. Subtract #2 from #1 and write the answer here: _____

4. Using a calculator, multiply #3 by 60 seconds and write the answer here: _____

5. Write the student's reading time in seconds here: _____

6. Using a calculator, divide #4 by #5 and write the answer here: _____

The answer in #6 is the reading rate (words read correctly) per minute.

To interpret this number, first, locate the column in the chart below that represents the time of the year when this test was administered. Then, circle the reading rate that most closely matches your student's reading rate for this passage. Read across to the left to find the student's percentile rank—that is, an estimation of where that reading rate falls within those of other students at that grade level at that time of year.

ORAL READING FLUENCY NORMS FOR GRADE 6

Percentile	Fall WCPM	Winter WCPM	Spring WCPM
90	177	195	204
75	153	167	177
50	127	140	150
25	98	111	122
10	68	82	93

From Hasbrouck and Tindal, 2004.

► Narrative Middle School Level: The Lady at the Jewelry Store

Introduction: The title of this story is "The Lady at the Jewelry Store." As they walk down a city street, Inez and Julio encounter a strange woman. Read to find out how the two of them react to meeting this woman. I will ask you questions about the passage after you finish reading.

Record the time at the beginning: _____.

"I wonder if she'll be there again tonight," said Inez, with a thoughtful expression coming to her face.

"Who?" asked Julio, looking goofy as always as his sneakers slapped the sidewalk between the darkened buildings.

"The old lady, the one who looked so cold sitting there. Don't you remember how she was shivering, and how you could hear her teeth chattering?"

Julio suddenly remembered then, and shuddered without making a comment. Yesterday on their way home from late play practice the two friends had seen the shabby profile of a woman huddled in the entrance of an out-of-business jewelry store. The lone streetlight illuminated just the woman's legs, enveloped in a greasy, thread-bare blanket with old newspapers spread over it. As the two friends had hurried past, they saw the gleaming reflection of the streetlight in the old derelict's open eyes. Inez had gasped, but Julio had pulled her quickly on.

Now it was another night, and she asked, out of sympathy mixed with curiosity, "What do you suppose she was doing there?"

"She's homeless, silly."

"I know that. But how would she occupy herself, alone in the cold and dark like an old hibernating bear? I wonder what she was thinking about. What she was feeling."

"She was probably feeling cold and thinking about getting warm," said Julio in a matter-of-fact manner. "Why do you worry about this stuff?"

"Because she's a human being. Suppose it was you sitting there?" said Inez.

"I wouldn't be sitting there, because when it's cold, I go inside. Duh."

The two of them continued along in silence, and when they were still three blocks from the out-of-business jewelry store Julio said, "You're right. Suppose there wasn't any place inside you could go."

"Wouldn't you have kids who could take care of you?" said Inez.

"Or friends to welcome you out of the cold?" said Julio.

"Maybe she tried those, but maybe she didn't have anywhere else to go," said Inez.

"We could ask her," said Julio.

"No," said Inez. They were in front of the out-of-business jewelry store now and in the doorway lay the stained blanket and one yellow rose.

Record the time at the end: _____.

This text has been rated at 1000L
It has 358 words

QUESTIONS

1. Where were Inez and Julio coming from when they passed the woman? (*play practice*) **Recall**

2. What was odd about the title of the story, "The Lady at the Jewelry Store"? (*The title suggests that the story will be about a lady with enough money to buy jewelry, and not a homeless woman.*) **Inference**

3. The story says "The lone streetlight illuminated just the woman's legs, enveloped in a greasy, thread-bare blanket." What does *enveloped* mean? (*wrapped up, enclosed*). **Vocabulary**

4. What do we know about Inez from this story? (*She's compassionate, caring. From the beginning she is concerned about the plight of the old woman.*) **Inference**

5. Why did Inez and Julio walk along for a time without speaking to each other? (*They were mad at each other; they disagreed, but didn't want to talk about it.*) **Inference**

6. What made Julio suddenly worry about the woman having no place to go? (*He thought it through; or he wanted to make peace with Inez.*) **Inference**

7. Why couldn't they ask the woman why she was homeless? (*She was gone when they thought to ask her.*) **Recall**

8. Why do you suppose the author said "in the shadowy doorway lay the stained blanket and one yellow rose"? (*He wanted to suggest the old woman had died, or had been rescued from the street, but he wanted to leave it unclear. There might be other creative and logical answers.*) **Inference**

Errors in oral reading accuracy: _____

Correct comprehension responses: _____

SCORING GUIDE FOR ORAL READING AND COMPREHENSION

(Circle the boxes that correspond to the student's scores)

	Oral Reading Accuracy	Reading Comprehension	Listening Comprehension
Independent Level	11 or fewer errors	7–8 correct responses	
Instructional Level	12–36 errors	6–7 correct responses	6–7 correct responses
Frustration Level	37 or more errors	5 or fewer correct responses	

COMPREHENSION SCORES, BY TYPE

	Recall Questions	Inference Questions	Vocabulary Questions
Student's Correct Answers			
Possible Correct Answers	2	5	1

READING RATE SCORING GUIDE FOR MIDDLE SCHOOL

If the results computed just above show that the student read this passage at his independent level, you may wish to calculate his reading rate and compare that to other readers at his grade level.

1. Here is the number of words in this passage: 358

2. Write the number of words read incorrectly here: _____

3. Subtract #2 from #1 and write the answer here: _____

4. Using a calculator, multiply #3 by 60 seconds and write the answer here: _____

5. Write the student's reading time in seconds here: _____

6. Using a calculator, divide #4 by #5 and write the answer here: _____

The answer in #6 is the reading rate (words read correctly) per minute.

To interpret this number, first, locate the column in the chart below that represents the time of the year when this test was administered. Then, circle the reading rate that most closely matches your student's reading rate for this passage. Read across to the left to find the student's percentile rank—that is, an estimation of where that reading rate falls within those of other students at that grade level at that time of year.

ORAL READING FLUENCY NORMS FOR MIDDLE SCHOOL

Percentile	Fall WCPM	Winter WCPM	Spring WCPM
90	180	192	202
75	156	165	177
50	128	136	150
25	102	109	123
10	79	88	98

From Hasbrouck and Tindal, 2004.

▶ Narrative High School Level: Liliana

Introduction: The title of this story is "Liliana." Some high schools used to practice "tracking"—encouraging some students to go to college, and other students not to. Read to find out what happens when Liliana was "tracked." I will ask you questions about the passage after you finish reading.

Record the time at the beginning: _____.

When Liliana's family immigrated to New York City from the Spanish-speaking Caribbean, she was selected for the non-academic track in high school, a course of instruction that led directly to work after graduation. This wasn't particularly unusual since in her barrio families generally struggled to accommodate themselves to an unfamiliar language and culture, and to keep their heads above water in an unforgiving urban environment. Students were fortunate merely to finish high school, and only occasionally would an individual consider pursuing further education at a college.

In the fall semester of her senior year, her guidance counselor called her for an interview. Liliana was tall and beautiful, so after a quick perusal of her file, the counselor did what presumably he often did: he suggested a vocation as a beautician. Liliana, however, didn't want to arrange other people's hair, or decorate their faces with cosmetics; she wanted to go to college.

"But you can't," said the counselor, reexamining the file with a sudden stab of uncertainty. "You haven't taken the right courses, and, besides, where would you go to college?"

Liliana had an answer prepared, because as a young girl, she had participated in a program called the Fresh Air Fund that dispatched urban children from New York City to spend the summer with families in the country. Her host family had taken her to investigate the campus of a nearby college.

Eight years later in the counselor's office, Liliana said, "William Smith College." The school was unfamiliar to him, but he reluctantly agreed to help Liliana apply for admission, reminding her that she would require serious financial assistance, of course.

Liliana was accepted to William Smith College and she was offered an unusually generous scholarship. She matriculated, and although she was often home-sick, and frequently she wondered what she was doing among so many students who were wealthier than herself, she worked hard, and managed not only to graduate but to achieve a high grade point average. Then she submitted an application to law school and was accepted.

Years later, her high school guidance counselor happened to encounter an article in the *New York Times* introducing the new legal advisor for the Fresh Air Fund: Liliana. A short while later he read about her again, when she had been appointed to the Board of Trustees of William Smith College.

Record the time at the end: _____.

This text has been rated at 1200L
It has 390 words

QUESTIONS

1. Why do you think that Liliana was put in non-academic track courses in high school? (*She had immigrated from Latin America and probably didn't speak English well.*) **Inference**

2. Why did the guidance counselor tell Liliana that she would need a big scholarship? (*He knew her family didn't have enough money to pay for college.*) **Inference**

3. Name three things that made Liliana successful. (*She had high ideals, she stood up for herself, and she worked hard.* [*Must provide at least two of these answers*]) **Inference**

4. The text says "Liliana was accepted to William Smith College and she was offered an unusually generous scholarship. She matriculated." What does *matriculated* mean? (*enrolled, signed up*) **Vocabulary**

5. What was the effect on Liliana of being at William Smith College? (*It was hard on her, but it gave her a chance to be a successful professional person.*) **Inference**

6. How was Liliana different from other students at the college? (*She was poorer than most.*) **Recall**

7. How did Liliana repay the assistance she received at the Fresh Air Fund many years before? (*She became a lawyer for the Fresh Air Fund.*) **Recall**

8. How did her guidance counselor finally learn that he had been wrong about Liliana and her future? (*He read about her in the* New York Times). **Inference**

Errors in oral reading accuracy: _____

Correct comprehension responses: _____

SCORING GUIDE FOR ORAL READING AND COMPREHENSION

(Circle the boxes that correspond to the student's scores)

	Oral Reading Accuracy	Reading Comprehension	Listening Comprehension
Independent Level	12 or fewer errors	7–8 correct responses	
Instructional Level	13–39 errors	6–7 correct responses	6–7 correct responses
Frustration Level	40 or more errors	5 or fewer correct responses	

COMPREHENSION SCORES, BY TYPE

	Recall Questions	Inference Questions	Vocabulary Questions
Student's Correct Answers			
Possible Correct Answers	2	5	1

READING RATE SCORING GUIDE FOR HIGH SCHOOL

If the results computed just above show that the student read this passage at his independent level, you may wish to calculate his reading rate and compare that to other readers at his grade level.

1. Here is the number of words in this passage: 390

2. Write the number of words read incorrectly here: _____

3. Subtract #2 from #1 and write the answer here: _____

4. Using a calculator, multiply #3 by 60 seconds and write the answer here: _____

5. Write the student's reading time in seconds here: _____

6. Using a calculator, divide #4 by #5 and write the answer here: _____

The answer in #6 is the reading rate (words read correctly) per minute.

To interpret this number, first, locate the column in the chart below that represents the time of the year when this test was administered. Then, circle the reading rate that most closely matches your student's reading rate for this passage. Read across to the left to find the student's percentile rank—that is, an estimation of where that reading rate falls within those of other students at that grade level at that time of year.

ORAL READING FLUENCY NORMS FOR HIGH SCHOOL

Percentile	Fall WCPM	Winter WCPM	Spring WCPM
90	195	209	213
75	171	183	191
50	143	156	165
25	116	125	138
10	87	94	111

Note: These are estimates, extrapolated from From Hasbrouck and Tindal, 2004.

SOCIAL STUDIES PASSAGES

FORM A

We go in cars. We go to the store. We go to buy food at the store.

We go to school. We go on the bus. We go to school to learn to read.

We go fast. We go fast on airplanes. We go to see Grandmother in another city.

We go slow. We go slowly on boats. We go to the beach or the lake.

Sometimes we walk. We walk slowly.

Sometimes we run. We run fast.

We go.

▶ ▶ ▶

Jan lives in the city. The city has many big buildings. People work in some of the buildings. In other buildings there are stores. Some buildings have apartments. Jan lives in an apartment. It is on the fourth floor. She goes up and down on the elevator.

There are many cars, trucks, and buses in the city. They make a lot of noise. Taxis honk their horns. People walk very fast because they are very busy. Some people ride on the bus. There are many people on the bus. Some can sit down, but others have to stand.

David lives in the country. There are houses and barns in the country. David lives in a farmhouse. There is no elevator in David's house because it has only one floor. There are not very many tall buildings in the country. There are fields in the country.

Most families in the country have a truck. People who live on farms have tractors, too. They use the tractor to plant their fields. Some of the fields have things growing, and there are animals in other fields. Most of our food comes from the country. It is quiet in the country.

▶ ▶ ▶

The Earth is made up of land and water. The Earth has forests, plains, mountains, and oceans.

There are many trees in the forest. Some forests are in cool parts of the world, where most of the trees are pine trees. Owls, squirrels, and deer live in this forest. Forests in warm parts of the world are called jungles. Monkeys, snakes, and birds live in this forest.

Tall grasses grow on the plains. The plains are very flat. There are no mountains on the plains. There are very few hills. Rabbits and foxes live there. Sometimes strong winds blow on the plains. Farmers grow wheat on the plains.

There are very tall mountains in many parts of the Earth. Big rivers flow through the mountains. There are lakes in the mountains. Snow falls high in the mountains. It is very cold in the winter. Deer and bears live in the mountains.

There is land near the ocean. We find bays and harbors on the seacoast. There are large cities where rivers come down to the ocean. Many plants and animals live underwater.

▶ ▶ ▶

It is 1927, and his name is Charles Lindbergh. Later they will call him the Lone Eagle. Later they will call him Lucky Lindy. But not now. Now it is May 20, 1927, and he is standing in the still-dark dawn. He watches rain drizzle down on the airfield. And on his small airplane. The airplane has a name painted on its side: Spirit of St. Louis.

Lindbergh is nearly as tall as the plane itself. And yet he is about to attempt what no one has done before: to fly—without a stop—from New York to Paris, France. Over 3,600 miles away. Across the Atlantic Ocean. Alone.

He climbs into the boxlike cockpit that will be his only home for many, many hours. He nods to a man on the ground. The man pulls down hard on the propeller. The engine coughs, and sputters to life. Lindbergh listens as the engine catches, gurgles, and roars. He listens like a doctor. A few friends are here to say good-bye. They are only a few feet away, and yet to Lindbergh how far off they seem. They look up at him and wave. "Good luck! Keep safe!"

He clicks on his small flashlight and peers out. Heavy ice has formed on the plane's wings. He cannot risk his instruments' icing up.

He points the Spirit of St. Louis back down. The wings quiver as they slice through the turbulent air. The fog continues, but now, at least, the air is warmer. The ice begins to melt and Lindbergh roars ahead, through the fog and clouds, to Paris over 2,000 miles away.

▶ ▶ ▶

Transportation links people in our world. In the past, most people traveled by using horses, wagons, and trains.

In 1893, Henry Ford built an engine that used gasoline. A few years later, he built what was called a "horseless carriage." It had a motor on a frame with bicycle wheels. Mr. Ford's first cars were expensive because they were built one by one.

Soon, Mr. Ford and his company started building many cars at the same time. They built a less expensive car that more people could buy. It was called the Model T. Cars today are different from the Model T. They are safer and more comfortable.

Trains also carry many of the things that we buy in our stores. They also carry basic materials such as petroleum, coal, and metal ores. Some trains carry passengers. But most people prefer to travel by airplane now.

For hundreds of years, inventors experimented with flying machines. Then, in 1903, the Wright brothers made the first successful powered airplane flight. Their airplane carried only one person. Today, people travel the world in jet airplanes. Large airplanes can carry hundreds of people. They can travel thousands of miles in a few hours.

Ships are another important means of transportation. Ships are not fast like airplanes and automobiles, but they can carry many goods at fairly low cost. Cruise ships carry passengers. People on cruise ships are not in a hurry to arrive at their destinations. If they were, they would go by airplane. Cruise ship passengers like to relax and enjoy the beauty of the ocean.

There are many ways to move people and goods around our planet. Some are fast and some are slow. Some are expensive, and some are not.

▶ ▶ ▶

iv

Countries around the world trade goods. Trade means to buy, sell, or exchange goods. Countries need to trade with each other to get goods they do not have, and to make money for things they need.

The United States sells some of the goods we produce, such as wheat and corn, to other countries. We also trade with other countries to get some of the goods we need and want. For example, some companies in the United States buy rubber for tires and other uses.

Transportation is a way of moving goods or people from place to place. Trains and trucks are two kinds of transportation people can use to move goods. Ships and airplanes are other kinds of transportation people use when they trade goods.

Chocolate is made from cocoa beans, and cocoa beans come from cacao trees. Cacao trees grow best in hot and rainy places. Hawaii is the only state in the United States where cocoa beans grow, and there are not enough cocoa beans grown in Hawaii for all our uses. We trade with other countries to get enough cocoa beans. The cocoa beans are shipped to factories. Here people and machines make the cocoa beans into chocolate products.

The United States used to be one of the most successful trading nations in the world. We used to sell more goods than we bought. Now the situation has reversed. We buy more things from other countries than we sell to them. One example is automobiles. Many Americans now prefer automobiles from Japan because of quality and price. This kind of change has many effects. Employment among autoworkers in the United States has dropped, but it has increased in Japan.

▶ ▶ ▶

The Chesapeake Bay received its name from a Native American word that means "Great Shellfish Bay." A bay is an offshoot of a sea or lake that cuts into a coastline. The Chesapeake Bay also has inlets that go into the shore. An inlet is a narrow opening in a coastline, and is usually smaller than a bay. Maryland surrounds part of the Chesapeake Bay. Maryland is one of the Middle Atlantic states. Other states in the region are Delaware, Pennsylvania, New Jersey, and New York.

The Chesapeake Bay is rich in crabs, oysters, clams, and other shellfish. Approximately two hundred different kinds of fish live in the bay as well. Because of this abundance, many families in the Chesapeake Bay area earn their living harvesting seafood. The people who fish the bay are called watermen. These men and women gather different varieties of seafood in different seasons.

The watermen are also admired for their contribution to American history. During the Revolutionary War, they helped the French fleet, who were America's allies, by guiding their ships around the complicated waterways of the bay. With the help of the watermen, American and French forces were able to trap the British army.

Nowadays, watermen who catch crabs are called "crabbers." Crabbers fish for crabs in the summer using crab pots. A crab pot isn't really a pot at all—it is a large wire cage with several sections, one of which contains bait. Crabs can swim into the pot to consume the bait, but they cannot swim out of it. To harvest crabs, a crabber hauls the crab pot aboard the fishing boat, shakes out the pot, and sorts the catch by size and type. Then the crabber takes the catch to market.

▶ ▶ ▶

vi

During the Middle Ages, Europe had few strong central governments. People formed their own social system to meet their need for protection and justice. Feudalism was a political, social, and economic system that began in the 800s, and it provided the needed protection for people. Feudalism resembled a social structure. At the top, there was the monarch, a king or queen who was the supreme ruler. The next level included lords who pledged their loyalty to the monarch and military support in the event of a war or conflict. In return, the monarch granted the lord an estate, which consisted of land and people.

The lord owned the land, and he also received a large percentage of the crops produced on the land, as well as all the income from those crops. He collected taxes, maintained order, enforced laws, and protected the serfs. Serfs were the people who lived on the land and farmed it. A saying of the time was "No land without a lord, and no lord without land."

Many lords had knights, who were warriors trained and prepared to fight on horseback. Knights had a code of behavior called chivalry. According to the code of chivalry, a true knight had deep faith, was ready to die for the church, gave generously to all, protected those weaker than him, and used his strength to stand against injustice. Between 1100 and 1300, most knights received some land from their lords.

Serfs, who are sometimes called peasants, formed the base of the society in the Middle Ages. Unlike kings, lords, and knights, who were bound to be faithful to one another, serfs had no such loyalty to anyone. Serfs were not slaves, yet could not become knights. They could not be bought or sold separate from the land. Even so, serfs were tied to the land they worked and could not leave it without the lord's permission.

▶ ▶ ▶

The Supreme Court occupies the highest level of the American judicial system, the level at which final judgments are made about the laws of the United States and about people's rights under the law. When the Supreme Court makes a decision or ruling, that ruling applies to everyone, not just to the people involved in the case. The Supreme Court is very powerful because it has the final say, even after the lower courts, Congress, and the President, about what is legal in the United States and what is not.

The Supreme Court is one of the three branches of the United States federal government. Its home in Washington, D.C., is a building so grand that it has been nicknamed "the Marble Palace." The nine judges, or justices, of the Supreme Court meet here to decide many of the important questions facing the people of this country. During its history, the Supreme Court has made decisions on questions of slavery, free speech, women's rights, racial discrimination, and the racial make-up of the public schools. These decisions have become a part of the law under which we live. They affect the everyday lives of millions of American citizens.

The United States Supreme Court is the highest court of law in the land, and even the President must obey its rulings. Like an ordinary law court, the Supreme Court settles arguments between people or between an individual and the government. And, like any other law court, it can only settle an argument that is presented in the form of a criminal or civil case. In a criminal case, someone is accused of breaking the law. In a civil case, two people or groups of people go to court to settle a dispute, such as both claiming ownership of a certain piece of land.

The Supreme Court's special job is to make sure that the Constitution of the United States is upheld by all branches of the government. If the Court finds that a state law or an act of Congress is in conflict with the Constitution, then that law or act can no longer stand. Even a presidential act can be found to be unlawful by the Supreme Court.

The Court does not, however, have the power to make people obey its rulings. It has to rely on the government and citizens to carry them out. Nevertheless, most people feel that if we believe in living by the Constitution, then, as President John Kennedy once said, "It's important that we support the Supreme Court decisions, even when we may not agree with them."

SOCIAL STUDIES PASSAGES RESPONSE SHEETS

FORM A

Introduction: The title of this passage is "We Go." It's about different ways people travel. Read carefully because I will ask you questions about it after you finish.

Record the time at the beginning: _____.

We go in cars. We go to the store. We go to buy food at the store.

We go to school. We go on the bus. We go to school to learn to read.

We go fast. We go fast on airplanes. We go to see Grandmother in another city.

We go slow. We go slowly on boats. We go to the beach or the lake.

Sometimes we walk. We walk slowly.

Sometimes we run. We run fast.

We go.

Record the time at the end: _____.

This text has been rated at 230L
It has 80 words

QUESTIONS

1. According to this passage, why do we go to school? (*to learn to read*) **Recall**

2. What are two ways to go fast that were mentioned in this story? (*airplanes, running*) **Recall**

3. What words does the author use to tell you about places to go that have water? (*beach, lake*) **Vocabulary**

4. Why do you think the people in this story go on an airplane to visit Grandmother? (*she lives far away; the city where she lives is too far to drive*) **Inference**

5. According to the story, how fast do boats go? (*slowly*) **Recall**

6. What is another way to go slowly? (*walking*) **Inference**

Errors in oral reading accuracy: _____

Correct comprehension responses: _____

SCORING GUIDE FOR ORAL READING AND COMPREHENSION

(Circle the boxes that correspond to the student's scores)

	Oral Reading Accuracy	Reading Comprehension	Listening Comprehension
Independent Level	2 or fewer errors	6 correct responses	
Instructional Level	3–8 errors	5 correct responses	5 correct responses
Frustration Level	9 or more errors	4 or fewer correct responses	

COMPREHENSION SCORES, BY TYPE

	Recall Questions	Inference Questions	Vocabulary Questions
Student's Correct Answers			
Possible Correct Answers	3	2	1

READING RATE SCORING GUIDE FOR GRADE 1

If the results computed just above show that the student read this passage at his independent level, you may wish to calculate his reading rate and compare that to other readers at his grade level.

1. Here is the number of words in this passage: 80

2. Write the number of words read incorrectly here: _____

3. Subtract #2 from #1 and write the answer here: _____

4. Using a calculator, multiply #3 by 60 seconds and write the answer here: _____

5. Write the student's reading time in seconds here: _____

6. Using a calculator, divide #4 by #5 and write the answer here: _____

The answer in #6 is the reading rate (words read correctly) per minute.

To interpret this number, first, locate the column in the chart below that represents the time of the year when this test was administered. Then, circle the reading rate that most closely matches your student's reading rate for this passage. Read across to the left to find the student's percentile rank— that is, an estimation of where that reading rate falls within those of other students at that grade level at that time of year.

ORAL READING FLUENCY NORMS FOR GRADE 1

Percentile	Fall WCPM	Winter WCPM	Spring WCPM
90		81	111
75		47	82
50		23	53
25		12	28
10		6	15

From Hasbrouck and Tindal, 2004.

Introduction: The title of this passage is "The City and the Country." It's about how the city and the country are different. Read carefully because I will ask you questions about it after you finish.

Record the time at the beginning: _____.

Jan lives in the city. The city has many big buildings. People work in some of the buildings. In other buildings there are stores. Some buildings have apartments. Jan lives in an apartment. It is on the fourth floor. She goes up and down on the elevator.

There are many cars, trucks, and buses in the city. They make a lot of noise. Taxis honk their horns. People walk very fast because they are very busy. Some people ride on the bus. There are many people on the bus. Some can sit down, but others have to stand.

David lives in the country. There are houses and barns in the country. David lives in a farmhouse. There is no elevator in David's house because it has only one floor. There are not very many tall buildings in the country. There are fields in the country.

Most families in the country have a truck. People who live on farms have tractors, too. They use the tractor to plant their fields. Some of the fields have things growing, and there are animals in other fields. Most of our food comes from the country. It is quiet in the country.

Record the time at the end: _____.

This text has been rated at 350L
It has 197 words

QUESTIONS

1. What did this story say that it was like in the city? (*many big buildings, stores, apartments; many cars and trucks; noisy; people walk fast; people ride buses [must identify two]*) **Recall**

2. When the text said "People shop in other buildings," what does *shop* mean? (*buy things*) **Vocabulary**

3. Why do you think some people have to stand up on city buses? (*so many people on the bus; the buses are full; all the seats are taken*) **Inference**

4. Why do you think so many people ride buses in the city? (*it's easier than driving in the city; there are so many cars and trucks; there is so much traffic*) **Inference**

5. How did the story say the country is different from the city? (*not many big buildings; there are houses, barns, and fields; it's quiet*) **Inference**

6. What does David's family drive in the country? (*a truck*) **Recall**

7. Why is it quieter in the country than in the city? (*not so many people; less traffic*) **Inference**

8. What did the story say fields were used for in the country? (*growing things and animals*) **Recall**

Errors in oral reading accuracy: _____

Correct comprehension responses: _____

SCORING GUIDE FOR ORAL READING AND COMPREHENSION

(Circle the boxes that correspond to the student's scores)

	Oral Reading Accuracy	Reading Comprehension	Listening Comprehension
Independent Level	6 or fewer errors	7–8 correct responses	
Instructional Level	7–20 errors	6–7 correct responses	6–7 correct responses
Frustration Level	21 or more errors	5 or fewer correct responses	

COMPREHENSION SCORES, BY TYPE

	Recall Questions	Inference Questions	Vocabulary Questions
Student's Correct Answers			
Possible Correct Answers	3	4	1

READING RATE SCORING GUIDE FOR GRADE 2

If the results computed just above show that the student read this passage at his independent level, you may wish to calculate his reading rate and compare that to other readers at his grade level.

1. Here is the number of words in this passage: 197

2. Write the number of words read incorrectly here: _____

3. Subtract #2 from #1 and write the answer here: _____

4. Using a calculator, multiply #3 by 60 seconds and write the answer here: _____

5. Write the student's reading time in seconds here: _____

6. Using a calculator, divide #4 by #5 and write the answer here: _____

The answer in #6 is the reading rate (words read correctly) per minute.

To interpret this number, first, locate the column in the chart below that represents the time of the year when this test was administered. Then, circle the reading rate that most closely matches your student's reading rate for this passage. Read across to the left to find the student's percentile rank— that is, an estimation of where that reading rate falls within those of other students at that grade level at that time of year.

ORAL READING FLUENCY NORMS FOR GRADE 2

Percentile	Fall WCPM	Winter WCPM	Spring WCPM
90	106	125	142
75	79	100	117
50	51	72	89
25	25	42	61
10	11	18	31

From Hasbrouck and Tindal, 2004.

Introduction: The title of this passage is "Regions of the Earth." It tells about the Earth and how the parts of the Earth are different. Read carefully because I will ask you questions about it after you finish.

Record the time at the beginning: _____.

The Earth is made up of land and water. The Earth has forests, plains, mountains, and oceans.

There are many trees in the forest. Some forests are in cool parts of the world, where most of the trees are pine trees. Owls, squirrels, and deer live in this forest. Forests in warm parts of the world are called jungles. Monkeys, snakes, and birds live in this forest.

Tall grasses grow on the plains. The plains are very flat. There are no mountains on the plains. There are very few hills. Rabbits and foxes live there. Sometimes strong winds blow on the plains. Farmers grow wheat on the plains.

There are very tall mountains in many parts of the Earth. Big rivers flow through the mountains. There are lakes in the mountains. Snow falls high in the mountains. It is very cold in the winter. Deer and bears live in the mountains.

There is land near the ocean. We find bays and harbors on the seacoast. There are large cities where rivers come down to the ocean. Many plants and animals live underwater.

Record the time at the end: _____.

This test has been rated at 450L
It has 182 words

QUESTIONS

1. According to this passage, what kind of tree is common in cool forests? (*pine*) **Recall**

2. What do we sometimes call forests in warm places? (*jungles*) **Recall**

3. Why do you think owls, squirrels, and deer are not found in jungles? (*It may be too warm/hot; they like cooler places to live.*) **Inference**

4. What would it be like to live on the plains? (*it would be flat; you could see a long way; few trees; lots of grass; windy*) **Inference**

5. Why do you think it is often windy on the plains? (*no mountains or hills to block the wind; no trees to block the wind*) **Inference**

6. What does the expression *"high in the mountains"* mean? (*at/near the tops of mountains*)
Vocabulary

7. Why do you think there are cities at places where rivers meet the ocean? (*people could travel on the rivers and ocean; there would be fresh water; it would be a good place to live*)
Inference

8. In the sentence, "We find bays and harbors on the seacoast," what are *bays and harbors*? (*places where the ocean comes into the land*)
Vocabulary

Errors in oral reading accuracy: _____

Correct comprehension responses: _____

SCORING GUIDE FOR ORAL READING AND COMPREHENSION

(Circle the boxes that correspond to the student's scores)

	Oral Reading Accuracy	Reading Comprehension	Listening Comprehension
Independent Level	5 or fewer errors	7–8 correct responses	
Instructional Level	6–18 errors	6–7 correct responses	6–7 correct responses
Frustration Level	19 or more errors	5 or fewer correct responses	

COMPREHENSION SCORES, BY TYPE

	Recall Questions	Inference Questions	Vocabulary Questions
Student's Correct Answers			
Possible Correct Answers	2	4	2

READING RATE SCORING GUIDE FOR GRADE 2

If the results computed just above show that the student read this passage at his independent level, you may wish to calculate his reading rate and compare that to other readers at his grade level.

1. Here is the number of words in this passage: 182

2. Write the number of words read incorrectly here: _____

3. Subtract #2 from #1 and write the answer here: _____

4. Using a calculator, multiply #3 by 60 seconds and write the answer here: _____

5. Write the student's reading time in seconds here: _____

6. Using a calculator, divide #4 by #5 and write the answer here: _____

The answer in #6 is the reading rate (words read correctly) per minute.

To interpret this number, first, locate the column in the chart below that represents the time of the year when this test was administered. Then, circle the reading rate that most closely matches your student's reading rate for this passage. Read across to the left to find the student's percentile rank—that is, an estimation of where that reading rate falls within those of other students at that grade level at that time of year.

ORAL READING FLUENCY NORMS FOR GRADE 2

Percentile	Fall WCPM	Winter WCPM	Spring WCPM
90	106	125	142
75	79	100	117
50	51	72	89
25	25	42	61
10	11	18	31

From Hasbrouck and Tindal, 2004.

► Social Studies 3rd Grade Level: Charles Lindbergh

Introduction: The title of this passage is "Charles Lindbergh." It tells about a famous aviator who flew a small airplane across the ocean many years ago. Read carefully because I will ask you questions about it after you finish.

Record the time at the beginning: _____.

It is 1927, and his name is Charles Lindbergh. Later they will call him the Lone Eagle. Later they will call him Lucky Lindy. But not now. Now it is May 20, 1927, and he is standing in the still-dark dawn. He watches rain drizzle down on the airfield. And on his small airplane. The airplane has a name painted on its side: Spirit of St. Louis.

Lindbergh is nearly as tall as the plane itself. And yet he is about to attempt what no one has done before: to fly—without a stop—from New York to Paris, France. Over 3,600 miles away. Across the Atlantic Ocean. Alone.

He climbs into the boxlike cockpit that will be his only home for many, many hours. He nods to a man on the ground. The man pulls down hard on the propeller. The engine coughs, and sputters to life. Lindbergh listens as the engine catches, gurgles, and roars. He listens like a doctor. A few friends are here to say good-bye. They are only a few feet away, and yet to Lindbergh how far off they seem. They look up at him and wave. "Good luck! Keep safe!"

He clicks on his small flashlight and peers out. Heavy ice has formed on the plane's wings. He cannot risk his instruments' icing up. He points the Spirit of St. Louis back down. The wings quiver as they slice through the turbulent air. The fog continues, but now, at least, the air is warmer. The ice begins to melt and Lindbergh roars ahead, through the fog and clouds, to Paris over 2,000 miles away.

Record the time at the end: _____.

This text has been rated at 610L
It has 271 words

QUESTIONS

1. In what year did the events in this story take place? (*1927*) **Recall**

2. In this story, what was Lindbergh's goal (what was he trying to accomplish)? (*fly nonstop from New York to Paris, alone*) **Recall**

3. Why do you think no one before Lindbergh had ever done this? (*it was too dangerous*) **Inference**

4. Why was Lindbergh later nicknamed "Lucky Lindy"? (*he must have made the flight successfully*) **Inference**

5. Why did Lindbergh's friends shout "Good luck!" to him? (*he would need good luck to make it; the flight is dangerous*) **Inference**

6. Why did Lindbergh's friends seem far away to him when they were standing just a few feet away? (*mentally he had already left them behind; he felt alone because of what he was trying to do*) **Inference**

7. In the sentence, "The wings quiver as they slice through the turbulent air," what does *turbulent* mean? (*rough, stormy, bumpy*) **Vocabulary**

8. How did Lindbergh keep his airplane from icing up (getting covered with ice) as he flew? (*he flew lower where the air was warmer*) **Inference**

Errors in oral reading accuracy: _____

Correct comprehension responses: _____

SCORING GUIDE FOR ORAL READING AND COMPREHENSION

(Circle the boxes that correspond to the student's scores)

	Oral Reading Accuracy	Reading Comprehension	Listening Comprehension
Independent Level	8 or fewer errors	7–8 correct responses	
Instructional Level	9–27 errors	6–7 correct responses	6–7 correct responses
Frustration Level	28 or more errors	5 or fewer correct responses	

COMPREHENSION SCORES, BY TYPE

	Recall Questions	Inference Questions	Vocabulary Questions
Student's Correct Answers			
Possible Correct Answers	2	5	1

READING RATE SCORING GUIDE FOR GRADE 3

If the results computed just above show that the student read this passage at his independent level, you may wish to calculate his reading rate and compare that to other readers at his grade level.

1. Here is the number of words in this passage: 271

2. Write the number of words read incorrectly here: _____

3. Subtract #2 from #1 and write the answer here: _____

4. Using a calculator, multiply #3 by 60 seconds and write the answer here: _____

5. Write the student's reading time in seconds here: _____

6. Using a calculator, divide #4 by #5 and write the answer here: _____

The answer in #6 is the reading rate (words read correctly) per minute.

To interpret this number, first, locate the column in the chart below that represents the time of the year when this test was administered. Then, circle the reading rate that most closely matches your student's reading rate for this passage. Read across to the left to find the student's percentile rank—that is, an estimation of where that reading rate falls within those of other students at that grade level at that time of year.

ORAL READING FLUENCY NORMS FOR GRADE 3

Percentile	Fall WCPM	Winter WCPM	Spring WCPM
90	128	146	162
75	99	120	137
50	71	92	107
25	44	62	78
10	21	36	48

From Hasbrouck and Tindal, 2004.

▶ Social Studies 4th Grade Level: Transportation

Introduction: The title of this passage is "Transportation." It's about people and other things being moved from one place to another. Read carefully because I will ask you questions about it after you finish.

Record the time at the beginning: _____ .

Transportation links people in our world. In the past, most people traveled by using horses, wagons, and trains.

In 1893, Henry Ford built an engine that used gasoline. A few years later, he built what was called a "horseless carriage." It had a motor on a frame with bicycle wheels. Mr. Ford's first cars were expensive because they were built one by one.

Soon, Mr. Ford and his company started building many cars at the same time. They built a less expensive car that more people could buy. It was called the Model T. Cars today are different from the Model T. They are safer and more comfortable.

Trains also carry many of the things that we buy in our stores. They also carry basic materials such as petroleum, coal, and metal ores. Some trains carry passengers.

But most people prefer to travel by airplane now.

For hundreds of years, inventors experimented with flying machines. Then, in 1903, the Wright brothers made the first successful powered airplane flight. Their airplane carried only one person. Today, people travel the world in jet airplanes. Large airplanes can carry hundreds of people. They can travel thousands of miles in a few hours.

Ships are another important means of transportation. Ships are not fast like airplanes and automobiles, but they can carry many goods at fairly low cost. Cruise ships carry passengers. People on cruise ships are not in a hurry to arrive at their destinations. If they were, they would go by airplane. Cruise ship passengers like to relax and enjoy the beauty of the ocean.

There are many ways to move people and goods around our planet. Some are fast and some are slow. Some are expensive, and some are not.

Record the time at the end: _____.

This test has been rated at 750L
It has 290 words

QUESTIONS

1. What caused the first cars to cost a lot of money? (*They were built one at a time.*) **Inference**

2. According to the author, why don't many people travel by train nowadays? (*They prefer airplanes.*) **Recall**

3. What advantages do ships have over airplanes in carrying freight? (*carry a lot; not expensive*) **Recall**

4. Why did Henry Ford call the first car a *horseless carriage*? (*It was like a carriage, but with an engine instead of a horse.*) **Vocabulary**

5. According to the article, how was the Wright brothers' airplane different from modern jet airplanes? (*It carried only one person, but jet airplanes carry hundreds of people at a time.*) **Recall**

6. According to the article, how are basic materials such as oil and minerals taken from place to place? (*by train*) **Recall**

7. If a passenger on a cruise ship were in a hurry, what would you recommend? Why? (*Take an airplane instead. It's faster; ships are for taking your time and enjoying the ocean.*) **Inference**

8. If you had to send enough oil from city to city to fuel hundreds of cars, which two kinds of transportation mentioned in the article would you *not* use? Why not? (*horses, automobiles, jet airplanes* [*must name two*]; *because they can't carry enough or they are too expensive*) **Inference**

Errors in oral reading accuracy: _____

Correct comprehension responses: _____

SCORING GUIDE FOR ORAL READING AND COMPREHENSION

(Circle the boxes that correspond to the student's scores)

	Oral Reading Accuracy	Reading Comprehension	Listening Comprehension
Independent Level	9 or fewer errors	7–8 correct responses	
Instructional Level	10–29 errors	6–7 correct responses	6–7 correct responses
Frustration Level	30 or more errors	5 or fewer correct responses	

COMPREHENSION SCORES, BY TYPE

	Recall Questions	Inference Questions	Vocabulary Questions
Student's Correct Answers			
Possible Correct Answers	4	3	1

READING RATE SCORING GUIDE FOR GRADE 4

If the results computed just above show that the student read this passage at his independent level, you may wish to calculate his reading rate and compare that to other readers at his grade level.

1. Here is the number of words in this passage: 290

2. Write the number of words read incorrectly here: _____

3. Subtract #2 from #1 and write the answer here: _____

4. Using a calculator, multiply #3 by 60 seconds and write the answer here: _____

5. Write the student's reading time in seconds here: _____

6. Using a calculator, divide #4 by #5 and write the answer here: _____

The answer in #6 is the reading rate (words read correctly) per minute.

To interpret this number, first, locate the column in the chart below that represents the time of the year when this test was administered. Then, circle the reading rate that most closely matches your student's reading rate for this passage. Read across to the left to find the student's percentile rank—that is, an estimation of where that reading rate falls within those of other students at that grade level at that time of year.

ORAL READING FLUENCY NORMS FOR GRADE 4

Percentile	Fall WCPM	Winter WCPM	Spring WCPM
90	145	166	180
75	119	139	152
50	94	112	123
25	68	87	98
10	45	61	72

From Hasbrouck and Tindal, 2004.

▶ Social Studies 5th Grade Level: Countries Trade and Move Goods

Introduction: The title of this passage is "Countries Trade and Move Goods." It's about trade among the nations of the world. Read carefully because I will ask you questions about it after you finish.

Record the time at the beginning: _____.

Countries around the world trade goods. Trade means to buy, sell, or exchange goods. Countries need to trade with each other to get goods they do not have, and to make money for things they need.

The United States sells some of the goods we produce, such as wheat and corn, to other countries. We also trade with other countries to get some of the goods we need and want. For example, some companies in the United States buy rubber for tires and other uses.

Transportation is a way of moving goods or people from place to place. Trains and trucks are two kinds of transportation people can use to move goods. Ships and airplanes are other kinds of transportation people use when they trade goods.

Chocolate is made from cocoa beans, and cocoa beans come from cacao trees. Cacao trees grow best in hot and rainy places. Hawaii is the only state in the United States where cocoa beans grow, and there are not enough cocoa beans grown in Hawaii for all our uses. We trade with other countries to get enough cocoa beans. The cocoa beans are shipped to factories. Here people and machines make the cocoa beans into chocolate products.

The United States used to be one of the most successful trading nations in the world. We used to sell more goods than we bought. Now the situation has reversed. We buy more things from other countries than we sell to them. One example is automobiles. Many Americans now prefer automobiles from Japan because of quality and price. This kind of change has many effects. Employment among autoworkers in the United States has dropped, but it has increased in Japan.

—Adapted with permission from "Countries Trade and Move Goods," *Scott Foresman Social Studies: People and Places* (2005). Glenview, IL: Scott Foresman, pp. 139–137.

Record the time at the end: _____.

This text has been rated at 850L
It has 283 words

QUESTIONS

1. What is the major purpose of trade? (*to get goods that your own country doesn't have*) **Recall**

2. What were four kinds of transportation mentioned in the article? (*trucks, trains, ships, and airplanes*) **Recall**

3. What are some possible causes of a drop in the amount of American goods that other countries buy? (*lower quality; higher prices*) **Inference**

4. Why does the United States have to buy rubber and cocoa from other countries? (*not enough produced in our own country*) **Inference**

5. What is the United States still successful in selling to other countries? (*wheat and corn*) **Recall**

6. Why can cocoa beans grow in Hawaii, but not in another state? (*warm and rainy*) **Inference**

7. When the author of the passage uses the word *goods*, what does that refer to? (*products that are bought and sold in trade*) **Vocabulary**

8. Why is it helpful to the United States to buy cocoa from other countries? (*It creates jobs for American workers.*) **Inference**

Errors in oral reading accuracy: _____

Correct comprehension responses: _____

SCORING GUIDE FOR ORAL READING AND COMPREHENSION

(Circle the boxes that correspond to the student's scores)

	Oral Reading Accuracy	Reading Comprehension	Listening Comprehension
Independent Level	8 or fewer errors	7–8 correct responses	
Instructional Level	9–28 errors	6–7 correct responses	6–7 correct responses
Frustration Level	29 or more errors	5 or fewer correct responses	

COMPREHENSION SCORES, BY TYPE

	Recall Questions	Inference Questions	Vocabulary Questions
Student's Correct Answers			
Possible Correct Answers	3	4	1

If the results computed just above show that the student read this passage at his independent level, you may wish to calculate his reading rate and compare that to other readers at his grade level.

1. Here is the number of words in this passage: 283

2. Write the number of words read incorrectly here: _____

3. Subtract #2 from #1 and write the answer here: _____

4. Using a calculator, multiply #3 by 60 seconds and write the answer here: _____

5. Write the student's reading time in seconds here: _____

6. Using a calculator, divide #4 by #5 and write the answer here: _____

The answer in #6 is the reading rate (words read correctly) per minute.

To interpret this number, first, locate the column in the chart below that represents the time of the year when this test was administered. Then, circle the reading rate that most closely matches your student's reading rate for this passage. Read across to the left to find the student's percentile rank—that is, an estimation of where that reading rate falls within those of other students at that grade level at that time of year.

ORAL READING FLUENCY NORMS FOR GRADE 5

Percentile	Fall WCPM	Winter WCPM	Spring WCPM
90	166	182	194
75	139	156	168
50	110	127	139
25	85	99	109
10	61	74	83

From Hasbrouck and Tindal, 2004.

Introduction: The title of this passage is "The Great Shellfish Bay." It tells about a large bay in the eastern part of the United States. You will find out how it got its name. Read carefully because I will ask you questions about it after you finish.

Record the time at the beginning: _____.

The Chesapeake Bay received its name from a Native American word that means "Great Shellfish Bay." A bay is an offshoot of a sea or lake that cuts into a coastline. The Chesapeake Bay also has inlets that go into the shore. An inlet is a narrow opening in a coastline, and is usually smaller than a bay. Maryland surrounds part of the Chesapeake Bay. Maryland is one of the Middle Atlantic states. Other states in the region are Delaware, Pennsylvania, New Jersey, and New York.

The Chesapeake Bay is rich in crabs, oysters, clams, and other shellfish. Approximately two hundred different kinds of fish live in the bay as well. Because of this abundance, many families in the Chesapeake Bay area earn their living harvesting seafood. The people who fish the bay are called watermen.

These men and women gather different varieties of seafood in different seasons.

The watermen are also admired for their contribution to American history. During the Revolutionary War, they helped the French fleet, who were America's allies, by guiding their ships around the complicated waterways of the bay. With the help of the watermen, American and French forces were able to trap the British army.

Nowadays, watermen who catch crabs are called "crabbers." Crabbers fish for crabs in the summer using crab pots. A crab pot isn't really a pot at all—it is a large wire cage with several sections, one of which contains bait. Crabs can swim into the pot to consume the bait, but they cannot swim out of it. To harvest crabs, a crabber hauls the crab pot aboard the fishing boat, shakes out the pot, and sorts the catch by size and type. Then the crabber takes the catch to market.

Record the time at the end: _____.

This text has been rated at 870L
It has 292 words

QUESTIONS

1. According to this passage, how did the Chesapeake Bay get its name? (*from a Native American word for "Great Shellfish Bay"*) **Recall**

2. According to this passage, how are inlets and bays similar? How are they different? (similar: *both are parts of the sea or a lake that cut into the shore*; different: *inlets are usually smaller than bays* [*must answer both parts correctly*]) **Recall**

3. In the sentence, "Because of this abundance, many families in the Chesapeake Bay area earn their living harvesting seafood," what does *abundance* mean? (*richness; lots and lots of something, in this case fish and seafood*) **Vocabulary**

4. According to this passage, how did watermen help win the Revolutionary War? (*guided the French fleet to defeat the British*) **Recall**

5. According to this passage, how does a crabber use a crab pot? (*the pot is a cage that he puts in the water; the crab swims in, but can't swim out; the crabber pulls the pot back into the boat and takes out the crabs*) **Recall**

6. Why is the Chesapeake Bay a good place to make a living from the sea? (*many kinds of fish and shellfish live there; because the fish and shellfish are so abundant*) **Inference**

7. Why might Chesapeake Bay watermen be interested in keeping the bay free of pollution? (*to protect the fishing; to protect their livelihood; so they could keep making a living from the sea*) **Inference**

8. Why do you think watermen catch different kinds of shellfish at different times during the year? (*some things may not be ready to catch, or large enough, at certain times of the year; they need to catch different kinds of shellfish so they don't catch too many of one kind*) **Inference**

Errors in oral reading accuracy: _____

Correct comprehension responses: _____

SCORING GUIDE FOR ORAL READING AND COMPREHENSION

(Circle the boxes that correspond to the student's scores)

	Oral Reading Accuracy	Reading Comprehension	Listening Comprehension
Independent Level	9 or fewer errors	7–8 correct responses	
Instructional Level	10–29 errors	6–7 correct responses	6–7 correct responses
Frustration Level	30 or more errors	5 or fewer correct responses	

COMPREHENSION SCORES, BY TYPE

	Recall Questions	Inference Questions	Vocabulary Questions
Student's Correct Answers			
Possible Correct Answers	4	3	1

READING RATE SCORING GUIDE FOR GRADE 6

If the results computed just above show that the student read this passage at his independent level, you may wish to calculate his reading rate and compare that to other readers at his grade level.

1. Here is the number of words in this passage: **292**

2. Write the number of words read incorrectly here: _____

3. Subtract #2 from #1 and write the answer here: _____

4. Using a calculator, multiply #3 by 60 seconds and write the answer here: _____

5. Write the student's reading time in seconds here: _____

6. Using a calculator, divide #4 by #5 and write the answer here: _____

The answer in #6 is the reading rate (words read correctly) per minute.

To interpret this number, first, locate the column in the chart below that represents the time of the year when this test was administered. Then, circle the reading rate that most closely matches your student's reading rate for this passage. Read across to the left to find the student's percentile rank—that is, an estimation of where that reading rate falls within those of other students at that grade level at that time of year.

ORAL READING FLUENCY NORMS FOR GRADE 6

Percentile	Fall WCPM	Winter WCPM	Spring WCPM
90	177	195	204
75	153	167	177
50	127	140	150
25	98	111	122
10	68	82	93

From Hasbrouck and Tindal, 2004.

► Social Studies Middle School Level: Feudalism

Introduction: The title of this passage is "Feudalism." In it you're going to read about how life several hundred years ago was different from life today. Read carefully because I will ask you questions about it after you finish.

Record the time at the beginning: _____.

During the Middle Ages, Europe had few strong central governments. People formed their own social system to meet their need for protection and justice. Feudalism was a political, social, and economic system that began in the 800s, and it provided the needed protection for people. Feudalism resembled a social structure. At the top, there was the monarch, a king or queen who was the supreme ruler. The next level included lords who pledged their loyalty to the monarch and military support in the event of a war or conflict. In return, the monarch granted the lord an estate, which consisted of land and people.

The lord owned the land, and he also received a large percentage of the crops produced on the land, as well as all the income from those crops. He collected taxes, maintained order, enforced laws, and protected the serfs. Serfs were the people who lived on the land and farmed it. A saying of the time was "No land without a lord, and no lord without land."

Many lords had knights, who were warriors trained and prepared to fight on horseback. Knights had a code of behavior called chivalry. According to the code of chivalry, a true knight had deep faith, was ready to die for the church, gave generously to all, protected those weaker than him, and used his strength to stand against injustice. Between 1100 and 1300, most knights received some land from their lords.

Serfs, who are sometimes called peasants, formed the base of the society in the Middle Ages. Unlike kings, lords, and knights, who were bound to be faithful to one another, serfs had no such loyalty to anyone. Serfs were not slaves, yet could not become knights. They could not be bought or sold separate from the land. Even so, serfs were tied to the land they worked and could not leave it without the lord's permission.

Record the time at the end: _____.

This text has been rated at 1020L
It has 317 words

QUESTIONS

1. Why did people in the Middle Ages have to form their own social systems? (*there were few strong central governments; for protection and justice*) **Recall**

2. According to this passage, around what year did the time period known as the Middle Ages begin? (*about 800*) **Recall**

3. What people were at the top, the middle, and the bottom of the social system of feudalism? (Top: *king or queen/ruler;* middle: *lords and their knights;* bottom: *serfs*) **Recall**

4. If you were a lord, what would you have to promise your ruler? (*to be loyal to him/her; to supply knights and fight on his/her side in a war*) **Inference**

5. How were serfdom and slavery similar, and how were they different? (similar: *serfs couldn't leave their land without lord's permission;* different: *serfs couldn't be bought or sold separate from the land* [*must answer both parts correctly*]) **Inference**

6. If you were a knight, how were you expected to behave? (*by the code of chivalry; to have deep faith, be ready to die for the church, give generously to all, fight injustice* [*must answer with at least two of these*]) **Inference**

7. If you were a lord who had just received an estate from your monarch, what would you expect to get? (*land and serfs who lived on it*) **Inference**

8. In the phrase, "Serfs were tied to the land they worked," what does *tied* mean? (*couldn't leave it, move away, or be sold; had to stay there always*) **Vocabulary**

Errors in oral reading accuracy: _____

Correct comprehension responses: _____

SCORING GUIDE FOR ORAL READING AND COMPREHENSION

(Circle the boxes that correspond to the student's scores)

	Oral Reading Accuracy	Reading Comprehension	Listening Comprehension
Independent Level	10 or fewer errors	7–8 correct responses	
Instructional Level	11–31 errors	6–7 correct responses	6–7 correct responses
Frustration Level	32 or more errors	5 or fewer correct responses	

COMPREHENSION SCORES, BY TYPE

	Recall Questions	Inference Questions	Vocabulary Questions
Student's Correct Answers			
Possible Correct Answers	3	4	1

READING RATE SCORING GUIDE FOR MIDDLE SCHOOL

If the results computed just above show that the student read this passage at his independent level, you may wish to calculate his reading rate and compare that to other readers at his grade level.

1. Here is the number of words in this passage: 317

2. Write the number of words read incorrectly here: _____

3. Subtract #2 from #1 and write the answer here: _____

4. Using a calculator, multiply #3 by 60 seconds and write the answer here: _____

5. Write the student's reading time in seconds here: _____

6. Using a calculator, divide #4 by #5 and write the answer here: _____

The answer in #6 is the reading rate (words read correctly) per minute.

To interpret this number, first, locate the column in the chart below that represents the time of the year when this test was administered. Then, circle the reading rate that most closely matches your student's reading rate for this passage. Read across to the left to find the student's percentile rank—that is, an estimation of where that reading rate falls within those of other students at that grade level at that time of year.

ORAL READING FLUENCY NORMS FOR MIDDLE SCHOOL

Percentile	Fall WCPM	Winter WCPM	Spring WCPM
90	180	192	202
75	156	165	177
50	128	136	150
25	102	109	123
10	79	88	98

From Hasbrouck and Tindal, 2004.

► Social Studies High School Level: Why Is the Supreme Court So Powerful?

Introduction: The title of this passage is "Why Is the Supreme Court So Powerful?" It talks about the most powerful court in the legal system of the United States. Read carefully because I will ask you questions about it after you finish.

Record the time at the beginning: _____.

The Supreme Court occupies the highest level of the American judicial system, the level at which final judgments are made about the laws of the United States and about people's rights under the law. When the Supreme Court makes a decision or ruling, that ruling applies to everyone, not just to the people involved in the case. The Supreme Court is very powerful because it has the final say, even after the lower courts, Congress, and the President, about what is legal in the United States and what is not.

The Supreme Court is one of the three branches of the United States federal government. Its home in Washington, D.C., is a building so grand that it has been nicknamed "the Marble Palace." The nine judges, or jus-

tices, of the Supreme Court meet here to decide many of the important questions facing the people of this country. During its history, the Supreme Court has made decisions on questions of slavery, free speech, women's rights, racial discrimination, and the racial make-up of the public schools. These decisions have become a part of the law under which we live. They affect the everyday lives of millions of American citizens.

The United States Supreme Court is the highest court of law in the land, and even the President must obey its rulings. Like an ordinary law court, the Supreme Court settles arguments between people or between an individual and the government. And, like any other law court, it can only settle an argument that is presented in the form of a criminal or civil case. In a criminal case, someone is accused of breaking the law. In a civil case, two people or groups of people go to court to settle a dispute, such as both claiming ownership of a certain piece of land.

The Supreme Court's special job is to make sure that the Constitution of the United States is upheld by all branches of the government. If the Court finds that a state law or an act of Congress is in conflict with the Constitution, then that law or act can no longer stand. Even a presidential act can be found to be unlawful by the Supreme Court.

The Court does not, however, have the power to make people obey its rulings. It has to rely on the government and citizens to carry them out. Nevertheless, most people feel that if we believe in living by the Constitution, then, as President John Kennedy once said, "It's important that we support the Supreme Court decisions, even when we may not agree with them."

Record the time at the end: _____.

This text has been rated at 1200L
It has 431 words

QUESTIONS

1. If you lost your case before the Supreme Court, to what other courts could you take your case? Why? (*None; it is the highest court in the land.*) **Inference**

2. Why do you think the Supreme Court has nine judges instead of one or two? (*so a majority would have to agree; so one person's opinion would not be too powerful; so there could not be a tie vote*) **Inference**

3. According to this passage, what are some issues the Supreme Court has decided that affect our everyday lives? (*slavery, free speech, women's rights, children's rights, racial discrimination [must identify three]*) **Recall**

4. Who must obey the Supreme Court's rulings? Who doesn't have to? (*everyone, even the President; no one is exempt*) **Inference**

5. What was a name given to the Supreme Court building in Washington? (*the "Marble Palace"*) **Recall**

6. How do civil and criminal cases differ? (civil: *two people or groups have a dispute or disagreement to settle;* criminal: *a person or group is accused of a crime/breaking a law*) **Inference**

7. What document guides the Supreme Court's decisions about the fairness of laws or acts? (*the U.S. Constitution*) **Recall**

8. In the phrase, "The Supreme Court has the final say about what is legal," what does *say* mean? (*judgment, decision, opinion*) **Vocabulary**

Errors in oral reading accuracy: _____

Correct comprehension responses: _____

SCORING GUIDE FOR ORAL READING AND COMPREHENSION

(Circle the boxes that correspond to the student's scores)

	Oral Reading Accuracy	Reading Comprehension	Listening Comprehension
Independent Level	13 or fewer errors	7–8 correct responses	
Instructional Level	14–43 errors	6–7 correct responses	6–7 correct responses
Frustration Level	44 or more errors	5 or fewer correct responses	

COMPREHENSION SCORES, BY TYPE

	Recall Questions	Inference Questions	Vocabulary Questions
Student's Correct Answers			
Possible Correct Answers	3	4	1

READING RATE SCORING GUIDE FOR HIGH SCHOOL

If the results computed just above show that the student read this passage at his independent level, you may wish to calculate his reading rate and compare that to other readers at his grade level.

1. Here is the number of words in this passage: 431

2. Write the number of words read incorrectly here: _____

3. Subtract #2 from #1 and write the answer here: _____

4. Using a calculator, multiply #3 by 60 seconds and write the answer here: _____

5. Write the student's reading time in seconds here: _____

6. Using a calculator, divide #4 by #5 and write the answer here: _____

The answer in #6 is the reading rate (words read correctly) per minute.

To interpret this number, first, locate the column in the chart below that represents the time of the year when this test was administered. Then, circle the reading rate that most closely matches your student's reading rate for this passage. Read across to the left to find the student's percentile rank—that is, an estimation of where that reading rate falls within those of other students at that grade level at that time of year.

ORAL READING FLUENCY NORMS FOR HIGH SCHOOL

Percentile	Fall WCPM	Winter WCPM	Spring WCPM
90	195	209	213
75	171	183	191
50	143	156	165
25	116	125	138
10	87	94	111

Note: These are estimates, extrapolated from Hasbrouck and Tindal, 2004.

SCIENCE PASSAGES

FORM A

You can do things to stay healthy. You can exercise and stay clean. You can eat good foods. You can get lots of sleep.

You get exercise when you run and play. It helps you stay well. It makes you strong too. Staying clean helps you be healthy. Germs can be on your hands. Germs can make you sick.

Good foods help you grow. They help you stay healthy. Too many fats and sweets are bad for you. You also need sleep to be healthy. You need eight to ten hours of sleep every night.

▶ ▶ ▶

All animals need food to live. Some animals eat only plants. Animals like horses, manatees, and goats eat only plants. Some animals eat other animals. Lions, wolves, and hawks eat other animals. Some animals, like bears and raccoons, eat both plants and animals.

Plants use sunshine to make food. The sun's energy helps green plants make food. Animals eat the plants. Then other animals eat those animals. This is called a food chain.

Plants like grass use the sun's energy to grow and make food. Mice eat the grass and its seeds. Foxes eat the mice. That is one food chain. Sunlight on a pond makes water plants grow. Small fish and snails eat the plants. Larger fish eat the small fish. Raccoons eat the snails and larger fish. That is another food chain. All living things need food, so all living things are parts of food chains.

▶ ▶ ▶

Matter is anything that takes up space. Everything in the world is made of matter. The sun and the planets are made of matter, too. Everything around you is made of matter. You are made of matter, too. All matter has mass. Mass is how much matter is in something. Large things have more mass than small things. A car has more mass than a baseball. Which has more mass: a grownup or a baby? A grownup has more mass, of course. A whale has a lot of mass, and a goldfish has little mass. Which has more mass: a dog or an ant? A dog has more mass, of course.

Mass and weight are not the same thing. A bucket of feathers and a bucket of rocks may have the same mass. But the bucket of rocks is heavier. A block of wood and a block of iron may have the same mass. But which is heavier? The block of iron is heavier, of course.

When you look at something, you see its color, shape, and size. These are called properties of matter. Properties tell you about an object. Another property of matter is temperature. Temperature means how warm or cold something is. Another property is texture, which means how rough or smooth something is. Yet another property is whether something will float or sink.

▶ ▶ ▶

Do you know what a life cycle is? All plants and animals have life cycles. A life cycle is all the stages in the life of a living thing. In an animal's life cycle, a baby is born and grows, becoming an adult. It has babies of its own kind, and finally it dies. Its babies start their own life cycles. There are about a million different kinds of insects. Many have the same kind of life cycle.

Insects are small animals with six legs. Grasshoppers, crickets, dragonflies, and cockroaches are insects. Insects have a life cycle with three stages. The first stage is the egg. Many insects lay their eggs in a hard egg case that keeps the eggs safe. The second stage is the nymph. A nymph hatches from an egg. A nymph is a baby insect that looks like its parents. But a nymph has no wings. It eats and grows. The outside of its body cannot stretch. Soon it becomes too small for the nymph. The growing nymph breaks open its old covering and sheds it.

A nymph can shed its covering several times as it grows. As it gets older, the nymph grows its adult body parts. Wings and legs are body parts. The third stage is the adult. That is when the insect is fully grown. The last time the nymph sheds its covering, it has become an adult. When an insect is an adult it can have its own babies.

▶ ▶ ▶

Sound is a kind of energy. You can hear sound. Sometimes you can even feel sound. The music of a violin, the crying of a baby, and the banging of a door are very different sounds. But they are all made the same way. Sounds are made when matter vibrates, or moves quickly back and forth. All sounds are made by vibration.

Parts of a musical instrument vibrate to make sounds. For example, when you hit a drum, the head of the drum vibrates. When you press a piano key, a striker inside the piano makes a wire string vibrate. When you strum a guitar string, or rub a bow across a violin's strings, the string vibrates and makes a sound.

People and many animals have vocal cords, or flaps of tissue, in their throats. Air makes the vocal cords vibrate and make sounds. Animals and humans can make a wide range of sounds. Humans can cry, speak, hum, sing, and scream. Animals can bark, howl, roar, chirp, and whine.

We hear sounds when the air vibrates. These vibrations are picked up by special parts of our ears. The vibration from a bird's throat moves through the air to your ear. Your eardrum and special ear bones vibrate. Nerves in your ear send signals to your brain. Each sound has its own pattern of vibrations. You recognize a sound as a bird singing, a baby crying, or your friend talking. Sound can also travel through water and hard substances like plastic, glass, and wood. That is how you can hear sounds underwater and through walls.

▶ ▶ ▶

iv

The basic unit of all living things is the cell. Animal or plant, large or small, all living things are made up of cells. All living things start life as a single cell, which divides and forms new cells, so that new cells come from existing cells.

Some living things like bacteria are made up of only one cell. A new organism is formed when the single cell divides into two separate cells, which is called cell division. Each organism can produce offspring all by itself. The single cell divides into two identical cells. Then each cell can divide again. Most single-celled organisms reproduce very quickly. For example, bacteria can divide every few minutes. In your body, a few bacteria that cause disease can become thousands in just hours, making you very sick.

Most living things are complex, or made up of many cells. Complex living things may be made up of billions of cells. When these cells divide, they do not separate. They stay together and keep on dividing. As this happens, the organism grows and changes. When the organism becomes an adult and stops growing, its cells divide at a slower rate. Throughout life, cells die or wear away. They must be replaced until the organism dies.

When a cell of a complex organism divides, it makes two copies of all its parts. All the information a cell needs to live and reproduce is stored inside the cell. The information is stored in cell parts called chromosomes that look like short threads. When a cell begins to divide, its chromosomes line up in the center. Each one separates or breaks in half. The halves move to opposite sides of the cell. When the cell divides,

v

each new cell will have identical chromosomes. Finally the cell wall divides and closes off each of the two new cells. Each new cell will have all the same parts and chromosomes as the original cell.

▶ ▶ ▶

v

All living things must get energy to live, but they differ in how they get energy. Green plants get energy from food that they make, using sunlight, carbon dioxide, and water to make a type of sugar. Green plants store this sugar in their roots, stems, and leaves until they need it. Because they make their own food, green plants are called producers. Most other living things can't make their own food, and they get energy by eating, or consuming, food. Their food is other living things. That is why they are called consumers.

Some consumers eat only plants, some only animals, and some both plants and animals. A consumer that eats only plants is called an herbivore, from an ancient word "herb" that means "plant." Cows, deer, rabbits, and caterpillars are examples of herbivores. A consumer that eats only other animals is called a carnivore, from an ancient word "carn" that means "flesh." Owls, lions, frogs, and bats are examples of carnivores. Consumers that eat both plants and animals are called omnivores, from an older word "omni" that means "all." Bears, raccoons, box turtles, and humans are examples of omnivores. Many kinds of birds are omnivores, because they eat seeds, insects, and worms. And some consumers get their food from the dead bodies and waste products of living things. These consumers help break down complex chemicals into simple chemicals and help dead things decay. They are called decomposers. Buzzards, fungi such as mold and mushrooms, some insects, and some bacteria are decomposers.

▶ ▶ ▶

vi

Orangutans are large mammals belonging to the primate group. Primates are divided into two main groups: one that includes humans, apes, and monkeys, and another that includes lemurs, tree shrews, and other smaller primates. The orangutan, whose name means "man of the forest," is a type of ape whose closest relatives are the gorilla and the chimpanzee.

Orangutans are arboreal, or tree-dwelling, animals whose habitat is the rain forests of Sumatra and Borneo in Southeast Asia. Orangutans spend their entire lives in the rain forest canopy, rarely descending to the ground. Because they live in dense foliage high above the ground, they are rarely seen in the wild. Native legends of Borneo refer to them as ghosts that can suddenly appear and disappear.

Orangutans are the largest arboreal animals. For example, adult orangutans range in height from three and a half to four and a half feet tall and weigh from 90 to 175 pounds in the wild. Females are generally smaller than males. In zoos, where food is plentiful, orangutans sometimes weigh nearly 300 pounds. Orangutans have arms twice the length of their bodies and feet that look like hands. They are covered with long reddish-brown fur. The fur on their backs and shoulders may be more than a foot long and resembles a cape. Males have long fur on their faces that looks like flowing beards and mustaches. The orangutan has no tail. Extremely flexible joints in its wrists, hips, and shoulders allow it to move more easily than any other ape. Orangutans have four fingers and a thumb on each foot, allowing them to grasp branches, food, and other objects easily.

Orangutans eat mostly fruit, which they pick and peel with their fingers. They also eat leaves, honey, eggs, termites, small lizards, baby birds, and many kinds of insects. They have been observed using sticks and long grasses to reach fruit and pluck termites from their nests. In zoos, they are known as escape artists, able to pick locks and escape from enclosures. In the wild, they build nests of sticks and leaves high in trees. Orangutans reproduce very slowly. The female gives birth to a single infant about every eight years. This is the longest interval between births of any animal. Infants stay with their mothers for about eight years, and the male and female stay together during that time. Males defend their territories and protect their families by making loud sounds and occasionally by fighting. Except when defending themselves, orangutans are both silent and peaceful. In spite of protective laws, orangutans are endangered in the wild. Baby orangutans are illegally captured and sold as pets.

▶ ▶ ▶

Certain features in rocks reveal how the rock formed and can be used to classify it. For example, all rocks can be classified into three general groups: igneous, sedimentary, and metamorphic rock.

Igneous rock is named for the Latin word for fire, because it is formed when magma, molten rock from beneath the Earth's crust, cools and solidifies. Volcanic rocks, rocks formed during and after volcanic eruption, are the most obvious kind of igneous rock. The rocks that immediately surround most volcanoes form as magma pours out of volcanic vents, cools, and hardens. Because of this, in some igneous rocks of this type, wavelike patterns of melted rock are preserved during cooling. Oddly shaped volcanic rock fragments and chunks may result from violent gas explosions. These explosions cause magma to splatter, rather than to flow, and can rip chunks out of the volcano's vent. Finally, what is commonly thought of as volcanic ash is really very fine rock particles. Settling in a dense blanket, intensely hot volcanic ash can weld or fuse together into a third kind of volcanic rock, called tuff. Igneous rock is most commonly seen on the Earth's surface near active or recently active volcanoes.

Sedimentary rock, the most common type, is named for the Latin word meaning settling. Sedimentary rock forms when layers of sediment on or near the Earth's surface, including sand, gravel, and mud, compress and harden into layers. Sediment of various kinds is a result of wind and water erosion. Sediment is constantly deposited by wind and water into river valleys, lakes, oceans, and crevices. As a layer of sediment thickens, the particles near the bottom of the pile become compacted. Minerals dissolved in water are deposited between particles of sediment. The layer of compacted sediment and the dissolved minerals eventually cement together. The two forces of compacting and cementing form sedimentary rock. Sedimentary rock covers more than 75% of Earth's surface. It is commonly seen in the layers visible on mountainsides, in canyons, and where highways have been excavated through rock.

Metamorphic rock is named for the Greek words that mean changing form. Metamorphic rock is formed within the Earth's crust when existing rocks are transformed into a new form by heat, pressure, or both. When sedimentary rock is deeply buried in the Earth's crust by earthquakes, volcanic eruption, and other geologic events, it is subjected to both pressure and heat. Eventually it may melt and become magma. But if it does not melt, it will undergo chemical changes as some of its minerals change form or are replaced by other minerals. This process is enhanced when the sedimentary rock contains water between its grains. Sedimentary rock containing water, such as limestone, is chemically changed by pressure and heat more quickly than drier rocks. Likewise, igneous rock, containing little water, must be subjected to much greater heat and pressure before it is changed. The most common kinds of metamorphic rocks are slate, mica, quartz, and certain minerals such as garnet. Metamorphic rocks are uncommon at the Earth's surface, and are most often located there as a result of explosions, mining, or other human processes.

▶ ▶ ▶

X

SCIENCE PASSAGES
RESPONSE SHEETS

FORM A

Science: 1st Grade Level: Staying Healthy

Introduction: The title of this passage is "Staying Healthy." It tells lots of things you can do to stay healthy. I will ask you questions about it after you finish.

Record the time at the beginning: _____.

You can do things to stay healthy. You can exercise and stay clean. You can eat good foods. You can get lots of sleep.

You get exercise when you run and play. It helps you stay well. It makes you strong too. Staying clean helps you be healthy. Germs can be on your hands. Germs can make you sick.

Good foods help you grow. They help you stay healthy. Too many fats and sweets are bad for you. You also need sleep to be healthy. You need eight to ten hours of sleep every night.

Record the time at the end: _____.

This text has been rated at 300L
It has 95 words

QUESTIONS

1. What did the article say you can do to stay healthy? (*exercise, stay clean, eat good foods, get lots of sleep* [*must identify 2*]) **Recall**

2. Why does washing your hands help you stay healthy? (*gets rid of germs; germs can make you sick*) **Inference**

3. Why are running and riding a bike good for you? (*they give you exercise*) **Inference**

4. How does eating good foods help you stay healthy? (*helps you grow*) **Recall**

5. In the sentence, "Too many fats and sweets are bad for you," what does *sweets* mean? (*sweet or sugary foods; candy, chocolate, etc.*) **Vocabulary**

6. How much sleep did the article say you need to stay healthy? (*8–10 hours/night*) **Recall**

Errors in oral reading accuracy: _____

Correct comprehension responses: _____

SCORING GUIDE FOR ORAL READING AND COMPREHENSION

(Circle the boxes that correspond to the student's scores)

	Oral Reading Accuracy	Reading Comprehension	Listening Comprehension
Independent Level	3 or fewer errors	6 correct responses	
Instructional Level	4–10 errors	5 correct responses	5 correct responses
Frustration Level	11 or more errors	4 or fewer correct responses	

COMPREHENSION SCORES, BY TYPE

	Recall Questions	Inference Questions	Vocabulary Questions
Student's Correct Answers			
Possible Correct Answers	3	2	1

READING RATE SCORING GUIDE FOR GRADE 1

If the results computed just above show that the student read this passage at his independent level, you may wish to calculate his reading rate and compare that to other readers at his grade level.

1. Here is the number of words in this passage: 95

2. Write the number of words read incorrectly here: _____

3. Subtract #2 from #1 and write the answer here: _____

4. Using a calculator, multiply #3 by 60 seconds and write the answer here: _____

5. Write the student's reading time in seconds here: _____

6. Using a calculator, divide #4 by #5 and write the answer here: _____

The answer in #6 is the reading rate (words read correctly) per minute.

To interpret this number, first, locate the column in the chart below that represents the time of the year when this test was administered. Then, circle the reading rate that most closely matches your student's reading rate for this passage. Read across to the left to find the student's percentile rank—that is, an estimation of where that reading rate falls within those of other students at that grade level at that time of year.

ORAL READING FLUENCY NORMS FOR GRADE 1

Percentile	Fall WCPM	Winter WCPM	Spring WCPM
90		81	111
75		47	82
50		23	53
25		12	28
10		6	15

From Hasbrouck and Tindal, 2004.

▶ Science 2nd Grade Level (2.1): The Food Chain

Introduction: The title of this passage is "The Food Chain." It tells about how plants and animals get their food. I will ask you questions about it after you finish.

Record the time at the beginning: _____.

All animals need food to live. Some animals eat only plants. Animals like horses, manatees, and goats eat only plants. Some animals eat other animals. Lions, wolves, and hawks eat other animals. Some animals, like bears and raccoons, eat both plants and animals.

Plants use sunshine to make food. The sun's energy helps green plants make food. Animals eat the plants. Then other animals eat those animals. This is called a food chain.

Plants like grass use the sun's energy to grow and make food. Mice eat the grass and its seeds. Foxes eat the mice. That is one food chain. Sunlight on a pond makes water plants grow. Small fish and snails eat the plants. Larger fish eat the small fish. Raccoons eat the snails and larger fish. That is another food

chain. All living things need food, so all living things are parts of food chains.

Record the time at the end: _____.

This text has been rated at 340L
It has 148 words

QUESTIONS

1. When plants are eaten by small animals, and the small animals are eaten by larger animals, what did the article call this? (*a food chain*) **Recall**

2. What was one animal the article said eats only plants? (*horses, manatees, or goats*) **Recall**

3. How is a food chain like a real chain? (Why is it called a food *chain*?) (*each part is linked/connected to the next part like links in a chain*) **Inference**

4. What would happen in a food chain if all the plants died? (*the chain would be broken; all the animals would eventually die*) **Inference**

5. Why do green plants need sunlight? (*to grow and make food*) **Inference**

6. What example did the article give of a food chain that starts with grass? (*mice eat grass; foxes eat mice*) **Recall**

7. In the sentence, "Some animals eat only plants," what does *only* mean? (*eat nothing except plants; nothing else but plants*) **Vocabulary**

8. Why are all living things parts of food chains? (*all living things need food to live*) **Inference**

Errors in oral reading accuracy: _____

Correct comprehension responses: _____

SCORING GUIDE FOR ORAL READING AND COMPREHENSION

(Circle the boxes that correspond to the student's scores)

	Oral Reading Accuracy	Reading Comprehension	Listening Comprehension
Independent Level	4 or fewer errors	7–8 correct responses	
Instructional Level	5–15 errors	6–7 correct responses	6–7 correct responses
Frustration Level	16 or more errors	5 or fewer correct responses	

COMPREHENSION SCORES, BY TYPE

	Recall Questions	Inference Questions	Vocabulary Questions
Student's Correct Answers			
Possible Correct Answers	3	4	1

READING RATE SCORING GUIDE FOR GRADE 2

If the results computed just above show that the student read this passage at his independent level, you may wish to calculate his reading rate and compare that to other readers at his grade level.

1. Here is the number of words in this passage: 148

2. Write the number of words read incorrectly here: _____

3. Subtract #2 from #1 and write the answer here: _____

4. Using a calculator, multiply #3 by 60 seconds and write the answer here: _____

5. Write the student's reading time in seconds here: _____

6. Using a calculator, divide #4 by #5 and write the answer here: _____

The answer in #6 is the reading rate (words read correctly) per minute.

To interpret this number, first, locate the column in the chart below that represents the time of the year when this test was administered. Then, circle the reading rate that most closely matches your student's reading rate for this passage. Read across to the left to find the student's percentile rank—that is, an estimation of where that reading rate falls within those of other students at that grade level at that time of year.

ORAL READING FLUENCY NORMS FOR GRADE 2

Percentile	Fall WCPM	Winter WCPM	Spring WCPM
90	106	125	142
75	79	100	117
50	51	72	89
25	25	42	61
10	11	18	31

From Hasbrouck and Tindal, 2004.

▶ Science: 2nd Grade Level (2.2): Matter

Introduction: The title of this passage is "Matter." It tells about the matter and mass of objects. I will ask you questions about it after you finish.

Record the time at the beginning: _____.

Matter is anything that takes up space. Everything in the world is made of matter. The sun and the planets are made of matter, too. Everything around you is made of matter. You are made of matter, too. All matter has mass. Mass is how much matter is in something. Large things have more mass than small things. A car has more mass than a baseball. Which has more mass: a grownup or a baby? A grownup has more mass, of course. A whale has a lot of mass, and a goldfish has little mass. Which has more mass: a dog or an ant? A dog has more mass, of course.

Mass and weight are not the same thing. A bucket of feathers and a bucket of rocks may have the same mass. But the bucket of rocks is heavier. A block of wood and a block of iron may have the same mass. But which is heavier? The block of iron is heavier, of course.

When you look at something, you see its color, shape, and size. These are called properties of matter. Properties tell you about an object. Another property of matter is temperature. Temperature means how warm or cold something is. Another property is texture, which means how rough or smooth something is. Yet another property is whether something will float or sink.

Record the time at the end: _____.

This text has been rated at 460L
It has 226 words

QUESTIONS

1. According to this article, what is matter? (*anything that takes up space*) **Recall**

2. Tell me two things in this room that are made up of matter. (*Answers will vary, but must name objects or living things: chair, table, book, pencil, self, etc.*) **Inference**

3. What did the article call how much matter is in something? (*mass*) **Recall**

4. Which has more mass, a book or a piece of paper? Why? (*the book; because larger things have more mass than smaller things; because it is larger/heavier/has more matter than the paper* [*must answer both parts*]) **Inference**

5. What are the properties of matter that were named in this article? (*color, shape, size, temperature, texture* [*must name three*]) **Recall**

6. In the sentence, "Another property is texture, which means how rough or smooth something is," what does *rough* mean? (*not smooth; uneven surface; not level*) **Vocabulary**

7. What properties of an object could you find out if you could feel the object but you couldn't see it? (*size, shape, temperature, texture* [*must name three*]) **Inference**

8. What property of an object would you find out about if you put the object in water? (*if it would float or sink*) **Inference**

Errors in oral reading accuracy: _____

Correct comprehension responses: _____

SCORING GUIDE FOR ORAL READING AND COMPREHENSION

(Circle the boxes that correspond to the student's scores)

	Oral Reading Accuracy	Reading Comprehension	Listening Comprehension
Independent Level	7 or fewer errors	7–8 correct responses	
Instructional Level	8–23 errors	6–7 correct responses	6–7 correct responses
Frustration Level	24 or more errors	5 or fewer correct responses	

COMPREHENSION SCORES, BY TYPE

	Recall Questions	Inference Questions	Vocabulary Questions
Student's Correct Answers			
Possible Correct Answers	3	4	1

READING RATE SCORING GUIDE FOR GRADE 2

If the results computed just above show that the student read this passage at his independent level, you may wish to calculate his reading rate and compare that to other readers at his grade level.

1. Here is the number of words in this passage: 226

2. Write the number of words read incorrectly here: _____

3. Subtract #2 from #1 and write the answer here: _____

4. Using a calculator, multiply #3 by 60 seconds and write the answer here: _____

5. Write the student's reading time in seconds here: _____

6. Using a calculator, divide #4 by #5 and write the answer here: _____

The answer in #6 is the reading rate (words read correctly) per minute.

To interpret this number, first, locate the column in the chart below that represents the time of the year when this test was administered. Then, circle the reading rate that most closely matches your student's reading rate for this passage. Read across to the left to find the student's percentile rank—that is, an estimation of where that reading rate falls within those of other students at that grade level at that time of year.

ORAL READING FLUENCY NORMS FOR GRADE 2

Percentile	Fall WCPM	Winter WCPM	Spring WCPM
90	106	125	142
75	79	100	117
50	51	72	89
25	25	42	61
10	11	18	31

From Hasbrouck and Tindal, 2004.

▶ Science 3rd Grade Level: Life Cycles of Insects

Introduction: The title of this passage is "Life Cycles of Insects." It tells about the lives of different kinds of insects. I will ask you questions about it after you finish.

Record the time at the beginning: _____.

Do you know what a life cycle is? All plants and animals have life cycles. A life cycle is all the stages in the life of a living thing. In an animal's life cycle, a baby is born and grows, becoming an adult. It has babies of its own kind, and finally it dies. Its babies start their own life cycles. There are about a million different kinds of insects. Many have the same kind of life cycle.

Insects are small animals with six legs. Grasshoppers, crickets, dragonflies, and cockroaches are insects. Insects have a life cycle with three stages. The first stage is the egg. Many insects lay their eggs in a hard egg case that keeps the eggs safe. The second stage is the nymph. A nymph hatches from an egg. A nymph is a baby insect that looks like its parents. But a nymph has no wings. It eats and grows. The outside of its body cannot stretch. Soon it becomes too small for the nymph. The growing nymph breaks open its old covering and sheds it.

A nymph can shed its covering several times as it grows. As it gets older, the nymph grows its adult body parts. Wings and legs are body parts. The third stage is the adult. That is when the insect is fully grown. The last time the nymph sheds its covering, it has become an adult. When an insect is an adult it can have its own babies.

Record the time at the end: _____.

This text has been rated at 600L
It has 247 words

QUESTIONS

1. According to this passage, what is a life cycle? (*all the stages in the life of a living thing*) **Recall**

2. How did this passage say that many insects are similar? (*they have the same kind of life cycle*) **Inference**

3. What are the three stages of an insect's life cycle? (*egg, nymph, adult*) **Recall**

4. Why do many insects lay their eggs in an egg case? (*keeps eggs safe/protects eggs*) **Recall**

5. In the phrase, "A nymph can shed its covering," what does *shed* mean? (*take off, remove, crawl out of*) **Vocabulary**

6. Why does a nymph shed its outer covering? (*because the covering has become too small; covering can't stretch as the nymph grows*) **Inference**

7. When the nymph sheds its covering for the last time, what has happened? (*it is an adult; it is fully grown*) **Inference**

8. What are two things an adult insect can do that a nymph can't do? (*fly; have babies*) **Inference**

Errors in oral reading accuracy: _____

Correct comprehension responses: _____

SCORING GUIDE FOR ORAL READING AND COMPREHENSION

(Circle the boxes that correspond to the student's scores)

	Oral Reading Accuracy	Reading Comprehension	Listening Comprehension
Independent Level	7 or fewer errors	7–8 correct responses	
Instructional Level	8–25 errors	6–7 correct responses	6–7 correct responses
Frustration Level	26 or more errors	5 or fewer correct responses	

COMPREHENSION SCORES, BY TYPE

	Recall Questions	Inference Questions	Vocabulary Questions
Student's Correct Answers			
Possible Correct Answers	3	4	1

READING RATE SCORING GUIDE FOR GRADE 3

If the results computed just above show that the student read this passage at his independent level, you may wish to calculate his reading rate and compare that to other readers at his grade level.

1. Here is the number of words in this passage: 247

2. Write the number of words read incorrectly here: _____

3. Subtract #2 from #1 and write the answer here: _____

4. Using a calculator, multiply #3 by 60 seconds and write the answer here: _____

5. Write the student's reading time in seconds here: _____

6. Using a calculator, divide #4 by #5 and write the answer here: _____

The answer in #6 is the reading rate (words read correctly) per minute.

To interpret this number, first, locate the column in the chart below that represents the time of the year when this test was administered. Then, circle the reading rate that most closely matches your student's reading rate for this passage. Read across to the left to find the student's percentile rank—that is, an estimation of where that reading rate falls within those of other students at that grade level at that time of year.

ORAL READING FLUENCY NORMS FOR GRADE 3

Percentile	Fall WCPM	Winter WCPM	Spring WCPM
90	128	146	162
75	99	120	137
50	71	92	107
25	44	62	78
10	21	36	48

From Hasbrouck and Tindal, 2004.

► Science 4th Grade Level: How Sound is Made

Introduction: The title of this passage is "How Sound Is Made." It tells about how different sounds are made and how we hear sounds. I will ask you questions about it after you finish.

Record the time at the beginning: _____.

Sound is a kind of energy. You can hear sound. Sometimes you can even feel sound. The music of a violin, the crying of a baby, and the banging of a door are very different sounds. But they are all made the same way. Sounds are made when matter vibrates, or moves quickly back and forth. All sounds are made by vibration.

Parts of a musical instrument vibrate to make sounds. For example, when you hit a drum, the head of the drum vibrates. When you press a piano key, a striker inside the piano makes a wire string vibrate. When you strum a guitar string, or rub a bow across a violin's strings, the string vibrates and makes a sound.

People and many animals have vocal cords, or flaps of tissue, in their throats. Air makes the vocal cords vibrate and make sounds. Animals and humans can make a wide range of sounds. Humans can cry, speak, hum, sing, and scream. Animals can bark, howl, roar, chirp, and whine.

We hear sounds when the air vibrates. These vibrations are picked up by special parts of our ears. The vibration from a bird's throat moves through the air to your ear. Your eardrum and special ear bones vibrate. Nerves in your ear send signals to your brain. Each sound has its own pattern of vibrations. You recognize a sound as a bird singing, a baby crying, or your friend talking. Sound can also travel through water and hard substances like plastic, glass, and wood. That is how you can hear sounds underwater and through walls.

Record the time at the end: _____.

This text has been rated at 750L
It has 265 words

QUESTIONS

1. What might happen if your eardrum or ear bones couldn't vibrate? (*you couldn't hear sounds*) **Inference**

2. According to this passage, how are all sounds alike? (*they are made the same way; they are made when something vibrates*) **Inference**

3. In the sentence, "Sounds are made when matter vibrates," what does *vibrate* mean? (*move quickly back and forth*) **Vocabulary**

4. How does a musical instrument make sounds? (*parts of the instrument vibrate*) **Recall**

5. How does a piano make a sound when a key is pressed? (*a striker inside the piano hits a wire and makes it vibrate*) **Recall**

6. How do people's vocal cords make sounds? (*air makes them vibrate*) **Recall**

7. According to this passage, what has to happen for us to hear sounds? (*vibrations travel through air to ears; eardrum and ear bones vibrate*) **Inference**

8. How is it possible to hear sounds underwater? (*vibrations travel through water*) **Inference**

Errors in oral reading accuracy: _____

Correct comprehension responses: _____

SCORING GUIDE FOR ORAL READING AND COMPREHENSION

(Circle the boxes that correspond to the student's scores)

	Oral Reading Accuracy	Reading Comprehension	Listening Comprehension
Independent Level	8 or fewer errors	7–8 correct responses	
Instructional Level	9–27 errors	6–7 correct responses	6–7 correct responses
Frustration Level	28 or more errors	5 or fewer correct responses	

COMPREHENSION SCORES, BY TYPE

	Recall Questions	Inference Questions	Vocabulary Questions
Student's Correct Answers			
Possible Correct Answers	3	4	1

READING RATE SCORING GUIDE FOR GRADE 4

If the results computed just above show that the student read this passage at his independent level, you may wish to calculate his reading rate and compare that to other readers at his grade level.

1. Here is the number of words in this passage: 265

2. Write the number of words read incorrectly here: _____

3. Subtract #2 from #1 and write the answer here: _____

4. Using a calculator, multiply #3 by 60 seconds and write the answer here: _____

5. Write the student's reading time in seconds here: _____

6. Using a calculator, divide #4 by #5 and write the answer here: _____

The answer in #6 is the reading rate (words read correctly) per minute.

To interpret this number, first, locate the column in the chart below that represents the time of the year when this test was administered. Then, circle the reading rate that most closely matches your student's reading rate for this passage. Read across to the left to find the student's percentile rank—that is, an estimation of where that reading rate falls within those of other students at that grade level at that time of year.

ORAL READING FLUENCY NORMS FOR GRADE 4

Percentile	Fall WCPM	Winter WCPM	Spring WCPM
90	145	166	180
75	119	139	152
50	94	112	123
25	68	87	98
10	45	61	72

From Hasbrouck and Tindal, 2004.

▶ Science 5th Grade Level: How Living Things Grow

Introduction: The title of this passage is "How Living Things Grow." It tells about how cells divide and organisms grow. I will ask you questions about it after you finish.

Record the time at the beginning: _____.

The basic unit of all living things is the cell. Animal or plant, large or small, all living things are made up of cells. All living things start life as a single cell, which divides and forms new cells, so that new cells come from existing cells.

Some living things like bacteria are made up of only one cell. A new organism is formed when the single cell divides into two separate cells, which is called cell division. Each organism can produce offspring all by itself. The single cell divides into two identical cells. Then each cell can divide again. Most single-celled organisms reproduce very quickly. For example, bacteria can divide every few minutes. In your body, a few bacteria that cause disease can become thousands in just hours, making you very sick.

Most living things are complex, or made up of many cells. Complex living things may be made up of billions of cells. When these cells divide, they do not separate. They stay together and keep on dividing. As this happens, the organism grows and changes. When the organism becomes an adult and stops growing, its cells divide at a slower rate. Throughout life, cells die or wear away. They must be replaced until the organism dies.

When a cell of a complex organism divides, it makes two copies of all its parts. All the information a cell needs to live and reproduce is stored inside the cell. The information is stored in cell parts called chromosomes that look like short threads. When a cell begins to divide, its chromosomes line up in the center. Each one separates or breaks in half. The halves move to opposite sides of the cell. When the cell divides, each new cell will have identical chromosomes.

Finally the cell wall divides and closes off each of the two new cells. Each new cell will have all the same parts and chromosomes as the original cell.

Record the time at the end: _____.

This text has been rated at 850L
It has 369 words

QUESTIONS

1. According to this passage, what do all living things have in common? (*made up of cells*) **Inference**

2. In the phrase, "A new organism is formed . . ." what does *organism* mean? (*living thing*) **Vocabulary**

3. How did the article say all living things start life? (*as a single cell*) **Recall**

4. How do living things that are made up of just one cell, like bacteria, reproduce themselves? (*the one cell divides into two cells*) **Recall**

5. How can just a few disease-causing bacteria make you sick in a short time? (*because they multiply very quickly; they reproduce every few minutes; a few can become thousands in just hours*) **Inference**

6. How does a complex living thing that is made up of millions of cells grow larger? (*its cells divide but stay together, so the organism gets larger*) **Recall**

7. How does cell division change when an organism becomes an adult? (*It stops growing; cells divide at a slower rate.*) **Recall**

8. When a cell divides, how does each new cell get identical chromosomes? (*Each chromosome breaks in half and one half goes into each new cell.*) **Inference**

Errors in oral reading accuracy: _____

Correct comprehension responses: _____

SCORING GUIDE FOR ORAL READING AND COMPREHENSION

(Circle the boxes that correspond to the student's scores)

	Oral Reading Accuracy	Reading Comprehension	Listening Comprehension
Independent Level	10 or fewer errors	7–8 correct responses	
Instructional Level	11–32 errors	6–7 correct responses	6–7 correct responses
Frustration Level	33 or more errors	5 or fewer correct responses	

COMPREHENSION SCORES, BY TYPE

	Recall Questions	Inference Questions	Vocabulary Questions
Student's Correct Answers			
Possible Correct Answers	4	3	1

READING RATE SCORING GUIDE FOR GRADE 5

If the results computed just above show that the student read this passage at his independent level, you may wish to calculate his reading rate and compare that to other readers at his grade level.

1. Here is the number of words in this passage: 369

2. Write the number of words read incorrectly here: _____

3. Subtract #2 from #1 and write the answer here: _____

4. Using a calculator, multiply #3 by 60 seconds and write the answer here: _____

5. Write the student's reading time in seconds here: _____

6. Using a calculator, divide #4 by #5 and write the answer here: _____

The answer in #6 is the reading rate (words read correctly) per minute.

To interpret this number, first, locate the column in the chart below that represents the time of the year when this test was administered. Then, circle the reading rate that most closely matches your student's reading rate for this passage. Read across to the left to find the student's percentile rank—that is, an estimation of where that reading rate falls within those of other students at that grade level at that time of year.

ORAL READING FLUENCY NORMS FOR GRADE 5

Percentile	Fall WCPM	Winter WCPM	Spring WCPM
90	166	182	194
75	139	156	168
50	110	127	139
25	85	99	109
10	61	74	83

From Hasbrouck and Tindal, 2004.

▶Science 6th Grade Level: How Living Things Get Energy

Introduction: The title of this passage is "How Living Things Get Energy." It tells about how plants and animals get the energy they need to live. I will ask you questions about it after you finish.

Record the time at the beginning: _____.

All living things must get energy to live, but they differ in how they get energy. Green plants get energy from food that they make, using sunlight, carbon dioxide, and water to make a type of sugar. Green plants store this sugar in their roots, stems, and leaves until they need it. Because they make their own food, green plants are called producers. Most other living things can't make their own food, and they get energy by eating, or consuming, food. Their food is other living things. That is why they are called consumers.

Some consumers eat only plants, some only animals, and some both plants and animals. A consumer that eats only plants is called an herbivore, from an ancient word "herb" that means "plant." Cows, deer, rabbits, and caterpillars are examples of herbivores. A consumer that eats only other animals is called a carnivore, from an ancient word "carn" that means "flesh." Owls, lions, frogs, and bats are examples of carnivores. Consumers that eat both plants and animals are called omnivores, from an older word "omni" that means "all." Bears, raccoons, box turtles, and humans are examples of omnivores. Many kinds of birds are omnivores, because they eat seeds, insects, and worms. And some consumers get their food from the dead bodies and waste products of living things. These consumers help break down complex chemicals into simple chemicals and help dead things decay. They are called decomposers. Buzzards, fungi such as mold and mushrooms, some insects, and some bacteria are decomposers.

Record the time at the end: _____.

This text has been rated at 950L
It has 253 words

QUESTIONS

1. According to this article, how do green plants get energy? (*they make it; use sunlight, carbon dioxide, and water to make sugar/food*) **Recall**

2. What term did the article use for living things that make their own food? (*producers*) **Recall**

3. What term did the article use for living things that get their food by eating other living things? (*consumers*) **Recall**

4. According to this article, how are cows, deer, rabbits, and caterpillars alike? (*they are plant eaters/herbivores*) **Inference**

5. According to this article, how are bears, raccoons, box turtles, humans, and some birds alike? (*they are omnivores/ they eat both plants and animals*) **Inference**

6. In the sentence, "Buzzards, fungi . . . some insects, and some bacteria are decomposers," what does *decomposers* mean? (*things that eat dead organisms and waste products; things that help dead things decay*) **Vocabulary**

7. Why are decomposers useful in nature? (*they clean up dead things; help dead things decay; help break down complex chemicals into simple ones*) **Inference**

8. How might being an omnivore help an animal survive? (*could eat many things; easier to find foods it could eat*) **Inference**

Errors in oral reading accuracy: _____

Correct comprehension responses: _____

SCORING GUIDE FOR ORAL READING AND COMPREHENSION

(Circle the boxes that correspond to the student's scores)

	Oral Reading Accuracy	Reading Comprehension	Listening Comprehension
Independent Level	8 or fewer errors	7–8 correct responses	
Instructional Level	9–25 errors	6–7 correct responses	6–7 correct responses
Frustration Level	26 or more errors	5 or fewer correct responses	

COMPREHENSION SCORES, BY TYPE

	Recall Questions	Inference Questions	Vocabulary Questions
Student's Correct Answers			
Possible Correct Answers	3	4	1

READING RATE SCORING GUIDE FOR GRADE 6

If the results computed just above show that the student read this passage at his independent level, you may wish to calculate his reading rate and compare that to other readers at his grade level.

1. Here is the number of words in this passage: 253

2. Write the number of words read incorrectly here: _____

3. Subtract #2 from #1 and write the answer here: _____

4. Using a calculator, multiply #3 by 60 seconds and write the answer here: _____

5. Write the student's reading time in seconds here: _____

6. Using a calculator, divide #4 by #5 and write the answer here: _____

The answer in #6 is the reading rate (words read correctly) per minute.

To interpret this number, first, locate the column in the chart below that represents the time of the year when this test was administered. Then, circle the reading rate that most closely matches your student's reading rate for this passage. Read across to the left to find the student's percentile rank—that is, an estimation of where that reading rate falls within those of other students at that grade level at that time of year.

ORAL READING FLUENCY NORMS FOR GRADE 6

Percentile	Fall WCPM	Winter WCPM	Spring WCPM
90	177	195	204
75	153	167	177
50	127	140	150
25	98	111	122
10	68	82	93

From Hasbrouck and Tindal, 2004.

▶ Science Middle School Level: Orangutans

Introduction: The title of this passage is "Orangutans." It tells about a rare and interesting animal, the orangutan. I will ask you questions about it after you finish.

Record the time at the beginning: _____.

Orangutans are large mammals belonging to the primate group. Primates are divided into two main groups: one that includes humans, apes, and monkeys, and another that includes lemurs, tree shrews, and other smaller primates. The orangutan, whose name means "man of the forest," is a type of ape whose closest relatives are the gorilla and the chimpanzee.

Orangutans are arboreal, or tree-dwelling, animals whose habitat is the rain forests of Sumatra and Borneo in Southeast Asia. Orangutans spend their entire lives in the rain forest canopy, rarely descending to the ground. Because they live in dense foliage high above the ground, they are rarely seen in the wild. Native legends of Borneo refer to them as ghosts that can suddenly appear and disappear.

Orangutans are the largest arboreal animals. For example, adult orangutans range in height from three and a half to four and a half feet tall and weigh from 90 to 175 pounds in the wild. Females are generally smaller than males. In zoos, where food is plentiful, orangutans sometimes weigh nearly 300 pounds. Orangutans have arms twice the length of their bodies and feet that look like hands. They are covered with long reddish-brown fur. The fur on their backs and shoulders may be more than a foot long and resembles a cape. Males have long fur on their faces that looks like flowing beards and mustaches. The orangutan has no tail. Extremely flexible joints in its wrists, hips, and shoulders allow it to move more easily than any other ape. Orangutans have four fingers and a thumb on each foot, allowing them to grasp branches, food, and other objects easily.

Orangutans eat mostly fruit, which they pick and peel with their fingers. They also eat leaves, honey, eggs, termites, small lizards, baby birds, and many kinds of insects. They have been observed using sticks and long grasses to reach fruit and pluck termites from their nests. In zoos, they are known as escape artists, able to pick locks and escape from enclosures. In the wild, they build nests of sticks and leaves high in trees. Orangutans reproduce very slowly. The female gives birth to a single infant about every eight years. This is the longest interval between births of any animal. Infants stay with their mothers for about eight years, and the male and female stay together during that time. Males defend their territories and protect their families by making loud sounds and occasionally by fighting. Except when defending themselves, orangutans are both silent and peaceful. In spite of protective laws, orangutans are endangered in the wild. Baby orangutans are illegally captured and sold as pets.

Record the time at the end: _____.

This text has been rated at 1010L
It has 440 words

QUESTIONS

1. What are the two main groups of primates? (one group: *humans, apes, monkeys*; another group: *lemurs, tree shrews*) **Recall**

2. What two other apes are orangutans most similar to? (*gorillas and chimpanzees*) **Recall**

3. In the sentence, "Orangutans are the largest arboreal animals," what does *arboreal* mean? (*tree-dwelling, live in trees*) **Vocabulary**

4. Why do you think native legends refer to orangutans as ghosts? (*they are rarely seen; they live in the forest canopy; they seem to appear and disappear suddenly*) **Inference**

5. What physical traits make orangutans able to live in rain forests? (*long arms, very flexible joints, feet like hands, can grasp easily*) **Inference**

6. What are two reasons that orangutans are endangered? (*they reproduce only once every eight years; their babies are captured and sold*) **Inference**

7. What did you read that might make you think orangutans are intelligent? (*they can pick locks and escape from zoo enclosures; they use sticks and grass as tools*) **Inference**

8. How do male orangutans defend their territories? (*making loud noises, then fighting*) **Recall**

Errors in oral reading accuracy: _____

Correct comprehension responses: _____

SCORING GUIDE FOR ORAL READING AND COMPREHENSION

(Circle the boxes that correspond to the student's scores)

	Oral Reading Accuracy	Reading Comprehension	Listening Comprehension
Independent Level	13 or fewer errors	7–8 correct responses	
Instructional Level	14–44 errors	6–7 correct responses	6–7 correct responses
Frustration Level	45 or more errors	5 or fewer correct responses	

COMPREHENSION SCORES, BY TYPE

	Recall Questions	Inference Questions	Vocabulary Questions
Student's Correct Answers			
Possible Correct Answers	3	4	1

READING RATE SCORING GUIDE FOR MIDDLE SCHOOL

If the results computed just above show that the student read this passage at his independent level, you may wish to calculate his reading rate and compare that to other readers at his grade level.

1. Here is the number of words in this passage: 440

2. Write the number of words read incorrectly here: _____

3. Subtract #2 from #1 and write the answer here: _____

4. Using a calculator, multiply #3 by 60 seconds and write the answer here: _____

5. Write the student's reading time in seconds here: _____

6. Using a calculator, divide #4 by #5 and write the answer here: _____

The answer in #6 is the reading rate (words read correctly) per minute.

To interpret this number, first, locate the column in the chart below that represents the time of the year when this test was administered. Then, circle the reading rate that most closely matches your student's reading rate for this passage. Read across to the left to find the student's percentile rank— that is, an estimation of where that reading rate falls within those of other students at that grade level at that time of year.

ORAL READING FLUENCY NORMS FOR MIDDLE SCHOOL

Percentile	Fall WCPM	Winter WCPM	Spring WCPM
90	180	192	202
75	156	165	177
50	128	136	150
25	102	109	123
10	79	88	98

From Hasbrouck and Tindal, 2004.

Introduction: The title of this passage is "Rocks." It talks about different kinds of rocks and how they are classified. Read carefully. I will ask you questions about it after you finish.

Record the time at the beginning: _____.

Certain features in rocks reveal how the rock formed and can be used to classify it. For example, all rocks can be classified into three general groups: igneous, sedimentary, and metamorphic rock.

Igneous rock is named for the Latin word for fire, because it is formed when magma, molten rock from beneath the Earth's crust, cools and solidifies. Volcanic rocks, rocks formed during and after volcanic eruption, are the most obvious kind of igneous rock. The rocks that immediately surround most volcanoes form as magma pours out of volcanic vents, cools, and hardens. Because of this, in some igneous rocks of this type, wavelike patterns of melted rock are preserved during cooling. Oddly shaped volcanic rock fragments and chunks may result from violent gas explosions. These explo-sions cause magma to splatter, rather than to flow, and can rip chunks out of the volcano's vent. Finally, what is commonly thought of as volcanic ash is really very fine rock particles. Settling in a dense blanket, intensely hot volcanic ash can weld or fuse together into a third kind of volcanic rock, called tuff. Igneous rock is most commonly seen on the Earth's surface near active or recently active volcanoes.

Sedimentary rock, the most common type, is named for the Latin word meaning settling. Sedimentary rock forms when layers of sediment on or near the Earth's surface, including sand, gravel, and mud, compress and harden into layers. Sediment of various kinds is a result of wind and water erosion. Sediment is constantly deposited by wind and water into river valleys, lakes, oceans, and crevices. As a layer of sediment thickens, the particles near the bottom of the pile become compacted. Minerals dissolved in water are deposited between particles of sediment. The layer of compacted sediment and the dissolved minerals eventually cement together. The two forces of compacting and cementing form sedimentary rock. Sedimentary rock covers more than 75% of Earth's surface. It is commonly seen in the layers visible on mountainsides, in canyons, and where highways have been excavated through rock.

Metamorphic rock is named for the Greek words that mean changing form. Metamorphic rock is formed within the Earth's crust when existing rocks are transformed into a new form by heat, pressure, or both. When sedimentary rock is deeply buried in the Earth's crust by earthquakes, volcanic eruption, and other geologic events, it is subjected to both pressure and heat. Eventually it may melt and become magma. But if it does not melt, it will undergo chemical changes as some of its minerals change form or are replaced by

other minerals. This process is enhanced when the sedimentary rock contains water between its grains. Sedimentary rock containing water, such as limestone, is chemically changed by pressure and heat more quickly than drier rocks. Likewise, igneous rock, containing little water, must be subjected to much greater heat and pressure before it is changed. The most common kinds of metamorphic rocks are slate, mica, quartz, and certain minerals such as garnet. Metamorphic rocks are uncommon at the Earth's surface, and are most often located there as a result of explosions, mining, or other human processes.

Record the time at the end: _____.

This text has been rated at 1200L
It has 522 words

QUESTIONS

1. Name two of the three types of rocks. (*igneous, sedimentary, metamorphic*) **Recall**

2. What term does the author use for molten rock or lava? (*magma*) **Vocabulary**

3. Why is water an important factor in the formation of sedimentary rocks? (*sediments are carried by or dissolved in water*) **Inference**

4. How is tuff formed? (*hot volcanic ash settles in a dense blanket, fusing together*) **Recall**

5. What does the prefix *meta* tell us about how metamorphic rocks are formed? (*meta = changing form*) **Vocabulary**

6. What kind of rock do we see most frequently? Why? (*sedimentary: 75% of Earth's surface; road cuts and canyons*) **Inference**

7. Why is a miner more likely than other people to find metamorphic rocks? (*metamorphic rock is found deep in the earth*) **Inference**

8. Why does it take more energy to change igneous rock into metamorphic rock than to change sedimentary rock into metamorphic rock? (*igneous rock contains less water than sedimentary rock*) **Inference**

Errors in oral reading accuracy: _____

Correct comprehension responses: _____

SCORING GUIDE FOR ORAL READING AND COMPREHENSION

(Circle the boxes that correspond to the student's scores)

	Oral Reading Accuracy	Reading Comprehension	Listening Comprehension
Independent Level	16 or fewer errors	7–8 correct responses	
Instructional Level	17–52 errors	6–7 correct responses	6–7 correct responses
Frustration Level	53 or more errors	5 or fewer correct responses	

COMPREHENSION SCORES, BY TYPE

	Recall Questions	Inference Questions	Vocabulary Questions
Student's Correct Answers			
Possible Correct Answers	2	4	2

READING RATE SCORING GUIDE FOR HIGH SCHOOL

If the results computed just above show that the student read this passage at his independent level, you may wish to calculate his reading rate and compare that to other readers at his grade level.

1. Here is the number of words in this passage: 522

2. Write the number of words read incorrectly here: _____

3. Subtract #2 from #1 and write the answer here: _____

4. Using a calculator, multiply #3 by 60 seconds and write the answer here: _____

5. Write the student's reading time in seconds here: _____

6. Using a calculator, divide #4 by #5 and write the answer here: _____

The answer in #6 is the reading rate (words read correctly) per minute.
   To interpret this number, first, locate the column in the chart below that represents the time of

the year when this test was administered. Then, circle the reading rate that most closely matches your student's reading rate for this passage. Read across to the left to find the student's percentile rank—that is, an estimation of where that reading rate falls within those of other students at that grade level at that time of year.

ORAL READING FLUENCY NORMS FOR HIGH SCHOOL

Percentile	Fall WCPM	Winter WCPM	Spring WCPM
90	195	209	213
75	171	183	191
50	143	156	165
25	116	125	138
10	87	94	111

Note: These are estimates, extrapolated from From Hasbrouck and Tindal, 2004.

PRE-PRIMER AND PRIMER PASSAGES

FORM B

See instructions for creating these books on page 424.

Pencils are yellow.

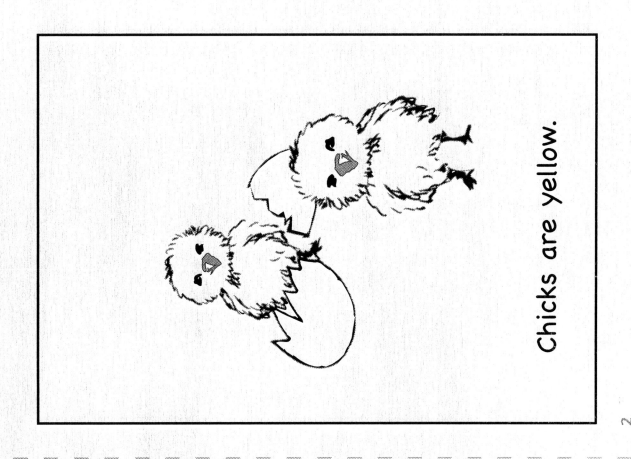

Chicks are yellow.

2

Flowers are yellow.

257

The sun is yellow.

4

3

Bananas are yellow.

258

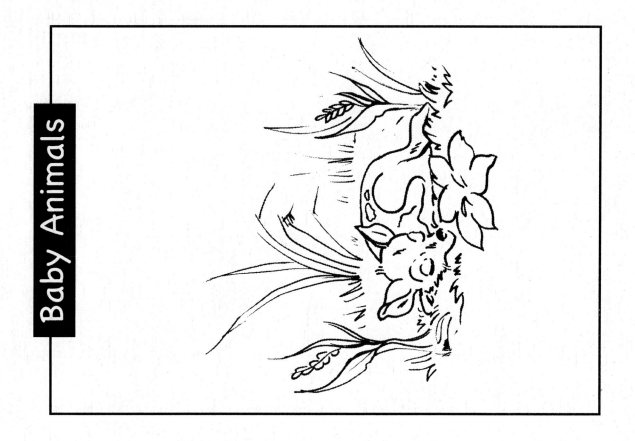

Baby snakes learn to crawl.

Baby birds learn to fly.

Baby deer learn to hide.

4

3

Baby turtles learn to swim.

Baby frogs learn to jump.

5

Baby monkeys learn to swing.

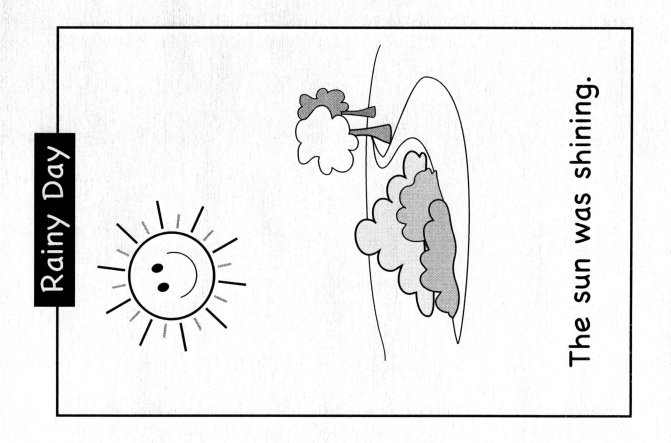

The sun was shining.

The sun went away.

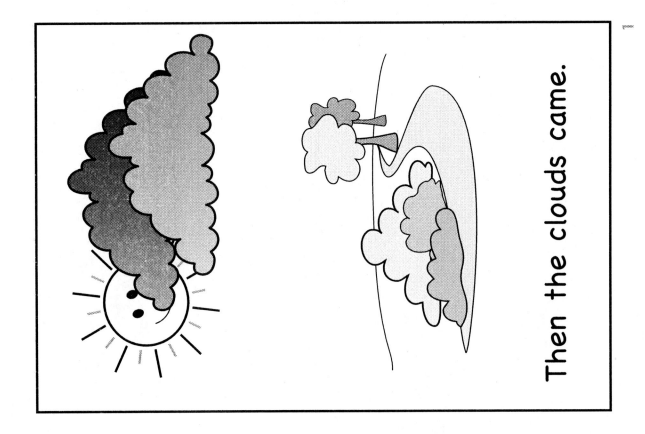

Then the clouds came.

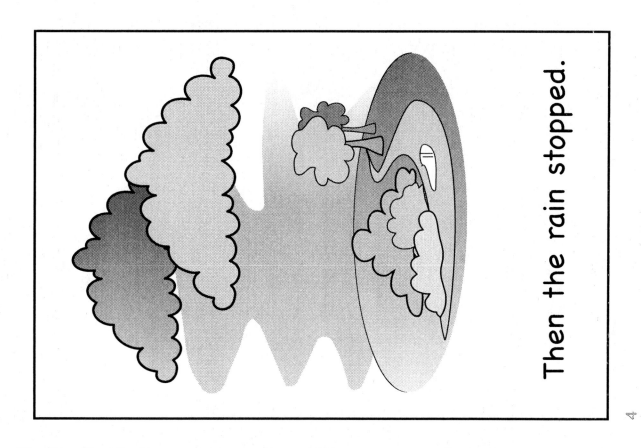

Then the rain stopped.

4

3

The rain came down.

265

A rainbow was in the sky.

The sun came back out.

Weather

What is the weather like outside? It may be warm or cool.

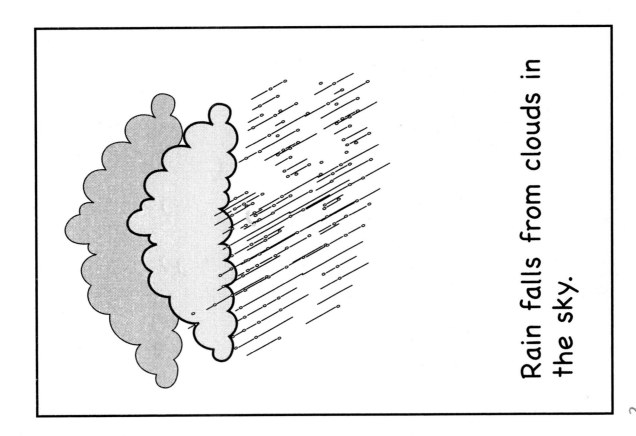

Rain falls from clouds in the sky.

It may be hot or cold.
It may be dry or wet.

If it is cold, rain can freeze. When rain freezes it turns into ice.

When it rains the ground gets wet. Plants and animals get wet.

Snow is frozen water.
When snowflakes melt,
they turn into water.

6

If it is very cold, snow
can fall from the clouds.

PRE-PRIMER AND PRIMER PASSAGES RESPONSE SHEETS

FORM B

▶ Pre-Primer A: What Is Yellow?

Teacher Prompts: Say, *"The title of this story is 'What Is Yellow?' It is about things that are yellow."* Walk through the pictures in the story. Help the student name the objects on each page. Go back to the beginning and say, *"Please read the story to me. Point to each word as you read."*

	Errors by Line
Pencils are yellow.	_____
Flowers are yellow.	_____
Chicks are yellow.	_____
Bananas are yellow.	_____
The sun is yellow.	_____
Total Errors	_____ **/16**

SCORING GUIDE FOR ORAL READING

(Circle the box that corresponds to the student's score)

	Oral Reading Accuracy
Independent Level	0 errors
Instructional Level	1–2 errors
Frustration Level	3 or more errors

▶ Pre-Primer B: Baby Animals

Teacher Prompts: Say, *"The title of this story is 'Baby Animals.' It is about what baby animals do."* Walk through the pictures in the story. Help the student name the animals and actions on each page. Go back to the beginning and say, *"Please read the story to me. Point to each word as you read."*

	Errors by Line
Baby birds learn to fly.	_____
Baby snakes learn to crawl.	_____
Baby turtles learn to swim.	_____
Baby deer learn to hide.	_____
Baby monkeys learn to swing.	_____
Baby frogs learn to jump.	_____
Total Errors	_____ /30

SCORING GUIDE FOR ORAL READING

(Circle the box that corresponds to the student's score)

	Oral Reading Accuracy
Independent Level	0–1 errors
Instructional Level	2–3 errors
Frustration Level	4 or more errors

▶ Pre-Primer C: A Rainy Day

Teacher Prompts: Say, *"The title of this story is 'A Rainy Day.' It is about some things that happened one rainy day."* Walk through the pictures in the story. Help the student tell what happens in each picture. On the last page ask, *"What sometimes happens after a rainstorm?"* Go back to the beginning and say, *"Please read the story to me. Point to each word as you read."*

	Errors by Line
The sun was shining.	_____
Then the clouds came.	_____
The sun went away.	_____
The rain came down.	_____
Then the rain stopped.	_____
The sun came back out.	_____
A rainbow was in the sky.	_____
Total Errors	_____ /31

SCORING GUIDE FOR ORAL READING

(Circle the box that corresponds to the student's score)

	Oral Reading Accuracy
Independent Level	0–2 errors
Instructional Level	3–4 errors
Frustration Level	5 or more errors

▶ Primer: Weather

Teacher Prompts: Say *"The title of this passage is 'Weather.' You will read about different kinds of weather."* Help the student tell what happens in each picture. Go back to the beginning and say, *"Please read the passage to me. Point to each word as you read."*

Record the time at the beginning: _____.

What is the weather like outside? It may be warm or cool. It may be hot or cold. It may be dry or wet.

Rain falls from clouds in the sky. When it rains the ground gets wet. Plants and animals get wet. If it is cold, rain can freeze. When rain freezes it turns into ice.

If it is very cold, snow can fall from the clouds. Snow is frozen water. When snowflakes melt, they turn into water.

Record the time at the end: _____.

(79 words)

QUESTIONS

1. When rain freezes, what does it turn into? (*ice*) **Recall**

2. What did the passage say snowflakes are made of? (*frozen water*) **Recall**

3. Could it ever rain when the sky is clear? Why not? (*no; rain falls from clouds*) **Inference**

4. What would the weather be like if the air and the ground were dry? (*it would be dry or clear; no rain or snow*) **Inference**

SCORING GUIDE FOR ORAL READING AND COMPREHENSION

(Circle the box that corresponds to the student's score)

	Oral Reading Accuracy	Reading Comprehension	Listening Comprehension
Independent Level	3 or fewer errors	4 correct responses	3–4
Instructional Level	4–8 errors	3 correct responses	6–7 correct responses
Frustration Level	9 or more errors	2 or fewer correct responses	

NARRATIVE PASSAGES

FORM B

Joe wanted to know many things.

"What keeps the birds up in the sky?" he asked, but his sister didn't know.

"Why can't birds fly backwards?" he asked. His sister didn't know.

"Why do birds have feathers?" he asked.

"I don't know!" said his sister.

"Now I want to know something," she asked.

"What do you want to know?" said Joe.

"Why do you ask so many questions?" asked his sister.

Joe thought for a minute.

"I don't know," he said.

▶ ▶ ▶

Carter was a small black dog. He lived with an inventor named Burt. Burt was bald and wanted more hair. He was inventing a new kind of juice to grow some.

Burt's first try made hair fall out. His second try made hair glow in the dark. His third try made hair disappear. Burt tried the new juice on Carter. All at once, Carter wasn't there. Except for his eyes and his nose.

Carter tried to chase cats. The cats didn't run. He tried to scare the mailman. The mailman looked around for a minute. Then kept on his rounds. Carter tried chasing trucks. But nobody saw him. It wasn't fun.

Carter put his paws on Burt's knees. Burt saw Carter's nose. Burt saw Carter's sad eyes. "You want me to change you back, don't you?"

Burt made new juice to try on Carter. His first try made Carter grow feathers. Other dogs thought he was a chicken. Burt's next try made Carter grow spines. Everybody stayed away from him.

Burt tried again. At last Carter grew hair. But it keeps growing. Now Carter has to go to the barber.

▶ ▶ ▶

Alicia loves baseball. Most of all, she loves batting. When kids can't bat, the other team shouts, "Easy out." But when Alicia bats the kids say, "Cover your heads!"

Alicia grabs the bat. She taps the plate, changes her grip, spreads her feet, and grins at the pitcher. Now she is ready.

The pitcher is scared of Alicia. He throws the ball to her right and he throws the ball to her left. Then he throws the ball over home plate. "Whack!" goes the bat. The ball jets toward the pitcher and he falls on his face. It flies over the fence and Alicia runs around the bases.

"Home run!" shouts the umpire. Then they hear a "smash." It comes from over the fence. Soon a woman walks through the gate holding a baseball, and the players all look sheepish. She walks past the pitcher and he shrugs.

"Who was batting?" she asks. The umpire points to Alicia. The woman walks up to Alicia. "What a girl!" she says as she hugs Alicia.

"Thanks, Mom."

"But we need another window. That's the fourth one this spring."

"Sorry, Mom."

"It's OK. We'll get a plastic one next time," said the woman.

▶ ▶ ▶

Mr. Flugle the baker was kind and funny. He had a tarantula named Harold, who slept all day in a cage behind the counter. A girl named Angela lived in the apartment block just down the street, and she stopped by every day after school. The aroma of hot cookies met her at the door. She always bought a cookie.

Angela and Mr. Flugle had a routine. She gave him two quarters, he put the quarters away, then he reached his hand over the counter and showed her his palm. No cookie. He showed her the back of his hand. No cookie. He touched her ear and there was a cookie! He had pulled a hot cookie out of her ear, or so it seemed. Mr. Flugle winked at Angela. She knew it was a trick, and one day she would figure out how he did it.

A boy named Andrew came in sometimes. He just wasn't raised right, and he stole cookies whenever Mr. Flugle's back was turned. One day Mr. Flugle bought a mirror. Andrew came into the shop, and when Mr. Flugle's back was turned, Andrew sneaked a cookie into his pocket.

"Hey, where's Harold?" said Mr. Flugle just then. "Boy, is there something in your pocket?" asked Mr. Flugle.

"Why, no," said Andrew, looking worried.

"Don't you feeling something wiggling in there?" Andrew's eyes got big as saucers.

"Look," said Mr. Flugle. He touched Andrew's pocket and the tarantula crawled out, or so it seemed.

"Yowee!" shouted Andrew, and he ran out of the door. Mr. Flugle winked at Angela. Then he put Harold back in his cage.

▶ ▶ ▶

Gerard's mother made wedding cakes, delicious cakes of every size, shape and flavor. Gerard's job was to make the cakes pretty, because he could make a plain cake look like a beautiful palace.

One day, a young man entered their cake shop. "I need a wedding cake," he said.

"You've come to the right place," said Gerard's mother. "Who is this cake for?"

The man clasped his hands to his chest. "I am marrying the most enchanting woman in the universe. Her eyes sparkle like stars in the night, her hair flows like a mountain stream, her lips . . ."

"That's enough about the lips," said Gerard's mother. "How many people are coming to the wedding?"

The man thought for a minute. "At least three hundred. She has a big family."

"The cake will be ready on Saturday," Gerard's mother said.

On Saturday morning, as Gerard was carving the last of the frosted roses, the door burst open and in came the same young man.

"Cancel the order!" the man shouted.

"What's wrong?" asked Gerard.

"Forget about the flowing hair! Forget about the dark eyes!"

"Did you change your mind about the wedding?" asked Gerard.

"Not about the wedding, just about the bride." The man gazed dreamily at the ceiling and whispered, "My new love is as lively as a gazelle, her hair is like a bonfire, her . . ."

iv

"Enough about the bonfires," said Gerard's mother. "What kind of cake do you want?"

Out on the street, they heard a noise that sounded like the baying of hounds, or three hundred angry wedding guests. The young man sweated and trembled and said, "Just make me a cake to go, and make it quick!"

▶ ▶ ▶

iv

Uncle Ezra had gotten too old to work on the farm. Now there was nothing to do but sit around on the porch, rock in his big chair, and stare down the hill toward the river. In the morning and in the evening he listened for the train that ran along the tracks down there. The North Texas Cannonball was the name of that train. In the morning it took passengers from New Orleans to Dallas, and in the evening it brought them from Dallas back to New Orleans.

The North Texas Cannonball was the most important thing in the old man's life. Twice each day he listened for the whistle, and the rumble of the engine, and the clicking of the wheels. He could almost see the passengers reclining in their comfortable seats and sipping their coffee and their tea. Uncle Ezra decided he had to have something to do with that train.

Before dawn one morning he walked through the fields down to the tracks and found a dried branch. And when he heard the whistle and the rumble of the engine, he set that branch on fire. The train rounded the curve, a quarter mile away. Uncle Ezra waved that burning branch over his head—"Whoosh! Whoosh! Whoosh!" Brakes squealed, cars banged one against another, and the North Texas Cannonball shuddered to a stop, right in front of Uncle Ezra.

The engineer jumped down. "Where is the emergency?" he shouted. "Is the trestle washed out up ahead?" Uncle Ezra rubbed the toe of one boot in the dirt and didn't say anything.

"What is it? Why did you stop the train?" the engineer demanded. "Speak up, old man. Those passengers have to get to Dallas. Why did you stop the train?"

At last Uncle Ezra thought of something. "Want to buy a 'possum?"

"A 'possum!" shouted the engineer. "You stopped this train to sell a 'possum?"

Just then a kindly conductor approached them. He said, "Take it easy, chief. You can see he's just a lonesome old man. Tell us, Uncle, how much do you want for that 'possum?"

"I don't know," said Uncle Ezra. "I haven't caught him yet."

▶ ▶ ▶

V

Carlo's mother stirred the eggs and deposited them next to the fried bananas on his plate. The tall, tanned woman wore trousers with baggy thighs, knee-high boots with a lustrous brown shine, and a black velvet hat hardened with steel.

Avoiding their prominent bandages, Carlo gently hoisted two cats off his chair and sat down. "Are you going horseback riding again today, Mom?"

"Yes," said his mother, keeping her back turned. "Can you get a lift home from school?"

"I suppose," said Carlo as she put the plate in front of him.

"You sure must like those horses," said Carlo.

"Why do you say that?" She still didn't look at him.

"You went riding four days this week."

His mother kept her back to him. She had quit her job as the town's chief of police last spring, and as summer evolved into autumn she showed no sign of returning to her former profession. It amazed Carlo to observe the trappings of the old life slip away. She stopped carrying a pistol on her waist, stopped getting midnight phone calls, and stopped driving a hundred miles an hour with a screaming siren. Late one afternoon she simply walked out of the police department and never went back.

Now her passion had become animals, and their house had gone from no cats to eleven. The cats came in all states of disrepair, from mangy to scarred to crippled. When she collected an injured creature, she said she would keep it long enough to nurse it back to full vigor. But once a cat was healthy, she couldn't bear to part with it, so with every passing week the healthy cats were joined by their needy kinsmen. Then had come the horses: his mother had bought an old stable out past the golf course where she boarded two cast-off horses. Carlo expected more.

Then the family diet changed. First, pepperoni gave way to mushrooms on the pizza. Then pasta with cheese replaced chicken casseroles, and then—what's this?—soy burgers replaced their meaty relatives. Today was the third time she'd served Carlo fried bananas with his eggs. Bacon had disappeared, and Carlo now suspected that the eggs' days were numbered.

▶ ▶ ▶

Richard was afraid to go to parties. When he attended one his hands perspired, then his chest, then his face and he became tongue-tied. Then he silently counted all the riveting things he couldn't think of to say. Because of this, Richard would do anything to avoid a party. Sometimes he'd even say he was going out of town, and then sequester himself in his darkened bedroom.

Richard's sister Deborah discovered his problem one summer when she dragged him along to her best friend's birthday party, and halfway through the evening she noticed her brother alone in a corner with his hair matted to his forehead and his hands fidgeting. Suddenly she could almost feel his discomfort, and the awareness made her own enjoyment evaporate.

She confronted him the next morning. "What was the matter with you last night?" she asked, but Richard grimaced with embarrassment and was silent. Deborah sat down at the family's computer, went online and typed "fear of parties" into a search engine, and then clicked on a web site about social anxiety.

"Hey!" she shouted, "I think I found your problem." Richard read over her shoulder that seven percent of all people panic when they go to parties. The site continued with a section called "What to do if you're scared to go to parties." There it offered a breathing exercise, in which the nervous person was advised to poke his finger in his stomach and breathe in and out while slowly counting to five. Normally he would keep up the exercise for five whole minutes, but the site conceded that the nervous victim might be allowed to quit sooner if the exercise made him nervous as well.

"See, Richard? You'll be the life of the party if you just walk into the center of the room, poke your hand in your stomach, count to five, and start breathing. Soon, everyone will be doing it!" Deborah teased playfully.

"Let's move on," said Richard, but he was smiling. The site also suggested that the anxious person fill a "comfort bag" with comforting objects, like a coloring book or a teddy bear, to bring to the party.

"A teddy bear?" Deborah snorted. "Why not put Sparky in your backpack and bring her along?" Sparky was the family's German shepherd.

Richard laughed, but that night he retrieved an old rabbit's foot keychain, and at the next party, he clutched it securely while he made conversation. It was easier to carry than a whole dog, he thought.

▶ ▶ ▶

The tenth graders in the library were quiet. The visiting author had become overwrought by the tale she was telling, and her abrupt silence had silenced the students. She asked their pardon, then cleared her throat, wiped her eyes, and continued her story.

A teenage girl and her family clung to survival in a Caribbean island village. Their country had been ruled by a decrepit and whimsical dictator, whose soldiers terrorized the countryside now that the dictator had died, stealing whatever shreds of sustenance remained to the people. Those citizens who stood up to them, who simply asked for clean water and decent work, were harassed and sometimes "disappeared," made to vanish into the night without any acknowledgement from the police or the military that they had ever existed. Hundreds upon hundreds of people attempted to flee the island in rickety boats of all descriptions, but frail as they were and close to starvation, many could not endure those many days' exposure to the elements. Sometimes whole boatloads of refugees were lost to Atlantic storms.

"Is that story real?" asked a student, during the questioning after, and the author explained that the events portrayed in her novel were indeed real, although she acknowledged that the characters were her own inventions.

When another student said, "Thank goodness this isn't happening to us," there was a long pause, and then a voice in the back of the room said, "I was there."

"Who?" asked a student.

"Me." The voice belonged to the reclusive boy in hand-me-down clothes who spoke shyly in whispers, and was as close to being anonymous as anyone in the school.

"You, Marcel?" asked the school principal.

"Yes, ma'am." The other students craned their necks to see who was talking.

"Can you tell us about it?" asked an incredulous girl sitting beside him.

"Yes. My father was the director of the high school in my town, and since he was opposed to the government, he did not discourage the students when they decided to show solidarity with the workers in a demonstration at the sugar refinery. Late one night there was a knock at our door, and when my mother opened it, there were soldiers . . ."

All eyes were now fixed firmly on Marcel as the fascinated students pressed their refugee-classmate for details of his odyssey, and the visiting author listened as attentively as any of them. Later as the novelist and principal approached the waiting limousine, the principal asked, "Is that why you wrote your book, so young people like Marcel would be real to their classmates?"

"Everyone has a story," the author replied. "And everyone needs people who will listen."

X

▶ ▶ ▶

NARRATIVE PASSAGES
RESPONSE SHEETS

FORM B

Introduction: The title of this story is "Joe Wants to Know." Sometimes a story can be just some talk between two people. Read this story to find out what kind of person Joe is, and how his sister feels about him. I will ask you questions about the passage after you finish reading.

Record the time at the beginning: _____.

Joe wanted to know many things.

"What keeps the birds up in the sky?" he

asked, but his sister didn't know.

"Why can't birds fly backwards?" he

asked. His sister didn't know.

"Why do birds have feathers?" he asked.

"I don't know!" said his sister.

"Now I want to know something," she

asked.

"What do you want to know?" said Joe.

"Why do you ask so many questions?"

asked his sister.

Joe thought for a minute.

"I don't know," he said.

Record the time at the end: _____.

This text has been rated at 300L
It has 81 words

QUESTIONS

1. What does Joe mostly want to know about? (*birds*) **Recall**

2. How does his sister feel about Joe's questions? (*She is irritated, impatient.*) **Inference**

3. Did Joe's sister know the answers to his questions? How do you know? (*No. She said, "I don't know."*) **Recall**

4. Why doesn't Joe's sister ask as many questions as Joe does? (*because she is not as curious; because she is older*) **Inference**

5. What did Joe's sister ask Joe? (*why he asked so many questions*) **Recall**

6. In the sentence, "'Why do birds have feathers?' said Joe," what are *feathers*? (*part of a bird's wing*) **Vocabulary**

Errors in oral reading accuracy: _____

Correct comprehension responses: _____

SCORING GUIDE FOR ORAL READING AND COMPREHENSION

(Circle the box that corresponds to the student's scores)

	Oral Reading Accuracy	Reading Comprehension	Listening Comprehension
Independent Level	2 or fewer errors	6 correct responses	
Instructional Level	3–8 errors	5 correct responses	6–7 correct responses
Frustration Level	9 or more errors	4 or fewer correct responses	

COMPREHENSION SCORES, BY TYPE

	Recall Questions	Inference Questions	Vocabulary Questions
Student's Correct Answers			
Possible Correct Answers	3	2	1

READING RATE SCORING GUIDE FOR GRADE 1

If the results computed just above show that the student read this passage at his independent level, you may wish to calculate his reading rate and compare that to other readers at his grade level.

1. Here is the number of words in this passage: 81

2. Write the number of words read incorrectly here: _____

3. Subtract #2 from #1 and write the answer here: _____

4. Using a calculator, multiply #3 by 60 seconds and write the answer here: _____

5. Write the student's reading time in seconds here: _____

6. Using a calculator, divide #4 by #5 and write the answer here: _____

The answer in #6 is the reading rate (words read correctly) per minute.

To interpret this number, first, locate the column in the chart below that represents the time of the year when this test was administered. Then, circle the reading rate that most closely matches your student's reading rate for this passage. Read across to the left to find the student's percentile rank—that is, an estimation of where that reading rate falls within those of other students at that grade level at that time of year.

ORAL READING FLUENCY NORMS FOR GRADE 1

Percentile	Fall WCPM	Winter WCPM	Spring WCPM
90		81	111
75		47	82
50		23	53
25		12	28
10		6	15

From Hasbrouck and Tindal, 2004.

► Narrative 2nd Grade Level (2.1): The Disappearing Dog

Introduction: The title of this story is "The Disappearing Dog." Carter, the dog in this story, lived with Burt. Burt was an inventor. Read to see what happened when Burt used some of his inventions on Carter. I will ask you questions about the story after you finish reading.

Record the time at the beginning: _____.

Carter was a small black dog. He lived with an inventor named Burt. Burt was bald and wanted more hair. He was inventing a new kind of juice to grow some.

Burt's first try made hair fall out. His second try made hair glow in the dark. His third try made hair disappear. Burt tried the new juice on Carter. All at once, Carter wasn't there. Except for his eyes and his nose.

Carter tried to chase cats. The cats didn't run. He tried to scare the mailman. The mailman looked around for a minute. Then kept on his rounds. Carter tried chasing trucks. But nobody saw him. It wasn't fun.

Carter put his paws on Burt's knees. Burt saw Carter's nose. Burt saw Carter's sad eyes. "You want me to change you back, don't you?"

Burt made new juice to try on Carter. His first try made Carter grow feathers. Other dogs thought he was a chicken. Burt's next try made Carter grow spines. Everybody stayed away from him.

Burt tried again. At last Carter grew hair. But it keeps growing. Now Carter has to go to the barber.

Record the time at the end: _____.

This text has been rated at 350L
It has 190 words

QUESTIONS

1. Why did Burt invent the juice? (*Burt was bald and wanted to grow new hair.*) **Recall**

2. Why didn't cats run when Carter chased them? (*They couldn't see him—they only saw his eyes and nose.*) **Recall**

3. What made people stay away from Carter? (*He grew sharp spines.*) **Recall**

4. The author said the mailman "kept on his rounds." What does *kept on his rounds* mean? (*kept going along his assigned route from house to house*) **Vocabulary**

5. In the sentence "He was inventing a new kind of juice to grow some," what does *inventing* mean? (*creating something that didn't exist before*) **Vocabulary**

6. What was the problem with Carter's new hair? (*It wouldn't stop growing.*) **Recall**

7. Why did you think Burt tried the juice on Carter but not on himself? (*He may have been afraid of trying it on himself. Scientists usually experiment on others. Accept either answer.*) **Inference**

8. How did Burt feel about Carter? How do you know? (*At first he treated him like an experimental animal—because he tried new medicines on him. Then he felt sorry for him—because he tried to improve his condition. Accept either or both answers.*) **Inference**

Errors in oral reading accuracy: _____

Correct comprehension responses: _____

SCORING GUIDE FOR ORAL READING AND COMPREHENSION

(Circle the boxes that correspond to the student's scores)

	Oral Reading Accuracy	Reading Comprehension	Listening Comprehension
Independent Level	6 or fewer errors	7–8 correct responses	
Instructional Level	7–19 errors	6–7 correct responses	6–7 correct responses
Frustration Level	20 or more errors	5 or fewer correct responses	

COMPREHENSION SCORES, BY TYPE

	Recall Questions	Inference Questions	Vocabulary Questions
Student's Correct Answers			
Possible Correct Answers	4	2	2

READING RATE SCORING GUIDE FOR GRADE 2

If the results computed just above show that the student read this passage at his independent level, you may wish to calculate his reading rate and compare that to other readers at his grade level.

1. Here is the number of words in this passage: 190

2. Write the number of words read incorrectly here: _____

3. Subtract #2 from #1 and write the answer here: _____

4. Using a calculator, multiply #3 by 60 seconds and write the answer here: _____

5. Write the student's reading time in seconds here: _____

6. Using a calculator, divide #4 by #5 and write the answer here: _____

The answer in #6 is the reading rate (words read correctly) per minute.

To interpret this number, first, locate the column in the chart below that represents the time of the year when this test was administered. Then, circle the reading rate that most closely matches your student's reading rate for this passage. Read across to the left to find the student's percentile rank—that is, an estimation of where that reading rate falls within those of other students at that grade level at that time of year.

Percentile	Fall WCPM	Winter WCPM	Spring WCPM
90	106	125	142
75	79	100	117
50	51	72	89
25	25	42	61
10	11	18	31

From Hasbrouck and Tindal, 2004.

Introduction: The title of this story is "Alicia at Bat." It's about an amazing young baseball player. Read to find out what happens when she hits one over the fence. I will ask you questions about the passage after you finish reading.

Record the time at the beginning: _____ .

Alicia loves baseball. Most of all, she loves batting. When kids can't bat, the other team shouts, "Easy out." But when Alicia bats the kids say, "Cover your heads!"

Alicia grabs the bat. She taps the plate, changes her grip, spreads her feet, and grins at the pitcher. Now she is ready.

The pitcher is scared of Alicia. He throws the ball to her right and he throws the ball to her left. Then he throws the ball over home plate. "Whack!" goes the bat. The ball jets toward the pitcher and he falls on his face. It flies over the fence and Alicia runs around the bases.

"Home run!" shouts the umpire. Then they hear a "smash." It comes from over the fence. Soon a woman walks through the gate holding a baseball, and the players all look sheepish. She walks past the pitcher and he shrugs.

"Who was batting?" she asks. The umpire points to Alicia. The woman walks up to Alicia. "What a girl!" she says as she hugs Alicia.

"Thanks, Mom."

"But we need another window. That's the fourth one this spring."

"Sorry, Mom."

"It's OK. We'll get a plastic one next time," said the woman.

Record the time at the end: _____ .

This text has been rated at 450L
It has 200 words

QUESTIONS

1. What did the other team say when Alicia came up to bat? (*"Cover your heads!"*) **Recall**

2. How did Alicia get ready to bat? (*grabs the bat, taps the plate, changes her grip, spreads her feet, and grins at the pitcher—The child should recall any two of the five.*) **Recall**

3. What did the woman mean when she said, "What a girl!"? (*that the girl was special, that she was proud of her*) **Vocabulary**

4. Why did the woman come onto the ball field? (*She found the ball; the ball broke something, probably a window.*) **Inference**

5. What do you think the players expected the woman to do when she walked onto the field? (*complain about the damage to her house; fuss at somebody*) **Inference**

6. What did the author mean when he said "The players all look *sheepish*"? (*guilty, ashamed*) **Vocabulary**

7. What else did the woman say Alicia had done that spring? (*broken three windows*) **Recall**

8. What do you think was most important to the woman in this story? (*her daughter was a good baseball player; she was proud of her daughter—either one*) **Inference**

Errors in oral reading accuracy: _____

Correct comprehension responses: _____

SCORING GUIDE FOR ORAL READING AND COMPREHENSION

(Circle the boxes that correspond to the student's scores)

	Oral Reading Accuracy	Reading Comprehension	Listening Comprehension
Independent Level	6 or fewer errors	7–8 correct responses	
Instructional Level	7–20 errors	6–7 correct responses	6–7 correct responses
Frustration Level	21 or more errors	5 or fewer correct responses	

COMPREHENSION SCORES, BY TYPE

	Recall Questions	Inference Questions	Vocabulary Questions
Student's Correct Answers			
Possible Correct Answers	3	3	2

READING RATE SCORING GUIDE FOR GRADE 2

If the results computed just above show that the student read this passage at his independent level, you may wish to calculate his reading rate and compare that to other readers at his grade level.

1. Here is the number of words in this passage: 200

2. Write the number of words read incorrectly here: _____

3. Subtract #2 from #1 and write the answer here: _____

4. Using a calculator, multiply #3 by 60 seconds and write the answer here: _____

5. Write the student's reading time in seconds here: _____

6. Using a calculator, divide #4 by #5 and write the answer here: _____

The answer in #6 is the reading rate (words read correctly) per minute.

To interpret this number, first, locate the column in the chart below that represents the time of the year when this test was administered. Then, circle the reading rate that most closely matches your student's reading rate for this passage. Read across to the left to find the student's percentile rank—that is, an estimation of where that reading rate falls within those of other students at that grade level at that time of year.

ORAL READING FLUENCY NORMS FOR GRADE 2

Percentile	Fall WCPM	Winter WCPM	Spring WCPM
90	106	125	142
75	79	100	117
50	51	72	89
25	25	42	61
10	11	18	31

From Hasbrouck and Tindal, 2004.

▶ Narrative 3rd Grade Level: Mr. Flugle, the Baker

Introduction: The title of this story is "Mr. Flugle, the Baker." Mr. Flugle and his young friend Angela share a love of magic tricks. Read to find out how they use magic to protect their bakery from dishonest fingers. I will ask you questions about the passage after you finish reading.

Record the time at the beginning: _____ .

Mr. Flugle the baker was kind and funny. He had a tarantula named Harold, who slept all day in a cage behind the counter. A girl named Angela lived in the apartment block just down the street, and she stopped by every day after school. The aroma of hot cookies met her at the door. She always bought a cookie.

Angela and Mr. Flugle had a routine. She gave him two quarters, he put the quarters away, then he reached his hand over the counter and showed her his palm. No cookie. He showed her the back of his hand. No cookie. He touched her ear and there was a cookie! He had pulled a hot cookie out of her ear, or so it seemed. Mr. Flugle winked at Angela. She knew it was a trick, and one day she would figure out how he did it.

A boy named Andrew came in sometimes. He just wasn't raised right, and he stole cookies whenever Mr. Flugle's back was turned. One day Mr. Flugle bought a mirror. Andrew came into the shop, and when Mr. Flugle's back was turned, Andrew sneaked a cookie into his pocket.

"Hey, where's Harold?" said Mr. Flugle just then. "Boy, is there something in your pocket?" asked Mr. Flugle.

"Why, no," said Andrew, looking worried.

"Don't you feeling something wiggling in there?" Andrew's eyes got big as saucers.

"Look," said Mr. Flugle. He touched Andrew's pocket and the tarantula crawled out, or so it seemed.

"Yowee!" shouted Andrew, and he ran out of the door. Mr. Flugle winked at Angela. Then he put Harold back in his cage.

Record the time at the end: _____ .

This text has been rated at 600L
It has 272 words

QUESTIONS

1. The text said, "The aroma of hot cookies met her at the door." What does *aroma* mean? (*the smell*) **Vocabulary**

2. How did Mr. Flugle let Angela know that he was teasing her? (*He winked.*) **Inference**

3. Why do you think Angela didn't ask Mr. Flugle how he did the cookie trick? (*It would spoil the fun—or she doesn't want him to know she doesn't believe he's magical.*) **Inference**

4. Where did Angela live? (*in an apartment down the street*) **Recall**

5. What caused Mr. Flugle to buy a mirror for his shop? (*He suspected that Andrew was stealing from him.*) **Inference**

6. Describe Harold. (*large hairy spider*) **Recall**

7. What was the effect on Andrew when he thought that a spider came out of his pocket? (*He was frightened into leaving the store.*) **Recall**

8. How did the author help you predict that Harold would have something to do with the stolen cookie? (*He said Harold's cage was empty. He'd already shown that Mr. Flugle could make things appear where they were not expected to be. Should provide either answer.*) **Inference**

Errors in oral reading accuracy: _____

Correct comprehension responses: _____

SCORING GUIDE FOR ORAL READING AND COMPREHENSION

(Circle the boxes that correspond to the student's scores)

	Oral Reading Accuracy	Reading Comprehension	Listening Comprehension
Independent Level	7 or fewer errors	7–8 correct responses	
Instructional Level	8–27 errors	6–7 correct responses	6–7 correct responses
Frustration Level	28 or more errors	5 or fewer correct responses	

COMPREHENSION SCORES, BY TYPE

	Recall Questions	Inference Questions	Vocabulary Questions
Student's Correct Answers			
Possible Correct Answers	3	4	1

READING RATE SCORING GUIDE FOR GRADE 3

If the results computed just above show that the student read this passage at his independent level, you may wish to calculate his reading rate and compare that to other readers at his grade level.

1. Here is the number of words in this passage: 272

2. Write the number of words read incorrectly here: _____

3. Subtract #2 from #1 and write the answer here: _____

4. Using a calculator, multiply #3 by 60 seconds and write the answer here: _____

5. Write the student's reading time in seconds here: _____

6. Using a calculator, divide #4 by #5 and write the answer here: _____

The answer in #6 is the reading rate (words read correctly) per minute.

To interpret this number, first, locate the column in the chart below that represents the time of the year when this test was administered. Then, circle the reading rate that most closely matches your student's reading rate for this passage. Read across to the left to find the student's percentile rank— that is, an estimation of where that reading rate falls within those of other students at that grade level at that time of year.

ORAL READING FLUENCY NORMS FOR GRADE 3

Percentile	Fall WCPM	Winter WCPM	Spring WCPM
90	128	146	162
75	99	120	137
50	71	92	107
25	44	62	78
10	21	36	48

From Hasbrouck and Tindal, 2004.

▶ Narrative 4th Grade Level, Form B: The Cake Decorator

Introduction: The title of this story is "The Cake Decorator." When you have a job sometimes you meet unusual people. This passage tells of someone Gerard met on the job. I will ask you questions about the passage after you finish reading.

Record the time at the beginning: _____.

Gerard's mother made wedding cakes, delicious cakes of every size, shape and flavor. Gerard's job was to make the cakes pretty, because he could make a plain cake look like a beautiful palace.

One day, a young man entered their cake shop. "I need a wedding cake," he said.

"You've come to the right place," said Gerard's mother. "Who is this cake for?"

The man clasped his hands to his chest. "I am marrying the most enchanting woman in the universe. Her eyes sparkle like stars in the night, her hair flows like a mountain stream, her lips . . ."

"That's enough about the lips," said Gerard's mother. "How many people are coming to the wedding?"

The man thought for a minute. "At least three hundred. She has a big family."

"The cake will be ready on Saturday," Gerard's mother said.

On Saturday morning, as Gerard was carving the last of the frosted roses, the door burst open and in came the same young man.

"Cancel the order!" the man shouted.

"What's wrong?" asked Gerard.

"Forget about the flowing hair! Forget about the dark eyes!"

"Did you change your mind about the wedding?" asked Gerard.

"Not about the wedding, just about the bride." The man gazed dreamily at the ceiling and whispered, "My new love is as lively as a gazelle, her hair is like a bonfire, her . . ."

"Enough about the bonfires," said Gerard's mother. "What kind of cake do you want?"

Out on the street, they heard a noise that sounded like the baying of hounds, or three hundred angry wedding guests. The young man sweated and trembled and said, "Just make me a cake to go, and make it quick!"

Record the time at the end: _____ .

This text has been rated at 750L
It has 280 words

QUESTIONS

1. Why did Gerard and his mother make a good team? (*She baked the cakes, and he decorated them.*) **Inference**

2. Why was Gerard's mother so interested in how many people would be coming to the wedding? (*The number of guests would let her know how big a cake to bake.*) **Inference**

3. How was the man's second bride different from the first one? (*The first had mysterious eyes and long flowing hair; the second was lively with hair like a bonfire.*) **Recall**

4. Why do you think that the wedding guests were angry? (*The man had cancelled the first wedding at the last minute.*) **Inference**

5. How did the author tell you that the man was afraid of the wedding guests? (*He was sweating and trembling, or they were chasing him.*) **Recall**

6. In the phrase, "They man gazed dreamily at the ceiling," what does *gazed* mean? (*stared; unfocused*) **Vocabulary**

7. When the man compares the woman's hair to a bonfire ("Her hair is like a bonfire") what is he saying about her hair? (*that it is of a bright color, perhaps wildly jutting in all directions*) **Vocabulary**

8. Describe the way Gerard's mother spoke to the man who ordered the cakes. (*She was brusque, business-like; she cut to the essentials.*) **Recall**

Errors in oral reading accuracy: _____

Correct comprehension responses: _____

SCORING GUIDE FOR ORAL READING AND COMPREHENSION

(Circle the boxes that correspond to the student's scores)

	Oral Reading Accuracy	Reading Comprehension	Listening Comprehension
Independent Level	8 or fewer errors	7–8 correct responses	
Instructional Level	9–28 errors	6–7 correct responses	6–7 correct responses
Frustration Level	29 or more errors	5 or fewer correct responses	

COMPREHENSION SCORES, BY TYPE

	Recall Questions	Inference Questions	Vocabulary Questions
Student's Correct Answers			
Possible Correct Answers	3	3	2

READING RATE SCORING GUIDE FOR GRADE 4

If the results computed just above show that the student read this passage at his independent level, you may wish to calculate his reading rate and compare that to other readers at his grade level.

1. Here is the number of words in this passage: 280

2. Write the number of words read incorrectly here: _____

3. Subtract #2 from #1 and write the answer here: _____

4. Using a calculator, multiply #3 by 60 seconds and write the answer here: _____

5. Write the student's reading time in seconds here: _____

6. Using a calculator, divide #4 by #5 and write the answer here: _____

The answer in #6 is the reading rate (words read correctly) per minute.

To interpret this number, first, locate the column in the chart below that represents the time of the year when this test was administered. Then, circle the reading rate that most closely matches your student's reading rate for this passage. Read across to the left to find the student's percentile rank—that is, an estimation of where that reading rate falls within those of other students at that grade level at that time of year.

ORAL READING FLUENCY NORMS FOR GRADE 4

Percentile	Fall WCPM	Winter WCPM	Spring WCPM
90	145	166	180
75	119	139	152
50	94	112	123
25	68	87	98
10	45	61	72

From Hasbrouck and Tindal, 2004.

Introduction: The title of this story is "Uncle Ezra and the Train." When people get old, especially if they live alone, they may find they have nothing much to do. In this story, read to find out what Uncle Ezra did to keep from being bored when he was an old man.

Record the time at the beginning: _____ .

Uncle Ezra had gotten too old to work on the farm. Now there was nothing to do but sit around on the porch, rock in his big chair, and stare down the hill toward the river. In the morning and in the evening he listened for the train that ran along the tracks down there. The North Texas Cannonball was the name of that train. In the morning it took passengers from New Orleans to Dallas, and in the evening it brought them from Dallas back to New Orleans.

The North Texas Cannonball was the most important thing in the old man's life. Twice each day he listened for the whistle, and the rumble of the engine, and the clicking of the wheels. He could almost see the passengers reclining in their comfortable seats and sipping their coffee and their tea.

Uncle Ezra decided he had to have something to do with that train.

Before dawn one morning he walked through the fields down to the tracks and found a dried branch. And when he heard the whistle and the rumble of the engine, he set that branch on fire. The train rounded the curve, a quarter mile away. Uncle Ezra waved that burning branch over his head— "Whoosh! Whoosh! Whoosh!" Brakes squealed, cars banged one against another, and the North Texas Cannonball shuddered to a stop, right in front of Uncle Ezra.

The engineer jumped down. "Where is the emergency?" he shouted. "Is the trestle washed out up ahead?" Uncle Ezra rubbed the toe of one boot in the dirt and didn't say anything.

"What is it? Why did you stop the train?" the engineer demanded. "Speak up, old man. Those passengers have to get to Dallas. Why did you stop the train?"

At last Uncle Ezra thought of something. "Want to buy a 'possum?"

"A 'possum!" shouted the engineer. "You stopped this train to sell a 'possum?"

Just then a kindly conductor approached them. He said, "Take it easy, chief. You can see he's just a lonesome old man. Tell us, Uncle, how much do you want for that 'possum?"

"I don't know," said Uncle Ezra. "I haven't caught him yet."

Record the time at the end: _____.

This text has been rated at 850L
It has 363 words

QUESTIONS

1. Describe the situation at the beginning of the story. Where did Uncle Ezra live, and who did he live with? (*Must answer both: He lived on a farm, and he lived alone.*) **Recall**

2. Why do you suppose Uncle Ezra didn't do anything all day? (*He was retired; he was too old to work.*) **Inference**

3. What was the one exciting thing in his life? (*the train that passed near his farm house two times a day*) **Recall**

4. What two cities did the train travel between? (*Dallas and New Orleans*) **Recall**

5. In the phrase "the passengers reclining in their comfortable seats," what does *reclining* mean? (*leaning back*) **Vocabulary**

6. How does the author tell you that the train stopped suddenly? (*Must recall two of these three: "Brakes squealed, cars banged one against another, and the [train] shuddered to a stop . . ."*) **Recall**

7. In the phrase "Is the trestle washed out up ahead?" what does *trestle* mean? (*a bridge for trains to pass over*) **Vocabulary**

8. What was the real reason Uncle Ezra stopped the train? (*Must say one of these three: he was bored and lonesome; he wanted to be important to someone or something; but he didn't really have a plan*) **Inference**

Errors in oral reading accuracy: _____

Correct comprehension responses: _____

SCORING GUIDE FOR ORAL READING AND COMPREHENSION

(Circle the boxes that correspond to the student's scores)

	Oral Reading Accuracy	Reading Comprehension	Listening Comprehension
Independent Level	11 or fewer errors	7–8 correct responses	
Instructional Level	12–36 errors	6–7 correct responses	6–7 correct responses
Frustration Level	37 or more errors	5 or fewer correct responses	

COMPREHENSION SCORES, BY TYPE

	Recall Questions	Inference Questions	Vocabulary Questions
Student's Correct Answers			
Possible Correct Answers	4	2	2

READING RATE SCORING GUIDE FOR GRADE 5

If the results computed just above show that the student read this passage at his independent level, you may wish to calculate his reading rate and compare that to other readers at his grade level.

1. Here is the number of words in this passage: 363

2. Write the number of words read incorrectly here: _____

3. Subtract #2 from #1 and write the answer here: _____

4. Using a calculator, multiply #3 by 60 seconds and write the answer here: _____

5. Write the student's reading time in seconds here: _____

6. Using a calculator, divide #4 by #5 and write the answer here: _____

The answer in #6 is the reading rate (words read correctly) per minute.

To interpret this number, first, locate the column in the chart below that represents the time of the year when this test was administered. Then, circle the reading rate that most closely matches your student's reading rate for this passage. Read across to the left to find the student's percentile rank—that is, an estimation of where that reading rate falls within those of other students at that grade level at that time of year.

ORAL READING FLUENCY NORMS FOR GRADE 5

Percentile	Fall WCPM	Winter WCPM	Spring WCPM
90	166	182	194
75	139	156	168
50	110	127	139
25	85	99	109
10	61	74	83

From Hasbrouck and Tindal, 2004.

Introduction: The title of this story is "The Former Chief of Police." We mostly think of adults as steady people; but sometimes, for reasons we don't always know about, adults can change their ways of thinking and acting. Read to find out what happens in Carlo's family when his mother changes. I will ask you questions about the passage after you finish reading.

Record the time at the beginning: _____ .

Carlo's mother stirred the eggs and deposited them next to the fried bananas on his plate. The tall, tanned woman wore trousers with baggy thighs, knee-high boots with a lustrous brown shine, and a black velvet hat hardened with steel.

Avoiding their prominent bandages, Carlo gently hoisted two cats off his chair and sat down. "Are you going horseback riding again today, Mom?"

"Yes," said his mother, keeping her back turned. "Can you get a lift home from school?"

"I suppose," said Carlo as she put the plate in front of him.

"You sure must like those horses," said Carlo.

"Why do you say that?" She still didn't look at him.

"You went riding four days this week."

His mother kept her back to him. She had quit her job as the town's chief of police last spring, and as summer evolved into autumn she showed no sign of returning to her former profession. It amazed Carlo to observe the trappings of the old life slip away. She stopped carrying a pistol on her waist, stopped getting midnight phone calls, and stopped driving a hundred miles an hour with a screaming siren. Late one afternoon she simply walked out of the police department and never went back.

Now her passion had become animals, and their house had gone from no cats to eleven. The cats came in all states of disrepair, from mangy to scarred to crippled. When she collected an injured creature, she said she would keep it long enough to nurse it back to full vigor. But once a cat was healthy, she couldn't bear to part with it, so with every passing week the healthy cats were joined by their needy kinsmen. Then had come the horses: his mother had bought an old stable out past the golf course where she boarded two cast-off horses. Carlo expected more.

Then the family diet changed. First, pepperoni gave way to mushrooms on the pizza. Then pasta with cheese replaced chicken casseroles, and then—what's this?—soy burgers replaced their meaty relatives. Today was the third time she'd served Carlo fried bananas with his eggs. Bacon had disappeared, and Carlo now suspected that the eggs' days were numbered.

Record the time at the end: _____.

This text has been rated at 930L
It has 366 words

QUESTIONS

1. At the beginning of the story, what do Carlo's mother's clothes tell you about her? (*that she likes horseback riding; that she is going riding*) **Inference**

2. Why do you think Carlo's mother won't look at him when Carlo asks her about going riding again? (*she is embarrassed or ashamed; she is going riding too much*) **Inference**

3. In the sentence, "She showed no sign of returning to her former profession," what does *former* mean? (*the one before now; the one she had before; her old job*) **Vocabulary**

4. What was Carlo's mom's new passion? (*animals; caring for animals*) **Recall**

5. How did Carlo's mother's behavior change after she quit her job? (*she started getting lots of animals and she changed the way the family ate*) **Recall**

6. Why do you think that Carlo's mother changed the family's diet? (*she didn't want them to eat meat/animal products—maybe she felt sorry for animals*) **Inference**

7. What food did the bananas replace? (*bacon*) **Recall**

8. The story said, "Carlo now suspected that the eggs' days were numbered." What does it mean to say their "days were numbered"? (*Soon there would be no more eggs.*) **Vocabulary**

Errors in oral reading accuracy: _____

Correct comprehension responses: _____

SCORING GUIDE FOR ORAL READING AND COMPREHENSION

(Circle the boxes that correspond to the student's scores)

	Oral Reading Accuracy	Reading Comprehension	Listening Comprehension
Independent Level	11 or fewer errors	7–8 correct responses	
Instructional Level	12–37 errors	6–7 correct responses	6–7 correct responses
Frustration Level	38 or more errors	5 or fewer correct responses	

COMPREHENSION SCORES, BY TYPE

	Recall Questions	Inference Questions	Vocabulary Questions
Student's Correct Answers			
Possible Correct Answers	3	3	2

READING RATE SCORING GUIDE FOR GRADE 6

If the results computed just above show that the student read this passage at his independent level, you may wish to calculate his reading rate and compare that to other readers at his grade level.

1. Here is the number of words in this passage: 366

2. Write the number of words read incorrectly here: _____

3. Subtract #2 from #1 and write the answer here: _____

4. Using a calculator, multiply #3 by 60 seconds and write the answer here: _____

5. Write the student's reading time in seconds here: _____

6. Using a calculator, divide #4 by #5 and write the answer here: _____

The answer in #6 is the reading rate (words read correctly) per minute.

To interpret this number, first, locate the column in the chart below that represents the time of the year when this test was administered. Then, circle the reading rate that most closely matches your student's reading rate for this passage. Read across to the left to find the student's percentile rank—that is, an estimation of where that reading rate falls within those of other students at that grade level at that time of year.

ORAL READING FLUENCY NORMS FOR GRADE 6

Percentile	Fall WCPM	Winter WCPM	Spring WCPM
90	177	195	204
75	153	167	177
50	127	140	150
25	98	111	122
10	68	82	93

From Hasbrouck and Tindal, 2004.

Narrative Middle School Level: Fear of Parties

Introduction: The title of this story is "Fear of Parties." Most people enjoy going out and seeing other people—but some people really don't like to socialize. Read to find out what Richard's sister does to help him overcome his fear of going to parties. I will ask you questions about the passage after you finish reading.

Record the time at the beginning: _____.

Richard was afraid to go to parties. When he attended one his hands perspired, then his chest, then his face and he became tongue-tied. Then he silently counted all the riveting things he couldn't think of to say. Because of this, Richard would do anything to avoid a party. Sometimes he'd even say he was going out of town, and then sequester himself in his darkened bedroom.

Richard's sister Deborah discovered his problem one summer when she dragged him along to her best friend's birthday party, and halfway through the evening she noticed her brother alone in a corner with his hair matted to his forehead and his hands fidgeting. Suddenly she could almost feel his discomfort, and the awareness made her own enjoyment evaporate.

She confronted him the next morning. "What was the matter with you last night?" she asked, but Richard grimaced with embarrassment and was silent. Deborah sat down at the family's computer, went online and typed "fear of parties" into a search engine, and then clicked on a web site about social anxiety.

"Hey!" she shouted, "I think I found your problem." Richard read over her shoulder that seven percent of all people panic when they go to parties. The site continued with a section called "What to do if you're scared to go to parties." There it offered a breathing exercise, in which the nervous person was advised to poke his finger in his stomach and breathe in and out while slowly counting to five. Normally he would keep up the exercise for five whole minutes, but the site conceded that the nervous victim might be allowed to quit sooner if the exercise made him nervous as well.

"See, Richard? You'll be the life of the party if you just walk into the center of the room, poke your hand in your stomach, count to five, and start breathing. Soon, everyone will be doing it!" Deborah teased playfully.

"Let's move on," said Richard, but he was smiling. The site also suggested that the anxious person fill a "comfort bag" with comforting objects, like a coloring book or a teddy bear, to bring to the party.

"A teddy bear?" Deborah snorted. "Why not put Sparky in your backpack and bring her along?" Sparky was the family's German shepherd.

Richard laughed, but that night he retrieved an old rabbit's foot keychain, and at the next party, he clutched it securely while he made conversation. It was easier to carry than a whole dog, he thought.

Record the time at the end: _____.

This text has been rated at 1020L
It has 418 words

QUESTIONS

1. What did Richard usually do when he was invited to a party? (*he didn't go; he hid in his room*) **Inference**

2. In phrase, "Then he silently counted all the riveting things he couldn't think of to say," what does *riveting* mean? (*very interesting*) **Vocabulary**

3. Why do you think Deborah helped Richard figure out what was wrong with him? (*she loved him; she wanted him to be more comfortable*) **Inference**

4. What did the story tell you about the meaning of "social anxiety"? (*a condition that makes people panic in social situations*) **Recall**

5. According to the story, what percent of people have social anxiety? (*7%*) **Recall**

6. Describe the suggestion for using breathing to help with social anxiety (*Put your finger in your stomach, breathe slowly and count to five*) **Recall**

7. Why did Richard and Deborah laugh at the idea of bringing a teddy bear or coloring book to a party? (*people would laugh at you; you would look silly*) **Inference**

8. How far along is Richard in solving his problem? Why do you think so? (*He went to another party and had a conversation; he seemed to have some control over his problem.*) **Inference**

Errors in oral reading accuracy: _____

Correct comprehension responses: _____

SCORING GUIDE FOR ORAL READING AND COMPREHENSION

(Circle the boxes that correspond to the student's scores)

	Oral Reading Accuracy	Reading Comprehension	Listening Comprehension
Independent Level	13 or fewer errors	7–8 correct responses	
Instructional Level	14–42 errors	6–7 correct responses	6–7 correct responses
Frustration Level	43 or more errors	5 or fewer correct responses	

COMPREHENSION SCORES, BY TYPE

	Recall Questions	Inference Questions	Vocabulary Questions
Student's Correct Answers			
Possible Correct Answers	3	4	1

READING RATE SCORING GUIDE FOR MIDDLE SCHOOL

If the results computed just above show that the student read this passage at his independent level, you may wish to calculate his reading rate and compare that to other readers at his grade level.

1. Here is the number of words in this passage: 418

2. Write the number of words read incorrectly here: _____

3. Subtract #2 from #1 and write the answer here: _____

4. Using a calculator, multiply #3 by 60 seconds and write the answer here: _____

5. Write the student's reading time in seconds here: _____

6. Using a calculator, divide #4 by #5 and write the answer here: _____

The answer in #6 is the reading rate (words read correctly) per minute.

To interpret this number, first, locate the column in the chart below that represents the time of the year when this test was administered. Then, circle the reading rate that most closely matches your student's reading rate for this passage. Read across to the left to find the student's percentile rank—that is, an estimation of where that reading rate falls within those of other students at that grade level at that time of year.

ORAL READING FLUENCY NORMS FOR MIDDLE SCHOOL

Percentile	Fall WCPM	Winter WCPM	Spring WCPM
90	180	192	202
75	156	165	177
50	128	136	150
25	102	109	123
10	79	88	98

From Hasbrouck and Tindal, 2004.

Narrative High School Level: Discovering Marcel

Introduction: The title of this story is "Discovering Marcel." How much do you really know about other students in your school? In this story, a visiting author teaches an important lesson. I will ask you questions about the passage after you finish reading.

Record the time at the beginning: _____.

The tenth graders in the library were quiet. The visiting author had become overwrought by the tale she was telling, and her abrupt silence had silenced the students. She asked their pardon, then cleared her throat, wiped her eyes, and continued her story.

A teenage girl and her family clung to survival in a Caribbean island village. Their country had been ruled by a decrepit and whimsical dictator, whose soldiers terrorized the countryside now that the dictator had died, stealing whatever shreds of sustenance remained to the people. Those citizens who stood up to them, who simply asked for clean water and decent work, were harassed and sometimes "disappeared," made to vanish into the night without any acknowledgement from the police or the military that they had ever existed. Hundreds upon hundreds of people attempted to flee the island in rickety boats of all descriptions, but frail as they were and close to starvation, many could not endure those many days' exposure to the elements. Sometimes whole boatloads of refugees were lost to Atlantic storms.

"Is that story real?" asked a student, during the questioning after, and the author explained that the events portrayed in her novel were indeed real, although she acknowledged that the characters were her own inventions.

When another student said, "Thank goodness this isn't happening to us," there was a long pause, and then a voice in the back of the room said, "I was there."

"Who?" asked a student.

"Me." The voice belonged to the reclusive boy in hand-me-down clothes who spoke shyly in whispers, and was as close to being anonymous as anyone in the school.

"You, Marcel?" asked the school principal.

"Yes, ma'am." The other students craned their necks to see who was talking.

"Can you tell us about it?" asked an incredulous girl sitting beside him.

"Yes. My father was the director of the high school in my town, and since he was opposed to the government, he did not discourage the students when they decided to show solidarity with the workers in a demonstration at the sugar refinery. Late one night there was a knock at our door, and when my mother opened it, there were soldiers . . ."

All eyes were now fixed firmly on Marcel as the fascinated students pressed their refugee-classmate for details of his odyssey, and the visiting author listened as attentively as any of them. Later as the novelist and principal approached the waiting limousine, the principal asked, "Is that why you wrote your book, so young people like Marcel would be real to their classmates?"

"Everyone has a story," the author replied. "And everyone needs people who will listen."

Record the time at the end: _____ .

This text has been rated at 1200L
It has 442 words

QUESTIONS

1. What was the setting of the author's story? (*a Caribbean island country that had been ruled by a dictator*) **Recall**

2. What things did the soldiers do to the citizens of that country? (*harassed them, made them disappear—must answer at least one*) **Recall**

3. In the passage, "The visiting author had become overwrought by the tale she was relating," what does *overwrought* mean? (*overwhelmed by emotion; suddenly made too sad to continue*) **Vocabulary**

4. In the phrase, ". . . the fascinated students pressed their refugee-classmate for details of his odyssey," what does *odyssey* mean? (*long and difficult trip*) **Vocabulary**

5. Why did the soldiers come for Marcel's father? (*He was a school director who did not discourage his students from taking part in protests against the government.*) **Recall**

6. What do you think happened to Marcel's father? (*He was probably "disappeared," taken away without any official acknowledgment and never allowed to return; possibly murdered— should answer any of these*) **Inference**

7. Why do you think Marcel had not told his story to his classmates? (*There was probably no occasion to tell them; before the author came, they wouldn't have known enough about the circumstances to understand his tale; or they might not have believed him; or he might have been too shy, or too upset by the memories to talk about them. Any of these answers is acceptable.*) **Inference**

8. Why did the author not seem to mind when Marcel became the center of attention instead of her? (*She wanted students like Marcel to be noticed in a good way by their classmates; she wanted them to have a chance to tell their stories.*) **Inference**

Errors in oral reading accuracy: _____

Correct comprehension responses: _____

SCORING GUIDE FOR ORAL READING AND COMPREHENSION

(Circle the boxes that correspond to the student's scores)

	Oral Reading Accuracy	Reading Comprehension	Listening Comprehension
Independent Level	13 or fewer errors	7–8 correct responses	
Instructional Level	14–44 errors	6–7 correct responses	6–7 correct responses
Frustration Level	43 or more errors	5 or fewer correct responses	

COMPREHENSION SCORES, BY TYPE

	Recall Questions	Inference Questions	Vocabulary Questions
Student's Correct Answers			
Possible Correct Answers	3	3	2

READING RATE SCORING GUIDE FOR HIGH SCHOOL

If the results computed just above show that the student read this passage at his independent level, you may wish to calculate his reading rate and compare that to other readers at his grade level.

1. Here is the number of words in this passage: 442

2. Write the number of words read incorrectly here: _____

3. Subtract #2 from #1 and write the answer here: _____

4. Using a calculator, multiply #3 by 60 seconds and write the answer here: _____

5. Write the student's reading time in seconds here: _____

6. Using a calculator, divide #4 by #5 and write the answer here: _____

The answer in #6 is the reading rate (words read correctly) per minute.

To interpret this number, first, locate the column in the chart below that represents the time of the year when this test was administered. Then, circle the reading rate that most closely matches your student's reading rate for this passage. Read across to the left to find the student's percentile rank—that is, an estimation of where that reading rate falls within those of other students at that grade level at that time of year.

ORAL READING FLUENCY NORMS FOR HIGH SCHOOL

Percentile	Fall WCPM	Winter WCPM	Spring WCPM
90	195	209	213
75	171	183	191
50	143	156	165
25	116	125	138
10	87	94	111

Note: These are estimates, extrapolated from Hasbrouck and Tindal, 2004.

SOCIAL STUDIES PASSAGES

FORM B

Trains are very big. Each has an engine and many cars. They carry many things that we need. They bring the food we eat. They bring the clothes we wear. They carry new cars, too. They carry all of the things we buy.

Some trains carry people. These trains are called passenger trains. Some passenger trains have sleeping cars. People can sleep there. A passenger train has a restaurant car, too. People can eat in the restaurant.

Passenger trains stop in stations. People get on the train in the station. They get off when they reach the place they want to go.

Trains go fast. They go on railroad tracks. They make a loud noise. Sometimes we hear the train's whistle. The whistle blows when the train crosses a street. The whistle tells us to be careful.

▶ ▶ ▶

Airplanes fly in the air. They go very fast. The pilot and the copilot fly them. Most airplanes carry people. They carry many people. Airplanes also carry their suitcases. Mothers and fathers go on airplanes. Children and grandparents go on airplanes. Dogs and cats go on airplanes, too. You can eat lunch on an airplane. You can drink milk, too.

Airplanes land at airports. People get on them at the airport. They all sit down in their seats. Then the airplane roars down the runway, and it takes off. It flies very far and very fast. It lands at another airport, and the people get off.

Airplanes make a loud noise. I like to listen to them. I like to look for the airplane high in the sky. Big airplanes fly very high. They fly higher than the clouds. On a clear day, I can see the airplane high in the sky. It looks very tiny because it is so high in the sky.

I like to watch airplanes. They fly over houses and mountains, and they fly across the ocean. Airplanes fly everywhere.

▶ ▶ ▶

I live in a big city with my parents, my little brother, and my grandmother. We live in a neighborhood where everyone gets together for holidays. My friends and I play in the park.

In my community, people help each other and they care about one another. Everyone works together. People have jobs and businesses in our community, and they go to work every day.

We have rules, too. The rules help everyone live safely in our community. The police help everyone to follow the rules.

Every day I go to school to learn from my teachers. I learn to read, and I learn to count. I learn how to stay healthy. All the other students in my class learn, too. Sometimes we learn in small groups. We learn together. I go to school on the bus.

In my community, I see the letter carrier deliver the mail. The police officer helps my little brother cross the street safely. My grandmother goes to the doctor. My mom and dad like to visit with the people at the store. They buy things for our family. I ride my bicycle.

We live near the fire station. I like to watch the fire fighters wash their truck. It is a big red truck with a long ladder. When there is a fire, they use their red lights and a siren. They use water to put out fires.

There are many kinds of people in a community. They all get along with each other.

▶ ▶ ▶

Young Ben Franklin only went to school for about two years, but he still wanted to learn. He loved to read, and he learned math by himself.

Then he learned the printing trade from his brother, and when he became older, he bought his own newspaper. It became very popular. Ben Franklin also wrote books. For example, he wrote a book called Poor Richard's Almanack, which provided practical wisdom and made Franklin famous. He was always interested in books. He began one of the first public libraries in the United States. He was also the first postmaster general of the United States.

Benjamin Franklin was an inventor, too. He invented the rocking chair and a special type of eyeglasses. He also invented the Franklin stove. This stove gave more heat with less wood. He invented the lightning rod, which protected tall buildings from lightning strikes. He discovered many things about electricity.

Benjamin Franklin wanted to help his country. He was one of the signers of the Declaration of Independence. Later, he went to talk to the king of France. He asked the king to help the colonies become free. The king said he would. With help from France, America won its war against England. Ben Franklin was a famous leader. He helped the colonies become free.

Ben Franklin was a very gifted man. He was very intelligent and successful. He made many contributions to our country. One of his greatest acts was to urge his country to abolish slavery and to stop the slave trade. He didn't live long enough to see this change.

▶ ▶ ▶

The dark room was very quiet. The only sounds were the creaking of iron beds, the breathing of sleeping boys, and a low tapping sound. One boy sat upright in a bed balancing a small board with papers on it across his knees. The boy pressed down on a piece of paper with a pointed instrument. It did not matter if the damp, cold room was dark. The boy could not see the dark. The boy was blind, and all the other boys in the room with him were also blind.

The boy was very tired, but he did not let himself fall asleep. He kept punching the paper with his pointed instrument. Fourteen-year-old Louis Braille spent many nights awake with his board and paper. He often worked until the new day began. Then it was time for lessons, and he had no more free time.

Louis had been working on this project for months. He had even taken it home during school vacation. There he worked outside in the warmth of the sun all summer. Passing villagers would say to each other: "Ah, there's young Louis at his pinpricks again!"

Louis was making little pinholes in his paper. These pinpricks would one day become the alphabet for blind people all over the world. Louis Braille did not know how successful his system of dots would become. After all, he was just a fourteen-year-old blind student in a special school in Paris. He knew, however, that there must be a way for blind people to read and write easily. In the end, his system is used worldwide, and it is named for him.

▶ ▶ ▶

iv

In the early 1500's Spain sent explorers to the Americas to find gold. The governor of Mexico heard reports of "Cities of Gold" to the north, and wanted to claim them for Spain. The cities were said to have walls of gold blocks, gates studded with jewels, and streets were paved with silver.

In 1540, the governor sent Francisco Vasquez de Coronado to search for Cibola, the golden cities. Coronado's party had more than a thousand men, many of whom were slaves. Coronado found Cibola, a simple Zuni pueblo near the present day border of New Mexico and Arizona. What had been said to be walls of gold turned out to be adobe shining in the desert sun. But Coronado did not give up.

Coronado sent search parties in different directions. One group went west in search of a large river, and they became the first Europeans to see the Colorado River and the Grand Canyon. They could not reach the river because it was at the bottom of the deep canyon. Another group found the Gulf of California. Another group went east to explore Pueblo villages. When they were on the Rio Grande River in what is now New Mexico they were attacked by Indian groups living in the area.

Meanwhile, Coronado's party heard about another city of riches called "Quivira." They went as far as present-day Kansas, but they found no gold. They found only herds of buffalo and Indian villages. They were the first Europeans to see buffalo. Coronado returned to Mexico and reported that there was no gold.

At the time, his expedition was called a failure. But, he had explored much of northern Mexico and what is now the American Southwest. He claimed the new lands for Spain.

▶ ▶ ▶

v

In 1955 a bus driver in Montgomery, Alabama, told a woman to give up her seat on the bus because a man wanted to sit down. The woman was tired from working all day, and she was tired of being treated as a second-class citizen. Rosa Parks was African American, and the man who wanted her seat was white. The bus driver was white, too. Because she refused to sit in the seats in the back of the bus that were reserved for African Americans, Rosa Parks was arrested for violating the law. In the past, she had often walked home from work so that she wouldn't have to sit in the back of the bus.

Rosa Parks was very committed to overcoming the rules of that era in the southern part of the United States. She went thirsty instead of drinking from the "colored only" drinking fountains. She climbed the stairs in buildings that had elevators for "whites only." She refused to accept second-class status.

After she was arrested, the African American community of her city supported her. A young minister named Dr. Martin Luther King was among her supporters. They began a boycott of the city bus system. They refused to ride the buses until the law requiring them to sit in the back of the bus was changed. For more than a year, African Americans did not ride the buses in Montgomery. They were the main customers of the bus system, and the boycott caused many problems for the city government. Finally, the Supreme Court ruled that segregation on public transportation was unconstitutional. A city could not reserve seats on the bus for people from one race. Rosa Parks earned the respect of the entire country.

▶ ▶ ▶

vi

We live in a global economy. That is a way of saying that people in one part of the world are exchanging services and goods with people who live in other parts of the world. Living in a global economy means that what happens in one country soon affects others. In our global economy, the products we buy come from all over the world. For example, today automobile makers sell their cars worldwide, however, when your grandparents started driving, most cars sold in the United States were American-made.

The global economy has made some people and nations very wealthy, but it has also caused problems for some workers, communities, and economies. A generation ago, workers' wages were compared to wages of other workers in the same industry, in the same country. For example, if you were a worker in North Carolina and you made shirts in a factory, your wages would be roughly the same as those of other workers in the textile industry in the United States. Today, however, shirts that are sold in the United States are made in countries where workers are paid far less. The shirt you are wearing now was probably made in one of those countries. American textile workers have had to choose between huge pay cuts to compete with lower-paid workers elsewhere, or finding some other line of work. Most have done the latter. Most of the clothes Americans wear today were made overseas.

Industries like the textile industry have had to shut down because of increased competition. They could no longer compete in the global economy. Increased competition often leads to lower prices for consumers. But lower prices can sometimes cause lower profits for industries. In the United States, automobile manufacturing is such an industry. We have far fewer jobs in this industry today than we did 50 years ago. The same is true of television. Color television was invented in the United States, but no televisions are manufactured in the United States today.

There are still sharp differences in wealth among countries. Wealthy nations include the United States, several European nations, and Japan. These nations are called developed nations. Their industries and economies are well-developed. There are other so-called developing countries whose economic activity still does not provide as much income for their workers. Many developing nations are in Africa and Asia.

▶ ▶ ▶

The Tlingit people are Native Americans who live along the southeastern coast of Alaska in the United States and along the northern coast of British Columbia in Canada. This area makes up the Tlingit cultural region, and the influence of Tlingit culture is strong throughout this area. The Tlingit had frequent battles with early Russian traders who settled in Alaska. There are approximately 15,000 Tlingit people living in Alaska today.

This region is rich in natural resources, such as vast forests and plentiful fish and game for fishing and hunting. For hundreds of years the Tlingit made good use of these resources, fishing for salmon and hunting deer and seals. They used large planks of wood to build giant homes, with figures often carved into their doorways. Tlingit families placed totem poles outside their homes, as well. Some Tlingit families still follow this tradition. A totem pole is a tall post, usually carved of cedar that has images of people and animals, often brightly painted. Totem poles traced the histories of families, and they resembled a family tree or family crest. They typically commemorated dead ancestors, using symbols to confirm the lineage and social rank of the owner and symbols to represent the owner's guardian animal.

The Tlingit lived in these large homes during winter, but they moved to smaller wooden homes near hunting and fishing grounds during the warmer months. They carved wooden dugout canoes from large logs for fishing and hunting. Because game and fish were so plentiful, the Tlingit were able to spend time making and trading traditional goods, such as blankets, copper tools and ornaments, exquisite baskets, spoons of horn and shell, and seal oil. They had a large trading network with other Native Americans, and they sometimes bought goods from one group to trade with another.

For example, one of the most prized Tlingit products, even today, is the Chilkat blanket. It was traditionally woven from the dyed wool of mountain goats and sheep. These colorful blankets have detailed designs of shapes and animals that tell stories, just as a totem pole might tell the story of a family.

X

SOCIAL STUDIES PASSAGES RESPONSE SHEETS

FORM B

▶ Social Studies 1st Grade Level: Trains

Introduction: The title of this passage is "Trains." It's about trains and how they help us. Read carefully because I will ask you questions about it after you finish.

Record the time at the beginning: _____.

Trains are very big. Each has an engine and many cars. They carry many things that we need. They bring the food we eat. They bring the clothes we wear. They carry new cars, too. They carry all of the things we buy.

Some trains carry people. These trains are called passenger trains. Some passenger trains have sleeping cars. People can sleep there. A passenger train has a restaurant car, too. People can eat in the restaurant.

Passenger trains stop in stations. People get on the train in the station. They get off when they reach the place they want to go.

Trains go fast. They go on railroad tracks. They make a loud noise. Sometimes we hear the train's whistle. The whistle blows when the train crosses a street. The whistle tells us to be careful.

Record the time at the end: _____.

This text has been rated at 300L
It has 137 words

QUESTIONS

1. What are three things the story mentioned that are carried on trains? (*food we eat; clothes we wear; new cars; all the things we buy in stores; people*) **Recall**

2. In the sentence, "These are called passenger trains," what does the word *passenger* mean? (*person who rides*) **Vocabulary**

3. What does a passenger train carry? (*people*) **Recall**

4. What things do people do in a train station? (*get on and off trains*) **Recall**

5. What would people do if a passenger train did not have a restaurant car? (*go hungry; wait until they got to their destination in order to eat*) **Inference**

6. Why do only passenger trains have sleeping cars and restaurant cars? (*because they carry people, and people need those things*) **Inference**

Errors in oral reading accuracy: _____

Correct comprehension responses: _____

SCORING GUIDE FOR ORAL READING AND COMPREHENSION

(Circle the boxes that correspond to the student's scores)

	Oral Reading Accuracy	Reading Comprehension	Listening Comprehension
Independent Level	4 or fewer errors	6 correct responses	
Instructional Level	5–14 errors	5 correct responses	5 correct responses
Frustration Level	15 or more errors	4 or fewer correct responses	

COMPREHENSION SCORES, BY TYPE

	Recall Questions	Inference Questions	Vocabulary Questions
Student's Correct Answers			
Possible Correct Answers	3	2	1

READING RATE SCORING GUIDE FOR GRADE 1

If the results computed just above show that the student read this passage at his independent level, you may wish to calculate his reading rate and compare that to other readers at his grade level.

1. Here is the number of words in this passage: 137

2. Write the number of words read incorrectly here: _____

3. Subtract #2 from #1 and write the answer here: _____

4. Using a calculator, multiply #3 by 60 seconds and write the answer here: _____

5. Write the student's reading time in seconds here: _____

6. Using a calculator, divide #4 by #5 and write the answer here: _____

The answer in #6 is the reading rate (words read correctly) per minute.

To interpret this number, first, locate the column in the chart below that represents the time of the year when this test was administered. Then, circle the reading rate that most closely matches your student's reading rate for this passage. Read across to the left to find the student's percentile rank—that is, an estimation of where that reading rate falls within those of other students at that grade level at that time of year.

ORAL READING FLUENCY NORMS FOR GRADE 1

Percentile	Fall WCPM	Winter WCPM	Spring WCPM
90		81	111
75		47	82
50		23	53
25		12	28
10		6	15

From Hasbrouck and Tindal, 2004.

▶ Social Studies 2nd Grade Level (2.1): Airplanes

Introduction: The title of this passage is "Airplanes." In it you're going to read about airplanes and what they are like. Read carefully because I will ask you questions about it after you finish.

Record the time at the beginning: _____.

Airplanes fly in the air. They go very fast. The pilot and the copilot fly them. Most airplanes carry people. They carry many people. Airplanes also carry their suitcases. Mothers and fathers go on airplanes. Children and grandparents go on airplanes. Dogs and cats go on airplanes, too. You can eat lunch on an airplane. You can drink milk, too.

Airplanes land at airports. People get on them at the airport. They all sit down in their seats. Then the airplane roars down the runway, and it takes off. It flies very far and very fast. It lands at another airport, and the people get off.

Airplanes make a loud noise. I like to listen to them. I like to look for the airplane high in the sky. Big airplanes fly very high. They fly higher than the clouds. On a clear day, I can see the airplane high in the sky. It looks very tiny because it is so high in the sky.

I like to watch airplanes. They fly over houses and mountains, and they fly across the ocean. Airplanes fly everywhere.

Record the time at the end: _____.

This text has been rated at 350L
It has 184 words

QUESTIONS

1. Who did this story say goes on airplanes? (*people; mothers and fathers; children; dogs*) **Recall**

2. What did the story say a pilot does? (*makes the airplane go/drives the airplane*) **Recall**

3. In the sentence, "Then the airplane roars down the runway and it takes off," what does *runway* mean? (*pavement where the plane takes off*) **Vocabulary**

4. According to the story, what happens at airports? (*airplanes land and take off; people get on and off*) **Recall**

5. In the sentence, "Then the airplane roars down the runway, and it takes off," what does *takes off* mean? (*leaves the ground; flies up into the air*) **Vocabulary**

6. Why would it be noisy to live near an airport? (*because the airplanes make a lot of noise*) **Inference**

7. If you were flying in a big airplane, what are some things you could see out the window? (*the land below; houses, mountains, and the ocean; the sky; clouds*) **Inference**

8. What are three things the story said airplanes can fly over? (*houses; mountains; the ocean; clouds*) **Recall**

Errors in oral reading accuracy: _____

Correct comprehension responses: _____

SCORING GUIDE FOR ORAL READING AND COMPREHENSION

(Circle the boxes that correspond to the student's scores)

	Oral Reading Accuracy	Reading Comprehension	Listening Comprehension
Independent Level	6 or fewer errors	7–8 correct responses	
Instructional Level	7–18 errors	6–7 correct responses	6–7 correct responses
Frustration Level	19 or more errors	5 or fewer correct responses	

COMPREHENSION SCORES, BY TYPE

	Recall Questions	Inference Questions	Vocabulary Questions
Student's Correct Answers			
Possible Correct Answers	4	2	2

READING RATE SCORING GUIDE FOR GRADE 2

If the results computed just above show that the student read this passage at his independent level, you may wish to calculate his reading rate and compare that to other readers at his grade level.

1. Here is the number of words in this passage: 184

2. Write the number of words read incorrectly here: _____

3. Subtract #2 from #1 and write the answer here: _____

4. Using a calculator, multiply #3 by 60 seconds and write the answer here: _____

5. Write the student's reading time in seconds here: _____

6. Using a calculator, divide #4 by #5 and write the answer here: _____

The answer in #6 is the reading rate (words read correctly) per minute.

To interpret this number, first, locate the column in the chart below that represents the time of the year when this test was administered. Then, circle the reading rate that most closely matches your student's reading rate for this passage. Read across to the left to find the student's percentile rank— that is, an estimation of where that reading rate falls within those of other students at that grade level at that time of year.

Percentile	Fall WCPM	Winter WCPM	Spring WCPM
90	106	125	142
75	79	100	117
50	51	72	89
25	25	42	61
10	11	18	31

From Hasbrouck and Tindal, 2004.

Social Studies 2nd Grade Level (2.2): What Is a Community?

Introduction: The title of this passage is "What Is a Community?" It's about a part of a city that we call a community. Read carefully because I will ask you questions about it after you finish.

Record the time at the beginning: _____.

I live in a big city with my parents, my little brother, and my grandmother. We live in a neighborhood where everyone gets together for holidays. My friends and I play in the park.

In my community, people help each other and they care about one another. Everyone works together. People have jobs and businesses in our community, and they go to work every day.

We have rules, too. The rules help everyone live safely in our community. The police help everyone to follow the rules.

Every day I go to school to learn from my teachers. I learn to read, and I learn to count. I learn how to stay healthy. All the other students in my class learn, too. Sometimes we learn in small groups. We learn together. I go to school on the bus.

In my community, I see the letter carrier deliver the mail. The police officer helps my little brother cross the street safely. My grandmother goes to the doctor. My mom and dad like to visit with the people at the store. They buy things for our family. I ride my bicycle.

We live near the fire station. I like to watch the fire fighters wash their truck. It is a big red truck with a long ladder. When there is a fire, they use their red lights and a siren. They use water to put out fires.

There are many kinds of people in a community. They all get along with each other.

Record the time at the end: _____.

This text has been rated at 450L
It has 250 words.

QUESTIONS

1. Who does the person telling this story live with? (*parents, brother, and grandmother* [*must be specific, not answer "family"*]) **Recall**

2. What makes you think holidays are happy times in his community? (*people get together*) **Inference**

3. Why are rules important in a community? (*they keep people safe*) **Inference**

4. What were some jobs that people have that were named in this story? (*teacher, mail/letter carrier, police officer, doctor, firefighters [must identify two]*) **Inference**

5. In what way did the story say the police officer helps the little brother? (*cross the street safely*) **Recall**

6. In the sentence, "I see the letter carrier deliver the mail," what does *deliver* mean? (*bring the mail to houses and businesses*) **Vocabulary**

7. What does the person telling the story like to watch the firefighters do? (*wash the fire truck*) **Recall**

8. How did the story describe the fire truck? (*red, has a long ladder, has red lights and a siren*) **Recall**

Errors in oral reading accuracy: _____

Correct comprehension responses: _____

SCORING GUIDE FOR ORAL READING AND COMPREHENSION

(Circle the box that corresponds to the student's scores)

	Oral Reading Accuracy	Reading Comprehension	Listening Comprehension
Independent Level	8 or fewer errors	7–8 correct responses	
Instructional Level	9–25 errors	6–7 correct responses	6–7 correct responses
Frustration Level	26 or more errors	5 or fewer correct responses	

COMPREHENSION SCORES, BY TYPE

	Recall Questions	Inference Questions	Vocabulary Questions
Student's Correct Answers			
Possible Correct Answers	4	3	1

READING RATE SCORING GUIDE FOR GRADE 2

If the results computed just above show that the student read this passage at his independent level, you may wish to calculate his reading rate and compare that to other readers at his grade level.

1. Here is the number of words in this passage: 250

2. Write the number of words read incorrectly here: _____

3. Subtract #2 from #1 and write the answer here: _____

4. Using a calculator, multiply #3 by 60 seconds and write the answer here: _____

5. Write the student's reading time in seconds here: _____

6. Using a calculator, divide #4 by #5 and write the answer here: _____

The answer in #6 is the reading rate (words read correctly) per minute.

To interpret this number, first, locate the column in the chart below that represents the time of the year when this test was administered. Then, circle the reading rate that most closely matches your student's reading rate for this passage. Read across to the left to find the student's percentile rank—that is, an estimation of where that reading rate falls within those of other students at that grade level at that time of year.

ORAL READING FLUENCY NORMS FOR GRADE 2

Percentile	Fall WCPM	Winter WCPM	Spring WCPM
90	106	125	142
75	79	100	117
50	51	72	89
25	25	42	61
10	11	18	31

From Hasbrouck and Tindal, 2004.

Introduction: The title of this passage is "Meet Benjamin Franklin." It's about a famous American who helped his country in many different ways. Read carefully because I will ask you questions about it after you finish.

Record the time at the beginning: _____.

Young Ben Franklin only went to school for about two years, but he still wanted to learn. He loved to read, and he learned math by himself.

Then he learned the printing trade from his brother, and when he became older, he bought his own newspaper. It became very popular. Ben Franklin also wrote books. For example, he wrote a book called Poor Richard's Almanack, which provided practical wisdom and made Franklin famous. He was always interested in books. He began one of the first public libraries in the United States. He was also the first postmaster general of the United States.

Benjamin Franklin was an inventor, too. He invented the rocking chair and a special type of eyeglasses. He also invented the Franklin stove. This stove gave more heat with less wood. He invented the lightning rod, which protected tall buildings from lightning strikes. He discovered many things about electricity.

Benjamin Franklin wanted to help his country. He was one of the signers of the Declaration of Independence. Later, he went to talk to the king of France. He asked the king to help the colonies become free. The king said he would. With help from France, America won its war against England. Ben Franklin was a famous leader. He helped the colonies become free.

Ben Franklin was a very gifted man. He was very intelligent and successful. He made many contributions to our country. One of his greatest acts was to urge his country to abolish slavery and to stop the slave trade. He didn't live long enough to see this change.

Record the time at the end: _____.

This text has been rated at 600L
It has 264 words

QUESTIONS

1. How do we know that Ben Franklin must have been very intelligent? (*he had only two years of schooling; educated self*) **Inference**

2. Name two things that Ben Franklin contributed to our daily lives. (*post office, library, eyeglasses, Franklin stove*) **Recall**

3. What was probably one of Franklin's greatest disappointments? (*slavery continued during his life*) **Inference**

4. Name one contribution that Franklin made to American independence. (*arranged help from France; signed Declaration of Independence*) **Inference**

5. What caused the Franklin stove to be a big improvement over previous stoves? (*more heat, less fuel*) **Inference**

6. The author talked about Franklin learning the printing trade. What did he mean by "trade"? (*type of job; a job in printing*) **Vocabulary**

7. What job did Ben Franklin hold before anyone else? (*postmaster general, in charge of post offices*) **Recall**

8. What evidence did the author provide about Ben Franklin's interests in reading and in books? (*wrote books, published newspaper, opened public library*) **Inference**

Errors in oral reading accuracy: _____

Correct comprehension responses: _____

SCORING GUIDE FOR ORAL READING AND COMPREHENSION

(Circle the boxes that correspond to the student's scores)

	Oral Reading Accuracy	Reading Comprehension	Listening Comprehension
Independent Level	8 or fewer errors	7–8 correct responses	
Instructional Level	9–26 errors	6–7 correct responses	6–7 correct responses
Frustration Level	27 or more errors	5 or fewer correct responses	

COMPREHENSION SCORES, BY TYPE

	Recall Questions	Inference Questions	Vocabulary Questions
Student's Correct Answers			
Possible Correct Answers	2	5	1

READING RATE SCORING GUIDE FOR GRADE 3

If the results computed just above show that the student read this passage at his independent level, you may wish to calculate his reading rate and compare that to other readers at his grade level.

1. Here is the number of words in this passage: 264

2. Write the number of words read incorrectly here: _____

3. Subtract #2 from #1 and write the answer here: _____

4. Using a calculator, multiply #3 by 60 seconds and write the answer here: _____

5. Write the student's reading time in seconds here: _____

6. Using a calculator, divide #4 by #5 and write the answer here: _____

The answer in #6 is the reading rate (words read correctly) per minute.

To interpret this number, first, locate the column in the chart below that represents the time of the year when this test was administered. Then, circle the reading rate that most closely matches your student's reading rate for this passage. Read across to the left to find the student's percentile rank—that is, an estimation of where that reading rate falls within those of other students at that grade level at that time of year.

ORAL READING FLUENCY NORMS FOR GRADE 3

Percentile	Fall WCPM	Winter WCPM	Spring WCPM
90	128	146	162
75	99	120	137
50	71	92	107
25	44	62	78
10	21	36	48

From Hasbrouck and Tindal, 2004.

► Social Studies 4th Grade Level: Louis Braille: Reading Text for the Blind

Introduction: The title of this passage is "Louis Braille: Reading Text for the Blind." It's about a young man whose life benefited the blind all over the world. Read carefully because I will ask you questions about it after you finish.

Record the time at the beginning: _____.

The dark room was very quiet. The only sounds were the creaking of iron beds, the breathing of sleeping boys, and a low tapping sound. One boy sat upright in a bed balancing a small board with papers on it across his knees. The boy pressed down on a piece of paper with a pointed instrument. It did not matter if the damp, cold room was dark. The boy could not see the dark. The boy was blind, and all the other boys in the room with him were also blind.

The boy was very tired, but he did not let himself fall asleep. He kept punching the paper with his pointed instrument. Fourteen-year-old Louis Braille spent many nights awake with his board and paper. He often worked until the new day began. Then it was time for lessons, and he had no more free time.

Louis had been working on this project for months. He had even taken it home during school vacation. There he worked outside in the warmth of the sun all summer. Passing villagers would say to each other: "Ah, there's young Louis at his pinpricks again!"

Louis was making little pinholes in his paper. These pinpricks would one day become the alphabet for blind people all over the world. Louis Braille did not know how successful his system of dots would become. After all, he was just a fourteen-year-old blind student in a special school in Paris. He knew, however, that there must be a way for blind people to read and write easily. In the end, his system is used worldwide, and it is named for him.

Record the time at the end: _____.

This text has been rated at 740L
It has 273 words

QUESTIONS

1. What was unusual about the boy working in his room late at night? (*it was dark, and he could still work because he was blind*) **Inference**

2. Tell one thing about the other boys in the room with him. (*they were asleep; they were blind*) **Recall**

3. How did the author tell you about how dedicated Louis Braille was to the task he was working on? (*tired, but kept working all night; worked at home on school vacation*) **Inference**

4. Why were the pinpricks on paper so important for blind people? (*they could feel them without seeing them*) **Inference**

5. Why was it important for blind people to be able to read and write? (*access to the knowledge of the world*) **Inference**

6. How did Louis Braille make the holes in the paper? (*pushed holes into paper with a pointed instrument*) **Recall**

7. What did the author mean when he wrote about the creaking of beds? (*the sound of the metal as the boys moved in their sleep*) **Vocabulary**

8. What difficulty would Louis probably often have in the classroom during his school lessons? (*tired from little sleep*) **Inference**

Errors in oral reading accuracy: _____

Correct comprehension responses: _____

SCORING GUIDE FOR ORAL READING AND COMPREHENSION

(Circle the boxes that correspond to the student's scores)

	Oral Reading Accuracy	Reading Comprehension	Listening Comprehension
Independent Level	8 or fewer errors	7–8 correct responses	
Instructional Level	9–27 errors	6–7 correct responses	6–7 correct responses
Frustration Level	28 or more errors	5 or fewer correct responses	

COMPREHENSION SCORES, BY TYPE

	Recall Questions	Inference Questions	Vocabulary Questions
Student's Correct Answers			
Possible Correct Answers	2	5	1

READING RATE SCORING GUIDE FOR GRADE 4

If the results computed just above show that the student read this passage at his independent level, you may wish to calculate his reading rate and compare that to other readers at his grade level.

1. Here is the number of words in this passage: 273

2. Write the number of words read incorrectly here: _____

3. Subtract #2 from #1 and write the answer here: _____

4. Using a calculator, multiply #3 by 60 seconds and write the answer here: _____

5. Write the student's reading time in seconds here: _____

6. Using a calculator, divide #4 by #5 and write the answer here: _____

The answer in #6 is the reading rate (words read correctly) per minute.

To interpret this number, first, locate the column in the chart below that represents the time of the year when this test was administered. Then, circle the reading rate that most closely matches your student's reading rate for this passage. Read across to the left to find the student's percentile rank—that is, an estimation of where that reading rate falls within those of other students at that grade level at that time of year.

ORAL READING FLUENCY NORMS FOR GRADE 4

Percentile	Fall WCPM	Winter WCPM	Spring WCPM
90	145	166	180
75	119	139	152
50	94	112	123
25	68	87	98
10	45	61	72

From Hasbrouck and Tindal, 2004.

▶ Social Studies 5th Grade Level: Coronado and His Search for Gold

Introduction: The title of this passage is "Coronado and His Search for Gold." It tells about a Spanish explorer named Francisco Vasquez de Coronado's trip in the Americas. Read carefully because I will ask you questions about it after you finish.

Record the time at the beginning: _____.

In the early 1500's Spain sent explorers to the Americas to find gold. The governor of Mexico heard reports of "Cities of Gold" to the north, and wanted to claim them for Spain. The cities were said to have walls of gold blocks, gates studded with jewels, and streets were paved with silver.

In 1540, the governor sent Francisco Vasquez de Coronado to search for Cibola, the golden cities. Coronado's party had more than a thousand men, many of whom were slaves. Coronado found Cibola, a simple Zuni pueblo near the present day border of New Mexico and Arizona. What had been said to be walls of gold turned out to be adobe shining in the desert sun. But Coronado did not give up.

Coronado sent search parties in different directions. One group went west in search of a large river, and they became the first Europeans to see the Colorado River and the Grand Canyon. They could not reach the river because it was at the bottom of the deep canyon. Another group found the Gulf of California. Another group went east to explore Pueblo villages. When they were on the Rio Grande River in what is now New Mexico they were attacked by Indian groups living in the area.

Meanwhile, Coronado's party heard about another city of riches called "Quivira." They went as far as present-day Kansas, but they found no gold. They found only herds of buffalo and Indian villages. They were the first Europeans to see buffalo. Coronado returned to Mexico and reported that there was no gold.

At the time, his expedition was called a failure. But, he had explored much of northern Mexico and what is now the American Southwest. He claimed the new lands for Spain.

Record the time at the end: _____ .

This text has been rated at 850L
It has 293 words

QUESTIONS

1. What was it about Cibola that attracted Spanish explorers? (*They were looking for gold.*) **Recall**

2. What was the effect on the governor of Mexico of hearing about golden cities to the north? (*He wanted to claim them for Spain.*) **Inference**

3. Why was the expedition dangerous for Coronado's men? (*They faced Indian attacks.*) **Inference**

4. Name two important discoveries that Coronado's expedition made. (*Colorado River, Grand Canyon, Gulf of California, buffalo [any two]*) **Recall**

5. What caused the governor of Mexico to be very disappointed? (*no gold*) **Inference**

6. The text said, "The walls of gold turned out to be adobe shining in the desert sun." What does *adobe* mean? (*a method of house construction that uses mud, dried in the sun*) **Vocabulary**

7. Why was Coronado considered to be a failure? (*no gold*) **Inference**

8. Why would modern government leaders think that Coronado was very successful? (*claimed important new lands for Spain*) **Inference**

Errors in oral reading accuracy: _____

Correct comprehension responses: _____

SCORING GUIDE FOR ORAL READING AND COMPREHENSION

(Circle the boxes that correspond to the student's scores)

	Oral Reading Accuracy	Reading Comprehension	Listening Comprehension
Independent Level	12 or fewer errors	7–8 correct responses	
Instructional Level	13–29 errors	6–7 correct responses	6–7 correct responses
Frustration Level	30 or more errors	5 or fewer correct responses	

COMPREHENSION SCORES, BY TYPE

	Recall Questions	Inference Questions	Vocabulary Questions
Student's Correct Answers			
Possible Correct Answers	2	5	1

READING RATE SCORING GUIDE FOR GRADE 5

If the results computed just above show that the student read this passage at his independent level, you may wish to calculate his reading rate and compare that to other readers at his grade level.

1. Here is the number of words in this passage: 293

2. Write the number of words read incorrectly here: _____

3. Subtract #2 from #1 and write the answer here: _____

4. Using a calculator, multiply #3 by 60 seconds and write the answer here: _____

5. Write the student's reading time in seconds here: _____

6. Using a calculator, divide #4 by #5 and write the answer here: _____

The answer in #6 is the reading rate (words read correctly) per minute.

To interpret this number, first, locate the column in the chart below that represents the time of the year when this test was administered. Then, circle the reading rate that most closely matches your student's reading rate for this passage. Read across to the left to find the student's percentile rank—that is, an estimation of where that reading rate falls within those of other students at that grade level at that time of year.

ORAL READING FLUENCY NORMS FOR GRADE 5

Percentile	Fall WCPM	Winter WCPM	Spring WCPM
90	166	182	194
75	139	156	168
50	110	127	139
25	85	99	109
10	61	74	83

From Hasbrouck and Tindal, 2004.

▶ Social Studies 6th Grade Level: Rosa Parks

Introduction: The title of this passage is "Rosa Parks." She was an American who is famous because of her courage. Read carefully because I will ask you questions about it after you finish.

Record the time at the beginning: _____.

In 1955 a bus driver in Montgomery, Alabama, told a woman to give up her seat on the bus because a man wanted to sit down. The woman was tired from working all day, and she was tired of being treated as a second-class citizen. Rosa Parks was African American, and the man who wanted her seat was white. The bus driver was white, too. Because she refused to sit in the seats in the back of the bus that were reserved for African Americans, Rosa Parks was arrested for violating the law. In the past, she had often walked home from work so that she wouldn't have to sit in the back of the bus.

Rosa Parks was very committed to overcoming the rules of that era in the southern part of the United States. She went thirsty instead of drinking from the "colored only" drinking fountains. She climbed the stairs in buildings that had elevators for "whites only." She refused to accept second-class status.

After she was arrested, the African American community of her city supported her. A young minister named Dr. Martin Luther King was among her supporters. They began a boycott of the city bus system. They refused to ride the buses until the law requiring them to sit in the back of the bus was changed. For more than a year, African Americans did not ride the buses in Montgomery. They were the main customers of the bus system, and the boycott caused many problems for the city government. Finally, the Supreme Court ruled that segregation on public transportation was unconstitutional. A city could not reserve seats on the bus for people from one race. Rosa Parks earned the respect of the entire country.

Record the time at the end: _____.

This text has been rated at 950L
It has 289 words

QUESTIONS

1. How did the author tell you how strongly Rosa Parks felt about being required to sit in the back of the bus? (*often walked home to avoid sitting in the back of the bus*) **Inference**

2. Name another way in which Rosa Parks showed her opposition to rules for African Americans in 1955? (*went thirsty instead of drinking from "colored only" drinking fountains; climbed stairs because of "whites only" elevators*) **Recall**

3. How do we know that what Rosa Parks did was very important at that time? (*Martin Luther King supported her*) **Inference**

4. What term did the author use to describe the status of Rosa Parks and other African American citizens at that time? (*second-class status*) **Vocabulary**

5. Who finally decided that it was not constitutional to require people of one race to sit at the back of the bus? (*Supreme Court*) **Recall**

6. How do we know that the African American community of Montgomery supported Rosa Parks? (*began a boycott of the bus system*) **Inference**

7. What term did the author use to describe the community action that African Americans took in Montgomery? (*boycott*) **Vocabulary**

8. Why was the bus boycott in Montgomery so successful? (*most riders before the boycott were African Americans*) **Inference**

Errors in oral reading accuracy: _____

Correct comprehension responses: _____

SCORING GUIDE FOR ORAL READING AND COMPREHENSION

(Circle the boxes that correspond to the student's scores)

	Oral Reading Accuracy	Reading Comprehension	Listening Comprehension
Independent Level	9 or fewer errors	7–8 correct responses	
Instructional Level	10–29 errors	6–7 correct responses	6–7 correct responses
Frustration Level	30 or more errors	5 or fewer correct responses	

COMPREHENSION SCORES, BY TYPE

	Recall Questions	Inference Questions	Vocabulary Questions
Student's Correct Answers			
Possible Correct Answers	2	4	2

READING RATE SCORING GUIDE FOR GRADE 6

If the results computed just above show that the student read this passage at his independent level, you may wish to calculate his reading rate and compare that to other readers at his grade level.

1. Here is the number of words in this passage: 289

2. Write the number of words read incorrectly here: _____

3. Subtract #2 from #1 and write the answer here: _____

4. Using a calculator, multiply #3 by 60 seconds and write the answer here: _____

5. Write the student's reading time in seconds here: _____

6. Using a calculator, divide #4 by #5 and write the answer here: _____

The answer in #6 is the reading rate (words read correctly) per minute.

To interpret this number, first, locate the column in the chart below that represents the time of the year when this test was administered. Then, circle the reading rate that most closely matches your student's reading rate for this passage. Read across to the left to find the student's percentile rank—that is, an estimation of where that reading rate falls within those of other students at that grade level at that time of year.

ORAL READING FLUENCY NORMS FOR GRADE 6

Percentile	Fall WCPM	Winter WCPM	Spring WCPM
90	177	195	204
75	153	167	177
50	127	140	150
25	98	111	122
10	68	82	93

From Hasbrouck and Tindal, 2004.

Introduction: The title of this passage is "Economies Without Borders." It tells how our global economy has no borders, even though there are many countries in the world. Read carefully because I will ask you questions about it after you finish.

Record the time at the beginning: _____.

We live in a global economy. That is a way of saying that people in one part of the world are exchanging services and goods with people who live in other parts of the world. Living in a global economy means that what happens in one country soon affects others. In our global economy, the products we buy come from all over the world. For example, today automobile makers sell their cars worldwide, however, when your grandparents started driving, most cars sold in the United States were American-made.

The global economy has made some people and nations very wealthy, but it has also caused problems for some workers, communities, and economies. A generation ago, workers' wages were compared to wages of other workers in the same industry, in the same country. For example, if you were a worker in North Carolina and you made shirts in a factory, your wages would be roughly the same as those of other workers in the textile industry in the United States. Today, however, shirts that are sold in the United States are made in countries where workers are paid far less. The shirt you are wearing now was probably made in one of those countries. American textile workers have had to choose between huge pay cuts to compete with lower-paid workers elsewhere, or finding some other line of work. Most have done the latter. Most of the clothes Americans wear today were made overseas.

Industries like the textile industry have had to shut down because of increased competition. They could no longer compete in the global economy. Increased competition often leads to lower prices for consumers. But lower prices can sometimes cause lower profits for industries. In the United States, automobile manufacturing is such an industry. We have far fewer jobs in this industry today than we did 50 years ago. The same is true of television. Color television was invented in the United States, but no televisions are manufactured in the United States today.

There are still sharp differences in wealth among countries. Wealthy nations include the United States, several European nations, and Japan. These nations are called developed nations. Their industries and economies are well-developed. There are other so-called developing countries whose economic activity still does not provide as much income for their workers. Many developing nations are in Africa and Asia.

Record the time at the end: _____ .

This text has been rated at 1020L
It has 391 words

QUESTIONS

1. In the phrase, "Most have done the latter," what does *latter* mean? (*the second or later item in a sequence*) **Vocabulary**

2. According to this passage, what does it mean to us as consumers to live in a global economy? (*we can buy things made in other countries; we can sell our products in other countries*) **Inference**

3. From what the article said, do you think you pay more or less for a shirt now that we have a global economy? (*less*) **Inference**

4. How has increased competition caused problems for some industries and countries? (*made some industries fail; lowered prices and profits*) **Recall**

5. How can lower prices for products be both a good thing and a bad thing? (good: *lower prices mean that consumers/buyers pay less for products*; bad: *lower prices lead to lower profits for industries*) **Inference**

6. What is an example of something invented in the United States, but no longer manufactured here? (*color television*) **Recall**

7. What U.S. industries were given as an example of an industry that has suffered from increased competition? (*U.S. automobile manufacturing/textile manufacturing*) **Recall**

8. What is the main difference between developed and developing countries? (*developed countries are usually rich and have well-developed economies; developing countries are usually not rich and have economies that are still developing*) **Inference**

Errors in oral reading accuracy: _____

Correct comprehension responses: _____

SCORING GUIDE FOR ORAL READING AND COMPREHENSION

(Circle the boxes that correspond to the student's scores)

	Oral Reading Accuracy	Reading Comprehension	Listening Comprehension
Independent Level	12 or fewer errors	7–8 correct responses	
Instructional Level	13–39 errors	6–7 correct responses	6–7 correct responses
Frustration Level	40 or more errors	5 or fewer correct responses	

COMPREHENSION SCORES, BY TYPE

	Recall Questions	Inference Questions	Vocabulary Questions
Student's Correct Answers			
Possible Correct Answers	3	4	1

READING RATE SCORING GUIDE FOR MIDDLE SCHOOL

If the results computed just above show that the student read this passage at his independent level, you may wish to calculate his reading rate and compare that to other readers at his grade level.

1. Here is the number of words in this passage: 391

2. Write the number of words read incorrectly here: _____

3. Subtract #2 from #1 and write the answer here: _____

4. Using a calculator, multiply #3 by 60 seconds and write the answer here: _____

5. Write the student's reading time in seconds here: _____

6. Using a calculator, divide #4 by #5 and write the answer here: _____

The answer in #6 is the reading rate (words read correctly) per minute.

To interpret this number, first, locate the column in the chart below that represents the time of the year when this test was administered. Then, circle the reading rate that most closely matches your student's reading rate for this passage. Read across to the left to find the student's percentile rank—that is, an estimation of where that reading rate falls within those of other students at that grade level at that time of year.

ORAL READING FLUENCY NORMS FOR MIDDLE SCHOOL

Percentile	Fall WCPM	Winter WCPM	Spring WCPM
90	180	192	202
75	156	165	177
50	128	136	150
25	102	109	123
10	79	88	98

From Hasbrouck and Tindal, 2004.

▶ Social Studies High School Level: The Tlingit

Introduction: The title of this passage is "The Tlingit." The Tlingit are a group of indigenous people who live on the northwest coast of Canada and Alaska. Read carefully because I will ask you questions about it after you finish.

Record the time at the beginning: _____.

The Tlingit people are Native Americans who live along the southeastern coast of Alaska in the United States and along the northern coast of British Columbia in Canada. This area makes up the Tlingit cultural region, and the influence of Tlingit culture is strong throughout this area. The Tlingit had frequent battles with early Russian traders who settled in Alaska. There are approximately 15,000 Tlingit people living in Alaska today.

This region is rich in natural resources, such as vast forests and plentiful fish and game for fishing and hunting. For hundreds of years the Tlingit made good use of these resources, fishing for salmon and hunting deer and seals. They used large planks of wood to build giant homes, with figures often carved into their doorways. Tlingit families placed totem poles outside their homes, as well. Some Tlingit families still follow this tradition. A totem pole is a tall post, usually carved of cedar that has images of people and animals, often brightly painted. Totem poles traced the histories of families, and they resembled a family tree or family crest. They typically commemorated dead ancestors, using symbols to confirm the lineage and social rank of the owner and symbols to represent the owner's guardian animal.

The Tlingit lived in these large homes during winter, but they moved to smaller wooden homes near hunting and fishing grounds during the warmer months. They carved wooden dugout canoes from large logs for fishing and hunting. Because game and fish were so plentiful, the Tlingit were able to spend time making and trading traditional goods, such as blankets, copper tools and ornaments, exquisite baskets, spoons of horn and shell, and seal oil. They had a large trading network with other Native Americans, and they sometimes bought goods from one group to trade with another.

For example, one of the most prized Tlingit products, even today, is the Chilkat blanket. It was traditionally woven from the dyed wool of mountain goats and sheep. These colorful blankets have detailed designs of shapes and animals that tell stories, just as a totem pole might tell the story of a family.

Record the time at the end: _____.

This text has been rated at 1200L
It has 354 words

QUESTIONS

1. Where do the Tlingit people live? (*southeast coast of Alaska and north coast of British Columbia, Canada*) **Recall**

2. What do traditional Tlingit winter homes look like? (*very large, made of wood, figures carved into doorways, totem poles outside*) **Recall**

3. What would you learn about a Tlingit family by looking at its totem pole? (*the family's story; the family's history; the family tree; the family crest*) **Inference**

4. Why did Tlingit families traditionally have two homes? (*one large one for winter, and one smaller one near the hunting/fishing grounds for summer*) **Inference**

5. Why were the Tlingit able to have time to make products to trade with other groups? (*because their land was so abundant; because game and fish were plentiful*) **Inference**

6. The text said the Tlingit "typically commemorated dead ancestors, using symbols to confirm the lineage and social rank of the owner." What does *lineage* mean? (*who their ancestors were, especially how prominent they were*) **Vocabulary**

7. In the phrase, "One of the most prized Tlingit products, even today, is the Chilkat blanket," what does *prized* mean? (*valuable; desirable*) **Vocabulary**

8. How are a Chilkat blanket and a Tlingit totem pole similar? (*both tell stories in pictures and designs [do not accept "Both are made by Tlingit."]*) **Inference**

Errors in oral reading accuracy: _____

Correct comprehension responses: _____

SCORING GUIDE FOR ORAL READING AND COMPREHENSION

(Circle the boxes that correspond to the student's scores)

	Oral Reading Accuracy	Reading Comprehension	Listening Comprehension
Independent Level	11 or fewer errors	7–8 correct responses	
Instructional Level	12–35 errors	6–7 correct responses	6–7 correct responses
Frustration Level	36 or more errors	5 or fewer correct responses	

COMPREHENSION SCORES, BY TYPE

	Recall Questions	Inference Questions	Vocabulary Questions
Student's Correct Answers			
Possible Correct Answers	2	4	2

READING RATE SCORING GUIDE FOR HIGH SCHOOL

If the results computed just above show that the student read this passage at his independent level, you may wish to calculate his reading rate and compare that to other readers at his grade level.

1. Here is the number of words in this passage: 354

2. Write the number of words read incorrectly here: _____

3. Subtract #2 from #1 and write the answer here: _____

4. Using a calculator, multiply #3 by 60 seconds and write the answer here: _____

5. Write the student's reading time in seconds here: _____

6. Using a calculator, divide #4 by #5 and write the answer here: _____

The answer in #6 is the reading rate (words read correctly) per minute.

To interpret this number, first, locate the column in the chart below that represents the time of the year when this test was administered. Then, circle the reading rate that most closely matches your student's reading rate for this passage. Read across to the left to find the student's percentile rank—that is, an estimation of where that reading rate falls within those of other students at that grade level at that time of year.

ORAL READING FLUENCY NORMS FOR HIGH SCHOOL

Percentile	Fall WCPM	Winter WCPM	Spring WCPM
90	195	209	213
75	171	183	191
50	143	156	165
25	116	125	138
10	87	94	111

Note: These are estimates, extrapolated from Hasbrouck and Tindal, 2004.

SCIENCE PASSAGES

FORM B

How are a bee, a fish, and a tree alike? They are all living things. How are a rock, a ball, and water alike? They are all nonliving things.

Plants and animals are living things. Living things can grow and change. They can grow from a seed, an egg, or a baby. Living things can be parents. A plant that has seeds is a parent. A bird that lays eggs is a parent. So is a dog that has puppies. Some living things can move. They can run, swim, fly, or crawl. Some living things do not move.

Nonliving things can't move. They can't grow. They can't be parents. They can't eat. They don't die because they were never alive.

▶ ▶ ▶

Plants are living things. Plants grow and change. They need food, water, and air. They can make other plants. The new plants are just like themselves. Plants do not eat like animals. They make their own food. Plants need light, water, and air to make food. They also need minerals to stay healthy. Minerals come from bits of rock and soil.

Plants have different shapes, sizes, and colors. Some plants are very small. Some plants are very large. Many plants have green leaves. Some plants are gray or brown. Some plants have flowers in many colors. Many plants have no flowers. Many plants grow straight up. Other plants grow flat on the ground. Some grow up walls and trees, or on rocks. Some plants grow on top of water, and others grow under water.

▶ ▶ ▶

Your heart and lungs are called organs. Your two lungs and your heart are in your chest. You use your two lungs to breathe. You use your heart to move your blood around your body. When you take a breath, your lungs take in air. Air has oxygen in it. Oxygen is a gas that your body needs to live. Oxygen goes into your lungs from the air you breathe. The oxygen has to get to all parts of your body. Oxygen gets to your body parts from your blood.

Blood carries oxygen and other things your body needs. Your heart pumps blood to all your body parts. Blood is pumped away from your heart in tubes called arteries. Your blood carries oxygen with it. When the oxygen is used up the blood goes back to your lungs. In your lungs the blood gets rid of the spent oxygen. It also gets rid of other gases. Your lungs take in fresh air, and your blood picks up more new oxygen. Your blood travels back to the heart in tubes called veins. The heart pumps the blood to your body parts and lungs, over and over again. Your heart and lungs work together to keep you healthy. They work when you are awake. They keep working when you are asleep.

▶ ▶ ▶

Work is what happens when a force makes something move. When you move an object you do work. Lifting, throwing, pushing, and carrying are all work. You also do work when you move yourself. Standing up and sitting down are work. So are raising your hand and wiggling your ears.

Force is how much work you do to move the object. It takes more force to move something heavy than something light. It takes more force to lift two books than just one book. It takes more force to carry a full trash can than an empty one. Size doesn't matter. It takes less force to lift a trash bag full of paper than a lunch bag full of rocks. The heavier something is, the more force it takes to move it.

Work also depends on how far you move something. It takes more work to carry a brick for a mile than a block. It takes more work to push a wagon a yard than a foot. It takes more work to throw a baseball 100 feet than 50 feet.

If you cannot move something, no work has been done. You could push and push, but you could not knock down a brick wall. The pushing was not work. The wall did not move. Work happens when something moves.

▶ ▶ ▶

The ocean is home to thousands of kinds of animals, and most of them live in a single part of the ocean. The ocean has four main habitats. Habitats are areas where plants and animals live.

One habitat you may know is the shoreline. Many kinds of plants, birds, fish, and ocean animals live near the shoreline. Many creatures must live in shallow water or on rocks. Some are clams, sea lions, and barnacles. Tide pools are a second ocean habitat, and they are like small saltwater ponds. They are left behind when the tide goes out. Small ocean animals like mussels, sea stars, and sea anemones live in tide pools. The tide floods the pools, bringing food to these animals, and when the tide goes out, the water is still and the animals rest.

A third habitat is called the light zone. It is not shallow, but light can still reach the bottom. Because of this, the light zone is filled with many kinds of plants. Many animals eat and hide in the plants. Thousands of kinds of fish live in the light zone. Jellyfish, crabs, turtles, dolphins, and sharks also live here, and sea birds hunt for food here.

The largest habitat is called the dark zone. This is the deepest part of the ocean. The water is dark and cold. Many interesting ocean animals live in darkness. Some have body parts that glow in the dark. Spots of light attract other fish, which they eat. The angler fish appears to have a fishing rod on its head. A glowing "fish" on the rod attracts other fish. Then the angler fish eats them.

▶ ▶ ▶

iv

The sun is a star located at the center of a group of planets including Earth. The sun, the planets, and their moons make up the solar system. Solar means "related to the sun." The sun is an average-sized star, but it looks brighter than other stars because it is closer to Earth. It takes only eight minutes for the sun's light to reach Earth. The next closest star is so far away that it takes over four years for its light to reach Earth.

The total surface of the sun is about 12,000 times greater than the surface of Earth. The sun has more than 300,000 times more mass than Earth.

Like all stars, the sun is a ball of extremely hot gases. Deep in the center of the sun, atoms combine to create nuclear power. The nuclear power creates huge amounts of energy, which is released as heat and light. On its surface, the sun's temperature is 2 million degrees Celsius, and it is so hot that it glows with yellow light. It can be seen for millions of miles in space. It is hotter than some stars and cooler than others. Its yellow light is medium-hot.

The hottest stars give off blue-white light, and the coolest stars are red. The sun gives off more light than some stars and less light than others. It is bigger than some stars and smaller than others. It looks bigger and brighter than any other star, but the sun is really just average.

▶ ▶ ▶

Today, most of the food we eat, the metals we need, and the energy we consume come from the land. But someday we may develop the means to find and use the ocean's great wealth. The ocean is a vast source of minerals and of many kinds of energy.

Many valuable minerals come from the ocean floor. In some places the ocean floor is covered with rounded lumps of minerals. These lumps are called nodules. They contain minerals like iron, cobalt, and manganese. Right now it is easier to mine these minerals on land. But already machines have been invented that can scoop up the nodules from the ocean floor and carry them to the surface.

The ocean floor also contains many small openings that look like chimneys. These openings are called vents. Hot water from inside the earth pours out the vents. The hot water contains dissolved minerals like lead, copper, iron, and zinc. When the hot water mixes with the cold ocean water, the minerals form crystals around the vents. Mining these mineral deposits is much harder and more expensive than mining them on land. But someday we may need these underwater mineral deposits.

There is one mineral that is already being harvested from the ocean, and has been for thousands of years. That mineral is salt, an important mineral that is used all over the world. The ocean is the world's largest source of salt. Most of the salt in the ocean is table salt. It is relatively easy to obtain salt from ocean water. For thousands of years people have built shallow pools of ocean water and allowed the water to evaporate. The salt crystals are left behind. There are also ways to separate the salt and water, leaving salt and fresh water behind. This process is called desalinization. The fresh water can be used in many ways. Many of the most heavily populated places in the world are located near oceans. Desalinated water can help provide the water people need.

▶ ▶ ▶

vi

Of the nine planets in our solar system, Saturn is the second largest and is about ten times the size of Earth. Seven flat rings made of ice particles surround Saturn. Saturn can be seen from Earth with the unaided eye, but its rings can only be seen with a telescope. Saturn was the farthest planet from Earth that astronomers in ancient times could see. It was named for the Roman god of farming. The planet has been viewed for thousands of years, but its rings were first discovered in the early 1600's.

Saturn's seven icy rings surround it at its equator, or widest part. They do not touch the planet's surface at any point, and they are made up of billions of pieces of ice. The pieces of ice range in size from particles the size of dust to chunks more than ten feet across. The rings are easily seen with a telescope because of their enormous size. They are more than 180,000 miles across, but they are less than 10,000 feet thick.

Besides its rings, Saturn is also circled by at least 18 satellites, or moons. The largest of Saturn's moons has been named Titan. Titan is a huge moon. It is more than 3,100 miles across, and is larger than the planets Mercury and Pluto. Titan orbits Saturn, and is 744 million miles away from Earth. Titan is one of the only moons in the entire solar system that is known to have an atmosphere.

In 1998 a French space probe was launched to explore Titan. Seven years later, in January 2005, it landed on Titan and began sending information back to Earth. Titan is the first moon other than Earth's moon to be explored. Titan's surface temperature is 274 degrees below zero. Photographs from the probe showed a rugged landscape of ridges, peaks, and channels that look like dry riverbeds. One scientist looking at the photos compared the Titan landscape to the Arizona desert. Clouds of methane gas surround Titan, and storms of liquid methane rain down on the surface. The liquid methane erodes, or wears away, the moon's surface and creates riverbeds just as water does on Earth. On Earth, methane is a gas, but Titan's intense cold turns methane gas to a liquid. On Earth, methane explodes and burns very easily, but on Titan there is no oxygen. Without oxygen, the methane cannot burn.

▶ ▶ ▶

Some types of pollution, such as contamination of water, have existed for hundreds of years. But acid rain is a recent form of pollution that has worsened in only the past few decades. Today it is a major danger to our world.

Acid rain is a byproduct of industry. Smog from cities and smoke from coal-burning factories contain sulfur dioxide and oxides from nitrogen, which enter the atmosphere and combine with other gases and chemicals already in the air. They form sulfuric acid, a highly corrosive acid. Sulfuric acid molecules are carried back to earth in rain and snow, falling on our soil and running into our water sources. This is referred to as acid rain.

How acid a substance is can be measured on the pH scale. On this scale a measure of 7 indicates that the substance is neutral, neither acid nor alkaline, and the lower the number, the more acid the substance is. All rain and snow are partly acid, because of the way raindrops and snowflakes form around dust particles. The average pH of rain in nature is about 5.6. But as you count down the pH scale toward 1, each lower number is about 10 times more acidic than the number above it. For example, water with a pH of 4.5 is more than ten times as acid as normal rain, which is alarming, since the average rainfall in the eastern United States today has a pH of 4.5 or even lower.

The eastern half of the United States is particularly at risk for acid rain because of the smog produced by its many large cities and the number of coal-burning factories and power plants in the industrial northeast. The acid rain produced in the atmosphere pours down on the entire eastern seaboard east of the Appalachian Mountains. Forests gradually turn brown and die; lakes and rivers may look sparkling clean, but are empty of fish and other organisms. Food chains are disrupted and wildlife dwindles. Two of our most popular national parks, Shenandoah National Park and Great Smoky Mountain National Park, are marked by browned, dying forests and lakes that are eerily empty of fish. Park officials frequently restock lakes and rivers for anglers, but fish not caught soon die.

Efforts to control acid rain by cleaning the air have largely failed. Car exhaust is cleaner today than in the past, but there are millions more vehicles on the roads. Factories and power plants built taller smokestacks, some over a thousand feet tall. But this just put the pollutants higher in the air, so now acid rain from Ohio falls as far away as Sweden. Companies have been slow to install "scrubbers" in smokestacks because of their expense.

▶ ▶ ▶

X

SCIENCE PASSAGES
RESPONSE SHEETS

FORM B

Introduction: The title of this passage is "Living and Nonliving Things." It tells about the ways living things and nonliving things are alike. I will ask you questions about it after you finish reading.

Record the time at the beginning: _____.

How are a bee, a fish, and a tree alike? They are all living things. How are a rock, a ball, and water alike? They are all nonliving things.

Plants and animals are living things. Living things can grow and change. They can grow from a seed, an egg, or a baby. Living things can be parents. A plant that has seeds is a parent. A bird that lays eggs is a parent. So is a dog that has puppies. Some living things can move. They can run, swim, fly, or crawl. Some living things do not move.

Nonliving things can't move. They can't grow. They can't be parents. They can't eat. They don't die because they were never alive.

Record the time at the end: _____.

This text has been rated at 300L
It has 120 words

QUESTIONS

1. What did the article say are some ways that living things are alike? (*they can grow and change; they can eat; they can be parents/have babies; some can move [must name 2]*) **Recall**

2. In the sentence, "Nonliving things can't move," what does *nonliving* mean? (*not living; not alive; were never alive [do not accept "dead" as correct]*) **Vocabulary**

3. What are three ways that the article said some living things can move? (*swim, run, crawl, fly*) **Recall**

4. Could you tell if something is living or nonliving if it does not move? Why? (*No; because some living things can't move*) **Inference**

5. Could you tell if something is living or nonliving if it has babies? Why? (*Yes; because only living things can have babies*) **Inference**

6. Why can't a nonliving thing ever die? (*because it was never alive/living*) **Inference**

Errors in oral reading accuracy: _____

Correct comprehension responses: _____

SCORING GUIDE FOR ORAL READING AND COMPREHENSION

(Circle the boxes that correspond to the student's scores)

	Oral Reading Accuracy	Reading Comprehension	Listening Comprehension
Independent Level	4 or fewer errors	6 correct responses	
Instructional Level	5–12 errors	5 correct responses	5 correct responses
Frustration Level	13 or more errors	4 or fewer correct responses	

COMPREHENSION SCORES, BY TYPE

	Recall Questions	Inference Questions	Vocabulary Questions
Student's Correct Answers			
Possible Correct Answers	2	3	1

READING RATE SCORING GUIDE FOR GRADE 1

If the results computed just above show that the student read this passage at his independent level, you may wish to calculate his reading rate and compare that to other readers at his grade level.

1. Here is the number of words in this passage: 120

2. Write the number of words read incorrectly here: _____

3. Subtract #2 from #1 and write the answer here: _____

4. Using a calculator, multiply #3 by 60 seconds and write the answer here: _____

5. Write the student's reading time in seconds here: _____

6. Using a calculator, divide #4 by #5 and write the answer here: _____

The answer in #6 is the reading rate (words read correctly) per minute.

To interpret this number, first, locate the column in the chart below that represents the time of the year when this test was administered. Then, circle the reading rate that most closely matches your student's reading rate for this passage. Read across to the left to find the student's percentile rank—that is, an estimation of where that reading rate falls within those of other students at that grade level at that time of year.

ORAL READING FLUENCY NORMS FOR GRADE 1

Percentile	Fall WCPM	Winter WCPM	Spring WCPM
90		81	111
75		47	82
50		23	53
25		12	28
10		6	15

From Hasbrouck and Tindal, 2004.

▶ Science 2nd Grade Level (2.1): Plants

Introduction: The title of this passage is "Plants." It tells about what plants need to live and how they are different. I will ask you questions about it after you finish reading.

Record the time at the beginning: _____.

Plants are living things. Plants grow and change. They need food, water, and air. They can make other plants. The new plants are just like themselves. Plants do not eat like animals. They make their own food. Plants need light, water, and air to make food. They also need minerals to stay healthy. Minerals come from bits of rock and soil.

Plants have different shapes, sizes, and colors. Some plants are very small. Some plants are very large. Many plants have green leaves. Some plants are gray or brown. Some plants have flowers in many colors. Many plants have no flowers. Many plants grow straight up. Other plants grow flat on the ground. Some grow up walls and trees, or on rocks. Some plants grow on top of water, and others grow under water.

Record the time at the end: _____.

This text has been rated at 350L
It has 134 words

QUESTIONS

1. What did the article say plants need to grow? (*food, water, and air*) **Recall**

2. What do plants need to make food? (*light, water, and air*) **Recall**

3. What might happen to a plant if it couldn't get any light? Why? (*It might die, because it couldn't make food.* [*must answer both parts*]) **Inference**

4. Where do plants get the minerals they need? (*from bits of rock and soil*) **Recall**

5. In the sentence, "Minerals come from bits of rock and soil," what does *soil* mean? (*dirt; the ground*) **Vocabulary**

6. Not all plants are green. What two other plant colors did the passage mention? (*gray and brown*) **Recall**

7. What are some ways that plants grow besides straight up from the ground? (*flat on the ground, up trees and walls, on rocks, on top of water, under water* [*must name at least 2*]) **Recall**

8. Why is it a good thing for plants to have many different shapes and sizes? (*so they can grow in different places or in different conditions*) **Inference**

Errors in oral reading accuracy: _____

Correct comprehension responses: _____

SCORING GUIDE FOR ORAL READING AND COMPREHENSION

(Circle the boxes that correspond to the student's scores)

	Oral Reading Accuracy	Reading Comprehension	Listening Comprehension
Independent Level	4 or fewer errors	7–8 correct responses	
Instructional Level	5–13 errors	6–7 correct responses	6–7 correct responses
Frustration Level	14 or more errors	5 or fewer correct responses	

COMPREHENSION SCORES, BY TYPE

	Recall Questions	Inference Questions	Vocabulary Questions
Student's Correct Answers			
Possible Correct Answers	5	2	1

READING RATE SCORING GUIDE FOR GRADE 2

If the results computed just above show that the student read this passage at his independent level, you may wish to calculate his reading rate and compare that to other readers at his grade level.

1. Here is the number of words in this passage: 134

2. Write the number of words read incorrectly here: _____

3. Subtract #2 from #1 and write the answer here: _____

4. Using a calculator, multiply #3 by 60 seconds and write the answer here: _____

5. Write the student's reading time in seconds here: _____

6. Using a calculator, divide #4 by #5 and write the answer here: _____

The answer in #6 is the reading rate (words read correctly) per minute.

To interpret this number, first, locate the column in the chart below that represents the time of the year when this test was administered. Then, circle the reading rate that most closely matches your student's reading rate for this passage. Read across to the left to find the student's percentile rank—that is, an estimation of where that reading rate falls within those of other students at that grade level at that time of year.

ORAL READING FLUENCY NORMS FOR GRADE 2

Percentile	Fall WCPM	Winter WCPM	Spring WCPM
90	106	125	142
75	79	100	117
50	51	72	89
25	25	42	61
10	11	18	31

From Hasbrouck and Tindal, 2004.

▶ Science 2nd Grade Level (2.2): Your Heart and Lungs

Introduction: The title of this passage is "Your Heart and Lungs." It tells about how your heart and lungs work. I will ask you questions about it after you finish reading.

Record the time at the beginning: _____.

Your heart and lungs are called organs. Your two lungs and your heart are in your chest. You use your two lungs to breathe. You use your heart to move your blood around your body. When you take a breath, your lungs take in air. Air has oxygen in it. Oxygen is a gas that your body needs to live. Oxygen goes into your lungs from the air you breathe. The oxygen has to get to all parts of your body. Oxygen gets to your body parts from your blood.

Blood carries oxygen and other things your body needs. Your heart pumps blood to all your body parts. Blood is pumped away from your heart in tubes called arteries. Your blood carries oxygen with it. When the oxygen is used up the blood goes back to your lungs. In your lungs the blood gets rid of the spent oxygen. It also gets rid of other gases.

Your lungs take in fresh air, and your blood picks up more new oxygen. Your blood travels back to the heart in tubes called veins. The heart pumps the blood to your body parts and lungs, over and over again. Your heart and lungs work together to keep you healthy. They work when you are awake. They keep working when you are asleep.

Record the time at the end: _____.

This text has been rated at 450L
It has 219 words

QUESTIONS

1. What substance in your body is important to both your heart and lungs? (*blood*) **Inference**

2. What two things do you use your heart and lungs to do? (*breathe and move blood*) **Recall**

3. How does oxygen get into your lungs? (*you breathe it in with air*) **Inference**

4. Why do we need to get blood to all parts of our bodies? (*all body parts need oxygen; blood carries oxygen*) **Inference**

5. What are the tubes called that carry blood away from your heart to your other body parts? (*arteries*) **Recall**

6. In the phrase, "Your blood gets rid of the spent oxygen," what does *spent* mean? (*used up*) **Vocabulary**

7. Where does your blood go when it needs more oxygen? (*back to the lungs to get more oxygen*) **Recall**

8. How is the way your blood moves like a wheel? (*it moves in a circle from heart to body parts to lungs and back to heart again, round and round*) **Inference**

Errors in oral reading accuracy: _____

Correct comprehension responses: _____

SCORING GUIDE FOR ORAL READING AND COMPREHENSION

(Circle the boxes that correspond to the student's scores)

	Oral Reading Accuracy	Reading Comprehension	Listening Comprehension
Independent Level	7 or fewer errors	7–8 correct responses	
Instructional Level	8–22 errors	6–7 correct responses	6–8 correct responses
Frustration Level	23 or more errors	5 or fewer correct responses	

COMPREHENSION SCORES, BY TYPE

	Recall Questions	Inference Questions	Vocabulary Questions
Student's Correct Answers			
Possible Correct Answers	3	4	1

READING RATE SCORING GUIDE FOR GRADE 2

If the results computed just above show that the student read this passage at his independent level, you may wish to calculate his reading rate and compare that to other readers at his grade level.

1. Here is the number of words in this passage: 219

2. Write the number of words read incorrectly here: _____

3. Subtract #2 from #1 and write the answer here: _____

4. Using a calculator, multiply #3 by 60 seconds and write the answer here: _____

5. Write the student's reading time in seconds here: _____

6. Using a calculator, divide #4 by #5 and write the answer here: _____

The answer in #6 is the reading rate (words read correctly) per minute.

To interpret this number, first, locate the column in the chart below that represents the time of the year when this test was administered. Then, circle the reading rate that most closely matches your student's reading rate for this passage. Read across to the left to find the student's percentile rank—that is, an estimation of where that reading rate falls within those of other students at that grade level at that time of year.

ORAL READING FLUENCY NORMS FOR GRADE 2

Percentile	Fall WCPM	Winter WCPM	Spring WCPM
90	106	125	142
75	79	100	117
50	51	72	89
25	25	42	61
10	11	18	31

From Hasbrouck and Tindal, 2004.

► Science 3rd Grade Level: What Is Work?

Introduction: The title of this passage is "What Is Work?" It tells about how your body does work. I will ask you questions about it after you finish reading.

Record the time at the beginning: _____.

Work is what happens when a force makes something move. When you move an object you do work. Lifting, throwing, pushing, and carrying are all work. You also do work when you move yourself. Standing up and sitting down are work. So are raising your hand and wiggling your ears.

Force is how much work you do to move the object. It takes more force to move something heavy than something light. It takes more force to lift two books than just one book. It takes more force to carry a full trash can than an empty one. Size doesn't matter. It takes less force to lift a trash bag full of paper than a lunch bag full of rocks. The heavier something is, the more force it takes to move it.

Work also depends on how far you move something. It takes more work to carry a brick for a mile than a block. It takes more work to push a wagon a yard than a foot. It takes more work to throw a baseball 100 feet than 50 feet.

If you cannot move something, no work has been done. You could push and push, but you could not knock down a brick wall. The pushing was not work. The wall did not move. Work happens when something moves.

Record the time at the end: _____.

This text has been rated at 610L
It has 220 words

QUESTIONS

1. According to this passage, what happens when work is done? (*something moves*)
   Inference

2. What were some activities that this article said are work? (*lifting, throwing, pushing, carrying, standing up, sitting down, raising your hand, wiggling your ears* [*must name at least 4*])
   Recall

3. According to this passage, what does *force* mean? (*how much work it takes to move something*) **Vocabulary**

4. Which takes more force to lift, a brick or an egg? Why? (*the brick; because it is heavier*)
   Inference

5. Which is more work, to carry a book across the classroom or to another classroom? Why? (*to another room; because it is more work to move something farther*) **Inference**

6. Ann's bookbag is heavier than Sarah's. Both girls carry their bookbags the same distance. Who used more force and why? (*Ann/the first girl/the girl with the heavier bag; because her bag was heavier*) **Inference**

7. What are two things that tell you how much work is done? (*the amount of weight and the distance the weight is moved*) **Recall**

8. A boy pushed on a locked door until he was tired, but he couldn't open it. Did he do work? How do you know? (*No; because the door didn't move [do not accept "because the door was locked"]*) **Inference**

Errors in oral reading accuracy: _____

Correct comprehension responses: _____

SCORING GUIDE FOR ORAL READING AND COMPREHENSION

(Circle the boxes that correspond to the student's scores)

	Oral Reading Accuracy	Reading Comprehension	Listening Comprehension
Independent Level	7 or fewer errors	7–8 correct responses	
Instructional Level	8–22 errors	6–7 correct responses	6–7 correct responses
Frustration Level	23 or more errors	5 or fewer correct responses	

COMPREHENSION SCORES, BY TYPE

	Recall Questions	Inference Questions	Vocabulary Questions
Student's Correct Answers			
Possible Correct Answers	2	5	1

READING RATE SCORING GUIDE FOR GRADE 3

If the results computed just above show that the student read this passage at his independent level, you may wish to calculate his reading rate and compare that to other readers at his grade level.

1. Here is the number of words in this passage: 220

2. Write the number of words read incorrectly here: _____

3. Subtract #2 from #1 and write the answer here: _____

4. Using a calculator, multiply #3 by 60 seconds and write the answer here: _____

5. Write the student's reading time in seconds here: _____

6. Using a calculator, divide #4 by #5 and write the answer here: _____

The answer in #6 is the reading rate (words read correctly) per minute.

To interpret this number, first, locate the column in the chart below that represents the time of the year when this test was administered. Then, circle the reading rate that most closely matches your student's reading rate for this passage. Read across to the left to find the student's percentile rank—that is, an estimation of where that reading rate falls within those of other students at that grade level at that time of year.

ORAL READING FLUENCY NORMS FOR GRADE 3

Percentile	Fall WCPM	Winter WCPM	Spring WCPM
90	128	146	162
75	99	120	137
50	71	92	107
25	44	62	78
10	21	36	48

From Hasbrouck and Tindal, 2004.

▶ Science 4th Grade Level: Life in the Ocean

Introduction: The title of this passage is "Life in the Ocean." It tells about the major habitats of the ocean and what lives in each one. I will ask you questions about it after you finish reading.

Record the time at the beginning: _____.

The ocean is home to thousands of kinds of animals, and most of them live in a single part of the ocean. The ocean has four main habitats. Habitats are areas where plants and animals live.

One habitat you may know is the shoreline. Many kinds of plants, birds, fish, and ocean animals live near the shoreline. Many creatures must live in shallow water or on rocks. Some are clams, sea lions, and barnacles. Tide pools are a second ocean habitat, and they are like small saltwater ponds. They are left behind when the tide goes out. Small ocean animals like mussels, sea stars, and sea anemones live in tide pools. The tide floods the pools, bringing food to these animals, and when the tide goes out, the water is still and the animals rest.

A third habitat is called the light zone. It is not shallow, but light can still reach the bottom. Because of this, the light zone is filled with many kinds of plants. Many animals eat and hide in the plants. Thousands of kinds of fish live in the light zone. Jellyfish, crabs, turtles, dolphins, and sharks also live here, and sea birds hunt for food here.

The largest habitat is called the dark zone. This is the deepest part of the ocean. The water is dark and cold. Many interesting ocean animals live in darkness. Some have body parts that glow in the dark. Spots of light attract other fish, which they eat. The angler fish appears to have a fishing rod on its head. A glowing "fish" on the rod attracts other fish. Then the angler fish eats them.

Record the time at the end: _____.

This text has been rated at 750L
It has 275 words

QUESTIONS

1. According to this passage, what is a habitat? (*an area where plants and animals live*) **Vocabulary**

2. How many main habitats did the passage say the ocean has? (*four*) **Recall**

3. What makes the shoreline a good habitat for many living things? (*has shallow water and rocks they need to live*) **Inference**

4. How do animals living in tide pools get their food? (*tide floods the pools and brings them food*) **Recall**

5. What is life in the light zone like? (*water is not shallow but light can reach the bottom; filled with plants; many fish and animals live there; birds hunt there*) **Recall**

6. Why do you think the light zone is home to so many fish and animals? (*lots of plants to eat and hide in; lots of food there*) **Inference**

7. What is the deepest part of the ocean called? Why is it called that? (*dark zone; too deep for light to reach it* [*must answer both parts*]) **Inference**

8. How do some fish in the dark zone attract other fish to eat? (*they have spots or body parts that glow in the dark*) **Inference**

Errors in oral reading accuracy: _____

Correct comprehension responses: _____

SCORING GUIDE FOR ORAL READING AND COMPREHENSION

(Circle the boxes that correspond to the student's scores)

	Oral Reading Accuracy	Reading Comprehension	Listening Comprehension
Independent Level	8 or fewer errors	7–8 correct responses	
Instructional Level	9–28 errors	6–7 correct responses	6–8 correct responses
Frustration Level	29 or more errors	5 or fewer correct responses	

COMPREHENSION SCORES, BY TYPE

	Recall Questions	Inference Questions	Vocabulary Questions
Student's Correct Answers			
Possible Correct Answers	3	4	1

READING RATE SCORING GUIDE FOR GRADE 4

If the results computed just above show that the student read this passage at his independent level, you may wish to calculate his reading rate and compare that to other readers at his grade level.

1. Here is the number of words in this passage: 275

2. Write the number of words read incorrectly here: _____

3. Subtract #2 from #1 and write the answer here: _____

4. Using a calculator, multiply #3 by 60 seconds and write the answer here: _____

5. Write the student's reading time in seconds here: _____

6. Using a calculator, divide #4 by #5 and write the answer here: _____

The answer in #6 is the reading rate (words read correctly) per minute.

To interpret this number, first, locate the column in the chart below that represents the time of the year when this test was administered. Then, circle the reading rate that most closely matches your student's reading rate for this passage. Read across to the left to find the student's percentile rank—that is, an estimation of where that reading rate falls within those of other students at that grade level at that time of year.

ORAL READING FLUENCY NORMS FOR GRADE 4

Percentile	Fall WCPM	Winter WCPM	Spring WCPM
90	145	166	180
75	119	139	152
50	94	112	123
25	68	87	98
10	45	61	72

From Hasbrouck and Tindal, 2004.

► Science 5th Grade Level: The Sun

Introduction: The title of this passage is "The Sun." It tells about the sun and how it gets its light and heat. I will ask you questions about it after you finish reading.

Record the time at the beginning: _____.

The sun is a star located at the center of a group of planets including Earth. The sun, the planets, and their moons make up the solar system. Solar means "related to the sun." The sun is an average-sized star, but it looks brighter than other stars because it is closer to Earth. It takes only eight minutes for the sun's light to reach Earth. The next closest star is so far away that it takes over four years for its light to reach Earth.

The total surface of the sun is about 12,000 times greater than the surface of Earth. The sun has more than 300,000 times more mass than Earth.

Like all stars, the sun is a ball of extremely hot gases. Deep in the center of the sun, atoms combine to create nuclear power. The nuclear power creates huge amounts of energy, which is released as heat and light. On its surface, the sun's temperature is 2 million degrees Celsius, and it is so hot that it glows with yellow light. It can be seen for millions of miles in space. It is hotter than some stars and cooler than others. Its yellow light is medium-hot.

The hottest stars give off blue-white light, and the coolest stars are red. The sun gives off more light than some stars and less light than others. It is bigger than some stars and smaller than others. It looks bigger and brighter than any other star, but the sun is really just average.

Record the time at the end: _____.

This text has been rated at 850L
It has 252 words

QUESTIONS

1. According to this article, what objects make up the solar system? (*the sun, planets that move around the sun, and moons that move around the planets*) **Recall**

2. What does the word *solar* mean in this article? (*related to the sun*) **Vocabulary**

3. How are the sun and all other stars alike? (*they are balls of hot gases*) **Inference**

4. According to this article, how does the sun create or get its energy? (*atoms combine to create nuclear power*) **Recall**

5. How does our sun compare to other stars in size and heat? (*it is average in size and heat; some suns are larger/smaller and some are hotter/cooler*) **Inference**

6. Why does our sun look larger and brighter to us than other stars do? (*we are closer to it than to any other star*) **Inference**

7. What is the relationship between a star's temperature and its color? (*the hotter the star is, the more blue-white its color; the cooler it is, the redder its color*) **Inference**

8. How can we tell that the next closest star is really very far away from Earth? (*it takes over four years for its light to reach Earth*) **Inference**

Errors in oral reading accuracy: _____

Correct comprehension responses: _____

SCORING GUIDE FOR ORAL READING AND COMPREHENSION

(Circle the boxes that correspond to the student's scores)

	Oral Reading Accuracy	Reading Comprehension	Listening Comprehension
Independent Level	8 or fewer errors	7–8 correct responses	
Instructional Level	9–25 errors	6–7 correct responses	6–8 correct responses
Frustration Level	26 or more errors	5 or fewer correct responses	

COMPREHENSION SCORES, BY TYPE

	Recall Questions	Inference Questions	Vocabulary Questions
Student's Correct Answers			
Possible Correct Answers	2	5	1

READING RATE SCORING GUIDE FOR GRADE 5

If the results computed just above show that the student read this passage at his independent level, you may wish to calculate his reading rate and compare that to other readers at his grade level.

1. Here is the number of words in this passage: 252

2. Write the number of words read incorrectly here: _____

3. Subtract #2 from #1 and write the answer here: _____

4. Using a calculator, multiply #3 by 60 seconds and write the answer here: _____

5. Write the student's reading time in seconds here: _____

6. Using a calculator, divide #4 by #5 and write the answer here: _____

The answer in #6 is the reading rate (words read correctly) per minute.

To interpret this number, first, locate the column in the chart below that represents the time of the year when this test was administered. Then, circle the reading rate that most closely matches your student's reading rate for this passage. Read across to the left to find the student's percentile rank—that is, an estimation of where that reading rate falls within those of other students at that grade level at that time of year.

ORAL READING FLUENCY NORMS FOR GRADE 5

Percentile	Fall WCPM	Winter WCPM	Spring WCPM
90	166	182	194
75	139	156	168
50	110	127	139
25	85	99	109
10	61	74	83

From Hasbrouck and Tindal, 2004.

▶ Science 6th Grade Level: Ocean Resources

Introduction: The title of this passage is "Ocean Resources." It tells about the mineral resources that are in the ocean. I will ask you questions about it after you finish reading.

Record the time at the beginning: _____.

Today, most of the food we eat, the metals we need, and the energy we consume come from the land. But someday we may develop the means to find and use the ocean's great wealth. The ocean is a vast source of minerals and of many kinds of energy.

Many valuable minerals come from the ocean floor. In some places the ocean floor is covered with rounded lumps of minerals. These lumps are called nodules. They contain minerals like iron, cobalt, and manganese. Right now it is easier to mine these minerals on land. But already machines have been invented that can scoop up the nodules from the ocean floor and carry them to the surface.

The ocean floor also contains many small openings that look like chimneys.

These openings are called vents. Hot water from inside the earth pours out the vents. The hot water contains dissolved minerals like lead, copper, iron, and zinc. When the hot water mixes with the cold ocean water, the minerals form crystals around the vents. Mining these mineral deposits is much harder and more expensive than mining them on land. But someday we may need these underwater mineral deposits.

There is one mineral that is already being harvested from the ocean, and has been for thousands of years. That mineral is salt, an important mineral that is used all over the world. The ocean is the world's largest source of salt. Most of the salt in the ocean is table salt. It is relatively easy to obtain salt from ocean water. For thousands of years people have built shallow pools of ocean water and allowed the water to evaporate. The salt crystals are left behind. There are also ways to separate the salt and water, leaving salt and fresh water behind. This

process is called desalinization. The fresh

water can be used in many ways. Many of the

most heavily populated places in the world

are located near oceans. Desalinated water

can help provide the water people need.

Record the time at the end: _____.

This text has been rated at 950L
It has 335 words

QUESTIONS

1. This article refers to the ocean's great wealth. What kind of wealth did the article say is in the ocean? (*minerals and energy resources*) **Inference**

2. What mineral did the article say is easy to get from the ocean? (*salt*) **Recall**

3. How have people gotten salt from the ocean for thousands of years? (*built shallow pools of ocean water and let water evaporate; salt is left behind*) **Recall**

4. In the phrase, "... leaving salt and fresh water behind," what does *fresh* mean? (*not salty; without salt*) **Vocabulary**

5. Why might it be useful to be able to make fresh water out of ocean water? (*could be used for crops; there would be enough water for everyone; could be used during dry periods*) **Inference**

6. The article described openings on the ocean floor. Why are the openings called chimneys? (*hot water pours out of them like smoke pours out of a chimney*) **Inference**

7. How are minerals from the ocean floor being mined today? (*machines scoop up lumps of minerals and carry them to the surface*) **Recall**

8. Why do you think we have not really used the ocean's resources yet? (*too hard to find and get at them; don't have the technology to find and get at them; easier to use resources on land*) **Inference**

Errors in oral reading accuracy: _____

Correct comprehension responses: _____

SCORING GUIDE FOR ORAL READING AND COMPREHENSION

(Circle the boxes that correspond to the student's scores)

	Oral Reading Accuracy	Reading Comprehension	Listening Comprehension
Independent Level	10 or fewer errors	7–8 correct responses	
Instructional Level	11–34 errors	6–7 correct responses	6–8 correct responses
Frustration Level	35 or more errors	5 or fewer correct responses	

COMPREHENSION SCORES, BY TYPE

	Recall Questions	Inference Questions	Vocabulary Questions
Student's Correct Answers			
Possible Correct Answers	3	4	1

If the results computed just above show that the student read this passage at his independent level, you may wish to calculate his reading rate and compare that to other readers at his grade level.

1. Here is the number of words in this passage: 335

2. Write the number of words read incorrectly here: _____

3. Subtract #2 from #1 and write the answer here: _____

4. Using a calculator, multiply #3 by 60 seconds and write the answer here: _____

5. Write the student's reading time in seconds here: _____

6. Using a calculator, divide #4 by #5 and write the answer here: _____

The answer in #6 is the reading rate (words read correctly) per minute.

To interpret this number, first, locate the column in the chart below that represents the time of the year when this test was administered. Then, circle the reading rate that most closely matches your student's reading rate for this passage. Read across to the left to find the student's percentile rank—that is, an estimation of where that reading rate falls within those of other students at that grade level at that time of year.

ORAL READING FLUENCY NORMS FOR GRADE 6

Percentile	Fall WCPM	Winter WCPM	Spring WCPM
90	177	195	204
75	153	167	177
50	127	140	150
25	98	111	122
10	68	82	93

From Hasbrouck and Tindal, 2004.

Introduction: The title of this passage is "Saturn and Titan." It tells facts about the planet Saturn and its largest moon. I will ask you questions about it after you finish reading.

Record the time at the beginning: _____.

Of the nine planets in our solar system, Saturn is the second largest and is about ten times the size of Earth. Seven flat rings made of ice particles surround Saturn. Saturn can be seen from Earth with the unaided eye, but its rings can only be seen with a telescope. Saturn was the farthest planet from Earth that astronomers in ancient times could see. It was named for the Roman god of farming. The planet has been viewed for thousands of years, but its rings were first discovered in the early 1600's.

Saturn's seven icy rings surround it at its equator, or widest part. They do not touch the planet's surface at any point, and they are made up of billions of pieces of ice. The pieces of ice range in size from particles the size of dust to chunks more than ten feet across. The rings are easily seen with a tele-

scope because of their enormous size. They are more than 180,000 miles across, but they are less than 10,000 feet thick.

Besides its rings, Saturn is also circled by at least 18 satellites, or moons. The largest of Saturn's moons has been named Titan. Titan is a huge moon. It is more than 3,100 miles across, and is larger than the planets Mercury and Pluto. Titan orbits Saturn, and is 744 million miles away from Earth. Titan is one of the only moons in the entire solar system that is known to have an atmosphere.

In 1998 a French space probe was launched to explore Titan. Seven years later, in January 2005, it landed on Titan and began sending information back to Earth. Titan is the first moon other than Earth's moon to be explored. Titan's surface temperature is 274 degrees below zero. Photographs from the probe showed a rugged landscape of ridges, peaks, and channels that look like dry riverbeds. One scientist looking at the photos compared the Titan landscape to the Arizona desert. Clouds of methane gas surround Titan, and storms of liquid methane rain down on the surface. The liquid methane erodes, or wears away, the moon's surface and creates riverbeds just as water does on Earth. On Earth, methane is a gas, but Titan's intense cold turns methane gas to a liquid. On Earth, methane explodes and burns very easily, but on Titan there is no oxygen. Without oxygen, the methane cannot burn.

Record the time at the end: _____.

This text has been rated at 1020L
It has 400 words

QUESTIONS

1. People on Earth have been able to see Saturn for thousands of years. Why did it take until the 1600's to discover Saturn's rings? (*you can only see the rings with a telescope; telescopes hadn't been invented yet*) **Inference**

2. Tell me three things you read about Saturn's rings. (*you can't see them without a telescope; made of billions of pieces of ice; ice ranges in size from particles the size of dust to ten-foot-wide chunks; surround Saturn's equator; do not touch planet's surface*) **Recall**

3. According to the article, what is the equator of a planet? (*its widest part*) **Vocabulary**

4. What are two things that make Titan unique/different from other moons in the solar system? (*huge size; has an atmosphere*) **Inference**

5. In what ways is Titan like Earth? (*looks like Arizona desert; has an atmosphere; has ridges and dry riverbeds; has clouds and rain; has surface erosion* [*must identify three*]) **Recall**

6. What are Titan's clouds and rain made of? (*methane*) **Recall**

7. Why doesn't methane explode and burn on Titan like it does on Earth? (*no oxygen; can't burn without oxygen*) **Recall**

8. Do you think there could be life as we know it on Titan? Why or why not? (*probably not; no oxygen; temperature is 200+ degrees below zero; atmosphere is methane*) **Inference**

Errors in oral reading accuracy: _____

Correct comprehension responses: _____

SCORING GUIDE FOR ORAL READING AND COMPREHENSION

(Circle the boxes that correspond to the student's scores)

	Oral Reading Accuracy	Reading Comprehension	Listening Comprehension
Independent Level	12 or fewer errors	7–8 correct responses	
Instructional Level	13–40 errors	6–7 correct responses	6–8 correct responses
Frustration Level	41 or more errors	5 or fewer correct responses	

COMPREHENSION SCORES, BY TYPE

	Recall Questions	Inference Questions	Vocabulary Questions
Student's Correct Answers			
Possible Correct Answers	4	3	1

READING RATE SCORING GUIDE FOR MIDDLE SCHOOL LEVEL

If the results computed just above show that the student read this passage at his independent level, you may wish to calculate his reading rate and compare that to other readers at his grade level.

1. Here is the number of words in this passage: 400

2. Write the number of words read incorrectly here: _____

3. Subtract #2 from #1 and write the answer here: _____

4. Using a calculator, multiply #3 by 60 seconds and write the answer here: _____

5. Write the student's reading time in seconds here: _____

6. Using a calculator, divide #4 by #5 and write the answer here: _____

The answer in #6 is the reading rate (words read correctly) per minute.

To interpret this number, first, locate the column in the chart below that represents the time of the year when this test was administered. Then, circle the reading rate that most closely matches your student's reading rate for this passage. Read across to the left to find the student's percentile rank—that is, an estimation of where that reading rate falls within those of other students at that grade level at that time of year.

ORAL READING FLUENCY NORMS FOR MIDDLE SCHOOL

Percentile	Fall WCPM	Winter WCPM	Spring WCPM
90	180	192	202
75	156	165	177
50	128	136	150
25	102	109	123
10	79	88	98

From Hasbrouck and Tindal, 2004.

Introduction: The title of this passage is "Acid Rain." It tells about the environmental hazards of acid rain and how it affects our public lands. I will ask you questions about it after you finish reading.

Record the time at the beginning: _____.

Some types of pollution, such as contamination of water, have existed for hundreds of years. But acid rain is a recent form of pollution that has worsened in only the past few decades. Today it is a major danger to our world.

Acid rain is a byproduct of industry. Smog from cities and smoke from coal-burning factories contain sulfur dioxide and oxides from nitrogen, which enter the atmosphere and combine with other gases and chemicals already in the air. They form sulfuric acid, a highly corrosive acid. Sulfuric acid molecules are carried back to Earth in rain and snow, falling on our soil and running into our water sources. This is referred to as acid rain.

How acid a substance is can be measured on the pH scale. On this scale a measure of 7 indicates that the substance is neutral, neither acid nor alkaline, and the lower the number, the more acid the substance is. All rain and snow are partly acid, because of the way raindrops and snowflakes form around dust particles. The average pH of rain in nature is about 5.6. But as you count down the pH scale toward 1, each lower number is about 10 times more acidic than the number above it. For example, water with a pH of 4.5 is more than ten times as acid as normal rain, which is alarming, since the average rainfall in the eastern United States today has a pH of 4.5 or even lower.

The eastern half of the United States is particularly at risk for acid rain because of the smog produced by its many large cities and the number of coal-burning factories and power plants in the industrial northeast. The acid rain produced in the atmosphere pours down on the entire eastern seaboard east of the Appalachian Mountains. Forests gradually turn brown and die; lakes and rivers may look sparkling clean, but are empty of fish and other organisms. Food chains are disrupted and wildlife dwindles. Two of our most popular national parks, Shenandoah National Park and Great Smoky Mountain National Park, are marked by browned, dying forests and lakes that are eerily empty of fish. Park officials frequently restock lakes and rivers for anglers, but fish not caught soon die.

Efforts to control acid rain by cleaning the air have largely failed. Car exhaust is cleaner today than in the past, but there are millions more vehicles on the roads. Factories and power plants built taller smokestacks, some over a thousand feet tall. But this just put the pollutants higher in the air, so now acid rain from Ohio falls as far away as Sweden. Companies have been slow to install "scrubbers" in smokestacks because of their expense.

Record the time at the end: _____.

This text has been rated at 1190L
It has 454 words

QUESTIONS

1. Why is acid rain a new or recent form of pollution? (*because it is produced by machines/industry*) **Inference**

2. How do cities and factories contribute to acid rain? (*smoke from factories and smog from cities and cars enter the air; smoke and smog combine with other chemicals to form sulfuric acid; the acid falls back to Earth in rain and snow*) **Inference**

3. What does a pH scale show? What does a low pH number mean? (*shows how acid a substance is; the lower the number, the more acid it is* [*must answer both parts*]) **Recall**

4. In the phrase, "Food chains are disrupted and wildlife dwindles," what does *dwindles* mean? (*disappears; dies off; populations become smaller*) **Vocabulary**

5. How much more acid is water with a pH of 4.2 than water with a pH of 5.2? Why? (*ten times more acid; each number is ten times more acid than the number above it*) **Recall**

6. Why is the eastern half of the United States more affected by acid rain than the western half? (*because there are more big cities and coal-burning power plants in the East, so there is more smog*) **Inference**

7. What signs of acid rain effects might you notice if you were camping in an eastern national park? (*browning trees, dead forests, lack of fish and other life forms in the lakes and streams*) **Inference**

8. Why have efforts to control acid rain mostly failed? (*because there are more cars and factories than ever; cities are larger; companies have not used scrubbers in smokestacks because of the expense*) **Inference**

Errors in oral reading accuracy: _____

Correct comprehension responses: _____

SCORING GUIDE FOR ORAL READING AND COMPREHENSION

(Circle the boxes that correspond to the student's scores)

	Oral Reading Accuracy	Reading Comprehension	Listening Comprehension
Independent Level	14 or fewer errors	7–8 correct responses	
Instructional Level	15–45 errors	6–7 correct responses	6–8 correct responses
Frustration Level	46 or more errors	5 or fewer correct responses	

COMPREHENSION SCORES, BY TYPE

	Recall Questions	Inference Questions	Vocabulary Questions
Student's Correct Answers			
Possible Correct Answers	2	5	1

READING RATE SCORING GUIDE FOR HIGH SCHOOL

If the results computed just above show that the student read this passage at his independent level, you may wish to calculate his reading rate and compare that to other readers at his grade level.

1. Here is the number of words in this passage: 454

2. Write the number of words read incorrectly here: _____

3. Subtract #2 from #1 and write the answer here: _____

4. Using a calculator, multiply #3 by 60 seconds and write the answer here: _____

5. Write the student's reading time in seconds here: _____

6. Using a calculator, divide #4 by #5 and write the answer here: _____

The answer in #6 is the reading rate (words read correctly) per minute.

To interpret this number, first, locate the column in the chart below that represents the time of the year when this test was administered. Then, circle the reading rate that most closely matches your student's reading rate for this passage. Read across to the left to find the student's percentile rank— that is, an estimation of where that reading rate falls within those of other students at that grade level at that time of year.

ORAL READING FLUENCY NORMS FOR HIGH SCHOOL

Percentile	Fall WCPM	Winter WCPM	Spring WCPM
90	195	209	213
75	171	183	191
50	143	156	165
25	116	125	138
10	87	94	111

Note: These are estimates, extrapolated from Hasbrouck and Tindal, 2004.

► ► ► Assessing Phonics Knowledge

► Administering the *Demtup Names Test*

The *Demtup Names Test* on pages 402–405 can be used to examine students' strengths and weaknesses in specific types of phonics skills in words they do not already know. It should be administered in a different sitting from the other parts of the *Developmental Literacy Inventory*.

GETTING READY TO TEST

FIND A QUIET PLACE AND PLAN FOR THE TIME NEEDED. Using the *Demtup Names Test* for the purpose of determining a student's ability to decode unknown words can take about ten minutes.

ARRANGE THE SPACE AND ASSEMBLE THE MATERIALS. Before you begin, assemble all of the materials you will need:

- a copy of the *Demtup Names Test* pages for the student to read
- a photocopy of the examiner's pages for recording the student's responses
- blank paper and pencils
- a tape recorder (optional)

Reassure the student. Before beginning, tell the student that you want to know how she figures out how to pronounce new and unknown words. (Avoid using the word "test.") There will be no grade. It is important for the student to do her best, even though there may be some activities she will not be sure about.

SIT BESIDE THE STUDENT. If you are right-handed, place the student to your left, with your materials for recording placed off to the right and out of the student's view. If you are left-handed, do the reverse.

ASSESSING PHONICS KNOWLEDGE IN UNKNOWN WORDS

BEGIN BY READING THESE INSTRUCTIONS TO THE CHILD. *Demtup is a planet far from Earth. The children there have very strange names. The children look strange, too. Read about the children from Demtup, but be sure to say their names correctly. It hurts their feelings if you don't.*

THEN HAND THE CHILD THE STUDENT'S VERSION OF THE *DEMTUP NAMES TEST* AND ASK THE CHILD TO READ EACH SENTENCE OUT LOUD. Tell the child that the children's names have to be sounded out, but that the rest of each sentence about strange children from the planet Demtup is easier to read.

On the score sheet, you will only score the Demtup names listed there. Do not score any other elements. You will ignore the part of each sentence that follows each name; those parts are not included on the score sheet. You may help a child with the part of a sentence that follows the Demtup names, if necessary, but not with the Demtup names themselves. Circle correctly read elements in the Demtup names. If the child makes an error, write what the child said above the element not read correctly. If the child successfully self-corrects in a phonics element within a Demtup name, you may give full credit. Again, ignore any errors in the part of each sentence that follows the Demtup name.

CONTINUE TESTING UNTIL THE STUDENT IS UNSUCCESSFUL ON FOUR CONSECUTIVE ITEMS

Suggestion for the Examiner

When a student makes a response, receive it in a way that is encouraging, but not evaluative: "Thank you. OK, let's go on." Avoid pointing out errors. Also avoid praising a student for correct answers. The tasks will soon get harder, the student will make errors, and the absence of praise may become unnerving to the student!

Suggestion for the Examiner

At least until you become proficient at marking the errors, you may want to tape record the session. If you do, put the tape recorder in an inconspicuous place, and use a long-playing tape so you won't have to change it while you are testing. You will still need to mark the errors while you test. The tape recording will serve as a backup to reinforce your accuracy.

ENTER THE RESULTS ON THE SCORE SUMMARY SHEET. Enter the number of correct responses on each line on the Score Summary Sheet. You may sum the scores at the bottom.

INTERPRETING THE RESULTS

The *Demtup Names Test* assesses a sample of phonics elements. The 78 test items provide an overview of a student's ability to decode unknown words that contain a variety of phonics elements ranging from simple letter-to-sound patterns to more complex patterns of onsets and rimes, root words, prefixes, and suffixes. It may be used to observe how the student decodes unknown words that contain major types of phonics elements. You may find, for example, that a student has a good mastery of initial consonant sounds, but that vowel sounds are difficult. You may find that individual consonant sounds are not difficult for a student, but that they are difficult when combined in consonant blends. These results may suggest general areas of phonics instruction that need to be reinforced.

The total score should be considered within the context of the student's grade level. A score of 24 at the end of the first grade may be quite good, but not at the end of the fifth grade. Use the results as a window into your understanding of the student's progress in phonics, not as an absolute goal to be reached immediately at any cost.

ASSESSING PHONICS KNOWLEDGE

THE *DEMTUP NAMES TEST*

Mab Tep lives on Demtup.

Wan Dub lives there, too.

Gom Cull has three eyes.

Fid Lag has only one eye.

Ret Sid has two noses.

Quin Yob likes to eat candy.

Vax Kon is her friend.

Cim Gen is ten years old.

Mabben Ebbit laughs at his friend.

Hess Mock has a bicycle.

Mancar Rabbitwood has a long name.

Rewant Catly runs very fast.

Trin Sprut is very happy.

Smet Grob has six arms.

Brack Plun likes to eat wood.

Phin Jath has a dog.

Pabo Lupet has four brothers.

Bine Mape lives in a big house.

Tay Noam is green.

Noy Aulon has four ears.

Ker Nur can fly.

Zink Fost is very sad.

Wran Knop can sing well.

Minition Prement likes his name.

Polynough Infosion doesn't like his name.

DEMTUP NAMES TEST SCORE SUMMARY SHEET

Introduction: Begin by reading the following: *"Demtup is a planet far from Earth. The children there have very strange names. The children look strange, too. Read about the children from Demtup, but be sure to say their names correctly. It hurts their feelings if you don't."* As the child reads aloud from the student copy, *circle* each correct element that is shown below on this scoring sheet. In the event of an incorrect response, write what the child said above the element. The words in the sentences that follow the Demtup names have been eliminated from the scoring sheet. They are not to be scored. Score only the elements on this page.

Mab Tep	onset /m/	rime /ab/	_____ /2 points
	onset /t/	rime /ep/	_____ /2 points
Wan Dub	onset /w/	rime /an/	_____ /2 points
	onset /d/	rime /ub/	_____ /2 points
Gom Cull	onset (hard) /g/	rime /om/	_____ /2 points
	onset (hard) /c/	rime /ull/	_____ /2 points
Fid Lag	onset /f/	rime /id/	_____ /2 points
	onset /l/	rime /ag/	_____ /2 points
Ret Sid	onset /r/	rime /et/	_____ /2 points
	onset /s/	rime /id/	_____ /2 points
Quin Yob	onset /qu/	rime /in/	_____ /2 points
	onset /y/	rime /ob/	_____ /2 points
Vax Kon	onset /v/	rime /ax/	_____ /2 points
	onset /k/	rime /on/	_____ /2 points
Cim Gen	onset (soft) /c/	rime /im/	_____ /2 points
	onset (soft) /g/	rime /en/	_____ /2 points
Mabben Ebbit	short /a/ in stressed syllable		_____ /1 point
	schwa (ə) in unstressed syllable		_____ /1 point
	short /e/ in stressed syllable		_____ /1 point
	schwa (ə) in unstressed syllable		_____ /1 point
Hess Mock	onset /h/	rime /ess/	_____ /2 points
	onset /m/	rime /ock/	_____ /2 points
Mancar Rabbitwood	Student should read *man, car, rabbit,* and *wood* as sight words without decoding		_____ /4 points

Rewant Catly	read prefix *re*, sight word *want* without decoding	_____/2 points
	sight word *cat*, and suffix *ly* without decoding	_____/2 points
Trin Sprut	onset /*tr*/	_____/1 point
	initial three-letter consonant blend /*spr*/, onset /*spr*/	_____/1 point
Smet Grob	onset /*sm*/	_____/1 point
	onset /*gr*/	_____/1 point
Brack Plun	onset /*br*/ rime /*ack*/	_____/2 points
	onset /*pl*/	_____/1 point
Phin Jath	onset /*ph*/	_____/1 point
	onset /*j*/ rime /*ath*/	_____/2 points
Pabo Lupet	long /*a*/ in open syllable	_____/1 point
	long /*u*/ in open syllable	_____/1 point
Bine Mape	onset /*b*/ rime /*ine*/	_____/2 points
	onset /*m*/ rime /*ape*/	_____/2 points
Tay Noam	onset /*t*/ rime /*ay*/	_____/2 points
	onset /*n*/ rime /*oam*/	_____/2 points
Noy Aulon	onset /*n*/ rime /*oy*/	_____/2 points
	rime /*au*/ onset /*l*/ rime /*on*/	_____/3 points
Ker Nur	onset /*k*/ rime /*er*/	_____/2 points
	onset /*n*/ rime /*ur*/	_____/2 points
Zink Fost	onset /*z*/ rime /*ink*/	_____/2 points
	onset /*f*/ rime /*ost*/	_____/2 points
Wran Knop	onset /*wr*/	_____/1 point
	onset /*kn*/	_____/1 point
Minition	prefix *mini* suffix *tion*	_____/2 points
Prement	pronounced without decoding prefix *pre* suffix *ment* pronounced without decoding	_____/2 points
Polynough Infosion	prefix *poly* final *ough*	_____/2 points
	prefix *in* suffix *sion*	_____/2 points
TOTAL POINTS		_____/91 points

▶ ▶ ▶ Using the Results of the *Developmental Literacy Inventory*

The *Developmental Literacy Inventory* consists of assessments of emergent literacy, along with word lists and text passages written at all levels from kindergarten through high school, as well as in different genres. These are followed by comprehension questions and scoring procedures to measure word recognition and reading rate. Each of these elements can be used separately and in combination to yield insights into many aspects of students' reading ability.

▶ Major Elements of the *Developmental Literacy Inventory*

1. EMERGENT LITERACY

A student who cannot yet read enough words to derive meaning from text is considered to be in the emergent stage of literacy. Such a student is learning fundamental concepts about the language represented by print and about print itself that will support her or him in learning to read. These concepts are assessed in the emergent literacy section of the *Developmental Literacy Inventory*. They include:

- **Print concepts**. The layout of books, the realization that reading is done from print and not from pictures, the orientation of print on a page, and knowledge of the terms "word" and "letter" are assessed. Students who lack these orienting concepts have been shown to have difficulty participating in reading instruction (Clay, 1975; Snow, et. al., 1999).
- **Alphabet knowledge**. Students are observed as they recognize randomly presented letters in both lower case and upper case, and as they write all of the letters of the alphabet. Knowing the letters of the alphabet helps children learn to read.
- **The concept of word**. The concept of word is the knowledge that spoken language comes in units of words, and that those units are represented in print by clusters of letters with spaces on either side. Having the concept of word enables students to track accurately between the words as they are spoken and the words as they are represented on the page.

- **Phonological awareness.** Spoken words are made up of syllables and smaller units called phonemes. Phonemes are the smallest speech sounds. In the word "cat," the phonemes are the sounds that correspond to the letters C, A, and T. Being aware of phonemes is not the same thing as auditory discrimination. Even infants can readily hear the difference between "pit" and "bit," but many school age students are not aware that either word is made up of three phonemes. Awareness of phonemes prepares children to explore the connections between letters and sounds in words.
- **Beginning word recognition.** Emergent readers can often recognize some words. Some of the words are those high frequency words to which they have had much exposure. Other words are easily decodable words such as "net," "bag," and "fig," which have predictable spellings. Children's reading of both sorts of words is assessed in the emergent literacy section of the *Developmental Literacy Inventory*.

2. WORD RECOGNITION

Recognizing words is not one ability, but several. At its simplest, word recognition consists of having a store of words in memory, called a **sight vocabulary**, that a reader recognizes instantly. It also includes the ability to recognize words that are not already in one's sight vocabulary by using phonics or decoding them, that is, using the associations between the letters and sounds in words to pronounce them. Word recognition also involves the use of context: using the meaning of the text and the grammatical environment of an unknown word to narrow down the possibilities and make the word easier to identify.

FLASHED AND UNTIMED WORD PRESENTATIONS. Assessment of students' word recognition ability begins with the word lists. Two sets of word lists are included (for pre-test and post-test presentations) that were written at graduated levels of difficulty from first grade through high school. The words may be presented to the student in two ways: flashed and untimed.

In the *flashed* presentation, the teacher covers the word with two index cards. He holds the cards edge to edge over the word, then pulls down the lower card to reveal the word, and covers the word again a quarter of a second later by pulling down the upper card. (See Figure 2 on page 425 in the Appendix.)

The word is first shown to the student in a flashed presentation. The student's response is recorded. If the student does not correctly identify the word, the examiner removes the cards from the word and lets the student look at the word again for as long as needed. The student's responses in this *untimed* condition are recorded.

Both the scores and the student's actual miscues for both kinds of presentations are recorded for later analysis. Comparing the student's flashed and untimed reading scores can indicate the size of a student's sight vocabulary—how many words the student can recognize instantly—and his or her decoding ability—how well the student is able to use letter-to-sound correspondences, or knowledge of phonics, to decipher words that are not in the student's sight vocabulary.

In addition to measuring the students' word recognition rates in the flashed, untimed, and in-context conditions, we may examine their word knowledge in more detail. One kind of examination is to categorize their word recognition errors by strategy or level. Another way is to test them on their recognition of unknown or new words—words that can only be read by associating their letters with sounds.

ANALYZING WORD RECOGNITION STRATEGIES. Children's approaches to reading words vary with their maturity and experience with reading. Uta Frith (1985) and Usha Goswami (2000) identified a set of four levels or stages of children's development of word recognition: **logographic, transitional alphabetic, alphabetic,** and **orthographic**. Based on our own research (Temple, Nathan, Burris, and Temple, 1993) and on the work of Shane Templeton, Darrell Morris, and others (see Templeton and Morris, 2000, for a summary) the present authors have added one more stage: **derivational reading.** These categories of word recognition enable the teacher to understand the thinking about words that underlies students' word recognition errors. With that understanding, the teacher can plan corrective instruction. Table 3 on page 419 in the Appendix explains the stages of word recognition.

Students' responses to the word recognition in isolation tasks can be categorized according to the classification system explained in Table 4 on page 421 in the Appendix.

The *Demtup Names Test*: A Test of Phonics. One of the dilemmas in testing phonics is that when known words are used, children pronounce words correctly, not necessarily because they have decoded them, but because they often recognize them on sight from previous exposures. On the other hand, a measure of phonics knowledge that uses words not already recognized by children will consist of a list of nonsense words, and they are harder to read than authentic words (Harris and Sipay, 1990). Cunningham (1990) developed a Names Test as a response to this problem, since even as adults we often read names that we have never seen before. There is no context, however, for the Cunningham Names Test.

For the *Developmental Reading Inventory*, we developed a measure that presents unknown words that sample phonic elements within a context of known words. It consists of a series of sentences about children from the fictitious planet Demtup. The sentences are designed to be read easily by children at almost any level from mid-first grade level up, especially those children who have reached the alphabetic stage or beyond (see Table 4 on page 421). Each sentence begins with the name of a child from Demtup. These names are strange and unknown to the readers being assessed. They are urged to pronounce the names correctly because children from Demtup are upset if their names are not pronounced correctly. A typical test item might say: *Glob Noy has ears on the top of his head.* This item seeks to find out if the student can read several letter-to-sound correspondences in one package: the onset /gl/ and the rime /ob/, and the onset /n/ and the rime /oy/. The student is not assessed on the words in the part of the sentence that follows the name, and the teacher can assist the child in reading the rest of the sentence without penalty. But the context in which the unknown names are placed provides a comfortable respite from decoding for the child being assessed. In addition, many of the sentences are designed to elicit a bit of laughter from the child being assessed during the test and to lower the pressure in this demanding task.

The *Demtup Names Test* (see pages 402–403) is not designed to be a complete measure of English phonics, but rather to sample the major phonics elements—onsets and rimes that include beginning consonants and vowels, consonant digraphs and consonant blends, long and short vowels, phonogram patterns, root words, and suffixes—that beginning and developing readers use to read unknown words. The elements are arranged in a sequence fairly typical of the order in which children acquire decoding skills (Gunning, 1990; Bear, et. al, 2005).

READING WORDS IN CONTEXT IN THE TEXT PASSAGE. When students read aloud the text passages, the examiner carefully attends to the reading, and marks the errors, pauses, repetitions, and self-corrections. A comparison of the student's **word recognition in context** scores with the student's **word recognition in isolation** scores will show the degree to which the student is using the context to narrow down possibilities and identify the words.

3. READING RATE AND FLUENCY

Reading fluency is a measure of the reader's smoothness, or "automaticity" in reading. Reading fluency is a combination of reading rate, accuracy, and intonation or expression. As Armbruster, Lehr, and Osborne wrote in *Put Reading First* (2001),

> Fluency is the ability to read a text accurately and quickly. When fluent readers read silently, they recognize words automatically. They group words quickly in ways that help them gain meaning from what they read. Fluent readers read aloud effortlessly and with expression. Their reading sounds natural, as if they are speaking. (p. 22)

Reading fluency matters for several reasons. First, fluency is the bridge between word recognition and comprehension (Osborne, Lehr, and Hiebert, 2006), because a reader who reads words effortlessly has more concentration available to comprehend a text than a reader who struggles to identify the words (Foorman and Mehta, 2002; Perfetti, 1985; Samuels and Farstrup, 2006). Second, fluency is an indicator of efficiency—of the ratio between efforts expended and results attained. Slow and disfluent readers will tire sooner than others and more quickly abandon their efforts.

To assess reading fluency, you can measure the number of words the student reads correctly per minute. The resulting score can be compared two ways: (1) against norms for reading rates at different grade levels (see Table 5 on page 422 in the Appendix), and (2) against that student's own reading rate at an earlier point in the year. By counting the words the student reads accurately, you can combine measures of reading rate and word recognition. Rate and accuracy scores are reported as WCPM, for "words correctly read per minute." They are determined by taking the total number of words the child read, subtracting the words read incorrectly, and dividing the resulting number by the amount of time it took the child to read the passage.

In the examiner's pages of the *Developmental Literacy Inventory,* a scoring procedure for calculating students' correct reading rates as WCPM is provided for you. You can plot those scores on a chart to determine if that rate is "average," " below average," or "above average" for the time of year that assessment was administered. The average reading rates were taken from Hasbrouck and Tindal's "Oral Reading Fluency Data" (2006).

It is to be expected that reading rates may be slower in the passages from social studies and science, since those passages may contain more unfamiliar information than the narrative passages.

Reading rates are widely used as indicators of students' reading fluency, especially when they take accuracy of word recognition into account. However, as we noted above, intonation or prosody—adding emphasis, emotional tone, and meaningful phrasing while reading—is also an important aspect of reading fluency. The National Assessment of Educational Progress, a large-scale assessment of students' reading in the United States, uses a four-point rubric to evaluate a student's reading fluency that takes into account phrasing (reading words in meaningful groups), syntax (reading with the grammar of the sentence in mind), and expression (making the voice higher or lower, faster or slower, louder or softer depending on the emotional tone of the text). NAEP's Oral Reading Fluency Scale is reproduced in Table 6 on pgae 423 in the Appendix. You may wish to use the NAEP measure to supplement the reading rate and accuracy measures contained in the *Developmental Literacy Inventory.*

4. COMPREHENSION

Reading comprehension, or understanding what is read, consists of several abilities. Students' world knowledge is needed to contextualize the new information they gain from the text. They need the ability to find main ideas and recall them later. They also need to be able to make inferences to construct meanings when ideas are not explicitly stated. And they need items of vocabulary or word meanings.

QUESTIONS REQUIRING RECALL. Some of the questions require the recall of important information. These address ideas that were explicitly mentioned in the text. Ideas for recall include main ideas, or key propositions, as well as supporting details that are important to the construction of the meaning. In the context of this test, the act of recall is a fairly broad range activity.

What is designated as a recall question may ask that a student tell you a piece of information using the words in which it is mentioned in the text. For example, **the text says:** *In Israel, the birthday girl or boy gets a beautiful crown of flowers. The mother places the royal crown on her child's head.* **The question asks:** *According to this passage, in what country does the birthday child wear a crown of flowers?*

A recall question may also ask a student to tell an idea that has been stated in the text, although the question may not take exactly the same form as the answer. For example, in a second grade passage, **the text says:** *Jan lives in the city. The city has many big buildings. People work in some of the buildings. In other buildings there are stores. Some buildings have apartments. . . . There are many cars, trucks, and buses in the city. They make a lot of noise. People walk very fast because they are very busy. Some people ride on the bus. There are many people on the bus. . . .* **The question asks:** *What did this story say that it was like in the city?* The passage does not use the words "What the city is like," but it does provide details about life in the city that the student is asked to recall.

QUESTIONS REQUIRING INFERENCES. Other questions that are asked after the students read the text require that readers make **inferences** in order to construct meaning where ideas are not stated explicitly. Making inferences, too, covers a range of activity.

In narratives, some inferences require that the readers infer motives for behavior. For example, in a sixth grade passage, **the text says:**

"Cast near the trunk, but not too close."

"I know, Dad," said Paco. But his first cast arched neatly and plopped on top of the trunk. Without commenting, his father paddled the canoe to the other side of the dead tree, extricated the lure from the bark, and gently tossed it into the water.

The question asks: *How did Paco feel about his father's advice? How do you know?*

When the text is informational, inference questions can require readers to derive an answer that is not given by applying logic to information that is given. For example, in a middle school level passage, **the text says:** *Industries like the textile industry have had to shut down because of increased competition. They could no longer compete in the global economy. Increased competition often leads to lower prices for consumers. But lower prices can sometimes cause lower profits for industries.* **The question asks:**

From what the article said, do you think you pay more or less for a shirt now that we have a global economy?

Inference questions in informational texts can also ask readers to make summary judgments and derive main ideas from several pieces of information that are provided in the text. For example, **the text says:** *A third habitat is called the light zone. It is not shallow, but light can still reach the bottom. Because of this, the light zone is filled with many kinds of plants. Many animals eat and hide in the plants. Thousands of kinds of fish live in the light zone. Jellyfish, crabs, turtles, dolphins, and sharks also live here and sea birds hunt for food here.*

The question asks: *Why do you think the light zone is home to so many fish and animals?*

QUESTIONS TAPPING VOCABULARY. Vocabulary knowledge is another important part of reading comprehension. There are two kinds of vocabulary knowledge. One kind is vocabulary knowledge that is stored in memory. This kind of knowledge actually covers a range of specificity. A person may have never heard the word "avaricious"; may have heard it but not know the meaning; may know that it refers to a person and has negative qualities; may know that it is a synonym for "greedy"; or may use it in her vocabulary with that meaning.

Another kind of vocabulary knowledge is the ability to infer word meanings from context. For example, in a fourth grade section is found this question: *In the sentence, "The wings quiver as they slice through the turbulent air," what does* turbulent *mean?* A student who did not know that the word meant "stormy" or "stirred up" could infer some of the meaning from the context. *Turbulent* refers to *air* that an airplane is flying through, and it is a condition that makes the wings of the airplane tremble.

It is not always clear from a student's answer whether he knew the word ahead of time or whether he worked out the meaning from context. In order to find out more information, the examiner can always ask the student how she or he knew what the word meant. The examiner may also ask the vocabulary questions both before and after the student reads the passage.

4. LISTENING COMPREHENSION

Comprehension of written text may be tested without the students having to read the text. In the case of developing readers, listening to a text is usually easier than reading it—since the activity of recognizing written words and constructing understanding from them is less practiced than listening to speech and constructing meaning from it. In reading assessment, testing listening comprehension offers an indication of the readers' highest potential for comprehending a text, and serves as the goal against which their performance in reading comprehension can be measured.

Listening comprehension is composed of the listener's world knowledge, knowledge of vocabulary, ability to find and remember main ideas and important details, ability to make inferences, and ability to follow the structure of a presentation according to the genre. If a reader's reading comprehension score falls significantly below his or her listening comprehension, it is safe to assume that focused reading instruction can help close the gap. But if the two kinds of performance approximate each other, the student's reading performance can be expected to improve as his or her general level of education and thinking power improve.

5. READING ACROSS GENRES

Much as the grammar of a sentence offers a way for speakers to encode meanings in orderly ways, or for hearers to unpack those meanings properly, **genres** of writing are created from recurring forms and patterns for encoding and decoding meanings on a larger scale than sentences.

Narratives supply characters with personalities and motives who interact with other characters within settings. The actions of the characters have consequences, and the consequences give meaning to the actions. Narratives usually are not true; another word for narrative is fiction. But because narratives are usually arranged in problems and solutions and consequences, they often turn out to be true in the sense that they tell us "this is what happens when this kind of person interacts with that kind of person"; or "this is what happens when a person has that kind of problem and tries this kind of action as a solution" (Kermode, 2005).

Authors of contemporary fiction for young people in America are exhorted not to preach to their readers (see Seuling, 2004, for example). Indeed, much of the literature children read these days depends heavily on the readers' ability to make inferences. The narrative passages in the *Developmental Literacy Inventory* form complete stories at the earlier levels, but are often fragments of stories at the upper levels. Comprehending them requires readers to follow plot structures, understand characterization, infer relationships between characters, or make connections between fictional events and real-life problems.

Expository or informational text is intended to be factual, in the sense that it should correspond to the ways things are or were in the real world. Thus, ideas from expository texts can be studied, remembered, and applied directly in the real world. Expository texts from different disciplines have different forms and functions.

In the **sciences**, expository texts may explain how things work, how things evolved, or how they are related to each other in classificatory systems. Science texts make very careful and limited uses of language, often to distinguish scientific terms from the looser uses of words in everyday speech.

The **social studies**, as they are taught in the United States, are composed of several disciplines: history, geography, civics, and economics, and sometimes sociology and anthropology. Social studies texts may recount the stories of people, places, or events that are important to a society's understanding of itself. They may explain governmental institutions or economic principles. Sometimes texts in the social studies read much like narratives, with their people, settings, problems, solutions, and consequences. Even so, these narratives will include important details that are considered true, and may be expected to be remembered. Other kinds of social studies texts read more like scientific texts, with their explanations of events or processes, their presentations of concepts in classificatory relationships, and their careful use of terms.

In the *Developmental Literacy Inventory*, complete sets of all three kinds of passages are included: narrative texts, scientific texts, and social studies texts. These three present a cross section of the reading that students are expected to do in school. In administering the *Developmental Literacy Inventory* it is recommended that students be tested in one genre to establish their reading levels. Then, the examiner may test them in passages from the other genres at their independent or instructional levels. This additional testing will yield a profile that will allow a comparison of the students' ability to read and comprehend across different genres of text.

6. ORAL AND SILENT READING

Students often differ in their silent and oral reading ability. The rate of reading is affected if students must read words orally, and comprehension may differ as well. In the testing situation, of course, students must read orally in order for the examiner to assess their accuracy in word recognition and other strategies. When students read silently, you can assess their reading rate and their comprehension.

At any level of text passages, you may ask the student to read a passage silently. It is recommended that you determine the instructional and independent reading levels with passages read orally first, and then ask the student to read a same-level passage silently. That passage is normally from a same-genre passage taken from the opposite form; although it may be a passage from a different genre, depending on the examiner's purposes.

▶ ▶ ▶ Appendix

▶ Tables and Figures

TABLE 1 Correlating Reading Levels

Grade level	DLI levels	Fountas/Pinnell Guided Reading levels	Reading Recovery levels	Lexiles	DRA levels
K		A	A, B		A
			1		1
		B	2		2
	Pre-Primer A	C	3		3
1.1	Pre-Primer B	C	4		4
	Pre-Primer C		5		
		D	6		6
			7		
		E	8		8
1.2			9		
		F	10		10
	Primer		11	200–299	
		G	12		12
			13		
	Grade 1	H	14		14
			15		
		I	16		16
2	Grade 2.1	J	18	300–399	20
		K	19		
	Grade 2.2	L	20	400–499	28
		M			
3	Grade 3	N	22	500–599	30
		O, P	24	600–699	34
					38
4	Grade 4	Q, R, S	26	700–799	40
5	Grade 5	T, U, V	28	800–899	44
6	Grade 6	W, X, Y	30	900–999	
7	Middle school	Z	32	1000–1100	
8	Grade 8	Z	34		
9–10				1100–1150	

TABLE 2 Indicators of Reading Levels

	Word Recognition in Isolation	Word Recognition in Context	Comprehension (Responses to Questions)
Independent Level	90%	97%	90%
Instructional level	70–89%	90–96%	70–89%
Frustration Level	Below 70%	Below 90%	Below 70%

TABLE 3 Stages in Children's Development of Phonics

The stages of children's development of word recognition have been described by Uta Frith (1985) and summarized by Usha Goswami (2000). According to these scholars, children go through a set of stages of word recognition that can be called logographic, transitional, alphabetic, and orthographic. After presenting these stages, we will lay out ideas for instruction that will help children at each stage.

Logographic Reading

Young children—preschoolers and kindergartners—who are just beginning to see familiar words around them tend to recognize words as whole displays. Children recognize McDonald's restaurants by their golden arches. They may recognize the word "look" by associating the two O's with eyes. Children in this stage may refer to the same object with different but related names, calling a Crest toothpaste label at one time "Crest" and at another time "toothpaste" (Harste, Woodward, & Burke, 1985). They are not yet reading the letters in the words, but are trying to find any identifiable feature that will help them remember the words, almost as if the words were faces. Logographic readers often give no response at all when faced with a word they do not know, because they do not yet have strategy for sounding out words.

Marsh, et al. (1981) called this stage of word recognition "glance and guess," because children look at a word and call it by the few names of words they know, or say nothing at all. They have no way to begin to recognize words by working through their letters.

Transitional Alphabetic Reading

More advanced children—usually in early first grade—begin to read words by their letters, but not by very many letters. The child might read the first consonant of a word and call it by the name of another word she or he knows that begins with that sound. It is as if a word such as "ball" appeared to children like this: **bxxx**. They might correctly read the word, especially if they are helped by the context, but they might readily confuse it with "bat," "bark," or "beep" (Morris, 1999).

Alphabetic Reading

By the middle of first grade and into early second grade, most children begin to read more and more letters in words. When they attempt to read a word, rather than calling out the name of another word that begins the same way, a child might sound out every letter, even if it means pronouncing something that doesn't make sense. A child might say, "We went to the fire sta-t-yon" instead of "fire station." With practice, students produce fewer nonsense word readings and read words more accurately.

(continues)

TABLE 3   Continued

Children are acquiring a growing body of sight words—words that they can read accurately and quickly without having to decode them. This rapid word identification occurs after a period of sounding out the words, or *phonological recoding*, as linguists call it. Ehri (1991) suggests that the earlier practice of reading words alphabetically—figuring them out letter by letter—lays down pathways to the memory that makes it easier for children to recognize the words when they see the words later. She explains:

> When readers practice reading specific words by phonologically recoding the words, they form access routes for those words into memory. The access routes are built using knowledge of grapheme–phoneme correspondences that connect letters in spellings to phonemes in the pronunciation of words. The letters are processed as visual symbols for the phonemes, and the sequence of letters is retained as an alphabetic, phonological representation of the word. The first time an unfamiliar word is seen, it is read by phonological recoding. This initiates an access route into memory. Subsequent readings of the word strengthen the access route until the connections between letters and phonemes are fully formed and the spelling is represented in memory. (Ehri, 1991, p. 402)

Orthographic Reading

By late first grade to the middle of second grade, most children are moving into another stage. Now they are looking at words in terms of spelling patterns—not just one letter to one sound, but also familiar patterns such as *-ake*, *-ight*, and later *-tion*. Children who can separate words into onsets and rimes and who are taught by means of word sorts (Bear, Invernizzi, Templeton, & Johnston, 2000; Gillet and Temple, 1979) can read by analogy; that is, if they can read "bake" and "take," they can also read "rake" and "stake." As they move further into the orthographic phase, children read not just by phonogram patterns, or onsets and rimes, as Trieman (1988) calls them, but increasingly by root words and even historical morphemes.

Derivational Reading

From about fourth or fifth grade and up, normally advancing readers enter a phase of word recognition that we call *derivational reading*. (This term is not from Uta Frith, but is derived from Chomsky and Halle, 1970, and Templeton, 1991.) Readers from late first grade and second grade recognize that words like "firehouse' and "groundskeeper" contain other words they know within them. From fourth grade and later, more proficient readers recognize that words like "telegraph," "telephone," "biology," and "biography" also contain word parts that they recognize: *-graph*, from a Greek word meaning "to write"; *tele-* from another Greek word meaning "at a distance." They recognize that "sanity" is related to "sane" and that "sign" is related to "signal." Derivational reading thus combines something of word recognition and vocabulary.

TABLE 4   Word Knowledge Levels by Error Type

Level of Word Recognition	Target Word	Typical Miscue or Reading Error	Description of the Error Type	Teaching Focus
Logographic Reading	plant Crest	Lee ("She's my friend. She has one of those [pointing to the L] in her name.") Toothpaste!	Student typically looks at the shape of the word and calls out any word she knows that it reminds her of.	The student should learn more sight words as wholes. The student should be made to pay attention to the beginning sounds in words and the letters that spell them.
Transitional Alphabetic Reading	plant Crest	Papa car	Student identifies a letter or two and thinks of words she knows that contains the same letter sound.	The student should continue to learn more sight words as wholes. Word study should focus on letter-to-sound correspondences on parts of words beyond the initial letter, especially short vowel sounds.
Alphabetic Reading	plant right	pee lay night rye gut	Student reads through words one letter at a time, making a sound for each letter.	Word study should point out conventional spellings for sounds, and also begin to introduce common spelling patterns for short vowel phonograms or rimes.
Orthographic Reading	plant right	pl, pl, ant, plant! ruh, ruh, -ight, right!	Student sees words as patterns: *onsets* and *rimes*	Word study should introduce more spelling patterns (onsets and rimes)
Derivational Reading	atmospheric luxurious	Atmos . . . lux or yus	Student doesn't recognize that the target word is derived from a familiar word.	Word study should focus on derivational relationships between words.

TABLE 5 Normal Reading Rates for Students in Grades 1–8, Fall, Winter, Spring

Grade	Percentile	Fall WCPM*	Winter WCPM*	Spring WCPM*	Avg. Weekly Improvement
1	90	—	81	111	1.9
	75	—	47	82	2.2
	50	—	**23**	**53**	**1.9**
	25	—	12	28	1.0
	10	—	6	15	0.6
2	90	106	125	142	1.1
	75	79	100	117	1.2
	50	**51**	**72**	**89**	**1.2**
	25	25	42	61	1.1
	10	11	18	31	0.6
3	90	128	146	162	1.1
	75	99	120	137	1.2
	50	**71**	**92**	**107**	**1.1**
	25	44	62	78	1.1
	10	21	36	48	0.8
4	90	145	166	180	1.1
	75	119	139	152	1.0
	50	**94**	**112**	**123**	**0.9**
	25	68	87	98	0.9
	10	45	61	72	0.8
5	90	166	182	194	0.9
	75	139	156	168	0.9
	50	**110**	**127**	**139**	**0.9**
	25	85	99	109	0.8
	10	61	74	83	0.7
6	90	177	195	204	0.8
	75	153	167	177	0.8
	50	**127**	**140**	**150**	**0.7**
	25	98	111	122	0.8
	10	68	82	93	0.8
7	90	180	192	202	0.7
	75	156	165	177	0.7
	50	**128**	**136**	**150**	**0.7**
	25	102	109	123	0.7
	10	79	88	98	0.6

TABLE 5 Continued

Grade	Percentile	Fall WCPM*	Winter WCPM*	Spring WCPM*	Avg. Weekly Improvement
8	90	185	199	199	0.4
	75	161	173	177	0.5
	50	**133**	**146**	151	**0.6**
	25	106	115	124	0.6
	10	77	84	97	0.6

(Hasbrouck and Tindal, 2006)

WCPM means "words correctly read per minute." The "average weekly improvement" figure was derived by dividing the number of words learned in a year by 32 weeks, except that the first grade figure was divided by 16 weeks. This figure represents the average increase in reading rate that may be expected at each grade level.

TABLE 6 Oral Reading Fluency Scale from the National Assessment of Educational Progress

Level 4	Reads primarily in larger, meaningful phrase groups. Although some regressions, repetitions, and deviations from text may be present, these do not appear to detract from the overall structure of the story. Preservation of the author's syntax is consistent. Some or most of the story is read with expressive interpretation.
Level 3	Reads primarily in three- or four-word phrase groups. Some smaller groupings may be present. However, the majority of phrasing seems appropriate and preserves the syntax of the author. Little or no expressive interpretation is present.
Level 2	Reads primarily in two-word phrases with some three- or four-word groupings. Some word-by-word reading may be present. Word groupings may seem awkward and unrelated to larger context of sentence or passage.
Level 1	Reads primarily word-by-word. Occasional two-word or three-word phrases may occur—but these are infrequent and/or they do not preserve meaningful syntax.

Source: U.S. Department of Education, National Center for Education Statistics. *Listening to Children Read Aloud*, 15. Washington, DC: 1995.

FIGURE 1   How to Make the Pre-Primer Books

Students reading the Pre-Primer level materials will read from small books, rather than from a single page of text. You can either remove the book pages from your inventory and use the original pages, or you can photocopy the pages and use the copies. Here is how you will make the little books.

1. For each book, remove the pages the student will read from your inventory or make a clear photo-copy of each page using single-sided copying.

2. Fold the cover sheet in half horizontally so that the title and illustration are on the outside. Set the folded cover aside. (For greater durability, you can laminate the cover sheet at this point.)

3. Fold each book page in half horizontally so that the pages are on the outside and the blank side of the sheet is on the inside. The fold should be to the right, so that the odd-numbered pages (1, 3, etc.) are facing up and the even-numbered pages (2, 4, etc.) are facing down. Fold each sheet in the same way.

4. Stack the folded pages so that the page numbers are in order; the odd-numbered pages should be facing up, with page 1 on top. All the folds should be on the right-hand side.

5. Insert all of the pages at one time into the cover. The folded edges of each sheet should be on the outside, or the right-hand side, of the book. (This makes turning the pages of the book easier for young readers, and also makes the books more durable.) Double-check that the pages are in the correct order and are all facing the right way.

6. Staple the cover two or three times vertically along the line on the left side of the cover. All the raw edges of the pages will be enclosed within the cover, and the readers will grasp the folded edges as they turn the pages.

7. Store each little book with copies of the corresponding examiner's pages that you will write on as the reader reads the book to you.

staple

fold pages

outer fold for cover

FIGURE 2 "Flashing" Words

The test examiner holds two index cards (thumbs underneath, fingers on top). She pulls down the lower card and immediately pulls the upper card down after it, so that the word appears very briefly between the cards. The whole exposure should take no more than a quarter of a second. Practice is needed in order to flash words smoothly.

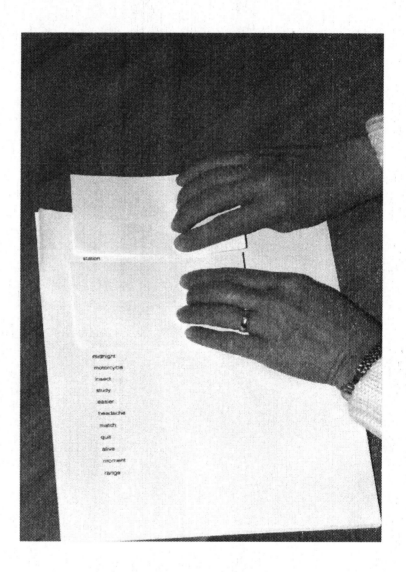

▶ ▶ ▶ References

Alexander, P. A., and Jetton, T. L. (2000). Learning from text: A multidimensional and developmental perspective. In M. L. Kamil, P. B. Mosenthal, P. D. Pearson, and R. Barr (Eds.), *Handbook of reading research, Volume III*. Mahwah, NJ: Lawrence Earlbaum Associates.

Armbruster, B. B., Lehr, F., and Osborn, J. (2001). *Put reading first: The research building blocks for teaching children to read. Kindergarten through grade 3*. Washington, D.C.: National Institute for Literacy.

Bear, D. R., Invernizzi, M., Templeton, S., and Johnston, F. (2007). *Words their way: Word study for phonics, vocabulary, and spelling instruction*. Upper Saddle River, NJ: Prentice Hall.

Betts, A. E. (1946). *Foundations of reading instruction, with emphasis on differentiated guidance*. Chicago: American Book Company.

Chomsky, N., and Halle, M. (1970). *The sound pattern of English*. New York: Macmillan.

Clay, M. M. (1975). *What did I write?* Portsmouth, NH: Heinemann.

Clay, M. M. (2000). *Concepts about print: What have children learned about the way we print language?* Portsmouth, NH: Heinemann.

Cunningham, P. (1990). The Names Test: A quick assessment of decoding ability. *The Reading Teacher, 44*: 124–129.

Deno, S. L., Fuchs, L. S., Marston, D., and Shin, J. (2001). Using curriculum-based measurement to establish growth standards for students with learning disabilities. *School Psychology Review, 30(4)*: 507–524.

Diamond, L. J. (2006, April). Triage for adolescent struggling readers. *The School Administrator*. http://www.aasa.org/publications/saarticledetail.cfm?ItemNumber=5870&snItemNumber=950

Duke, N. K. (2004). The case for informational text. *Educational Leadership, 61*(6): 40–44.

Ehri, L. (1991). Development of the ability to read words. In R. Barr, M. Kamil, P. Mosenthal, and P. D. Pearson, *Handbook of reading research, Vol. 2*. New York: Longman.

Foorman, B. R., and Mehta, P. (2002, November). *Definitions of fluency: Conceptual and methodological challenges.* PowerPoint presentation at A Focus on Fluency Forum, San Francisco, CA. Available at www.prel.org/programs/rel/fluency/Foorman.ppt

Frith, U. (1985). Beneath the surface of developmental dyslexia. In K. E. Patterson, J. C. Marshall, and M. Coltheart (Eds.), *Surface dyslexia* (pp. 301–330). London: Erlbaum.

Gillet, J., and Temple, C. (1978, December). Developing word knowledge: A cognitive view, *Reading World 18*(2):132–140.

Gillet, J. W., Temple, C., and Crawford, A. (2008). *Understanding reading problems: Assessment and instruction* (7th Ed.). New York: Longman.

Gipe, J. P. (2006). *Multiple paths to literacy: Assessment and differentiated instruction for diverse learners, K–12* (6th ed.). Upper Saddle River, NJ: Merrill Prentice Hall.

Goswami, U. (2000). Phonological and lexical processes. In M. L. Kamil, P. B. Mosenthal, P. D. Pearson, and R. Barr (Eds.), *Handbook of reading research, Volume III.* Mahwah, NJ: Lawrence Erlbaum.

Gunning, T. G. (2000). *Phonological awareness and primary phonics.* Boston: Allyn and Bacon.

Harris, A. J., and Sipay, E. R. (1990). *How to increase reading ability* (9th ed.). New York: Longman.

Harste, J., Woodward, V., and Burke, C. (1985). *Language stories and literacy lessons.* Portsmouth, NH: Heinemann.

Hasbrouck, J., and Tindal, G. (2006). Oral reading fluency norms: A valuable assessment tool for reading teachers. *The Reading Teacher 56*(7): 636–644.

Hiebert, E. H. (2003, April). *The role of text in developing fluency: A comparison of two interventions.* Paper presented at the annual meeting of the American Educational Research Association, Chicago, IL.

Hiebert, E. H., and Fisher, C. W. (2002, May). *Text matters in developing fluent reading.* Paper presented at the annual meeting of the International Reading Association, San Francisco, CA.

Hoffman, J. V., McCarthey, S. J., Abbott, J., Christian, C., Corman, L., Curry, C., Dressman, M., Elliot, B., Maherne, D., and Stahle, D. (1994). So what's new in the new basals? A focus on first grade. *Journal of Reading Behavior, 26:* 47–73.

Johnson, K. R. (1977). Personal communication.

Johnston, F. R., Invernizzi, M. A., and Juel, C. (1998). *Book buddies: Guidelines for volunteer tutors of emergent and early readers.* New York: Guilford.